Power Verbs for Managers and Executives

Power Verbs for Managers and Executives

for

Managers and Executives

Hundreds of Verbs and Phrases to Communicate More Dynamically and Effectively

Michael Lawrence Faulkner
with Michelle Faulkner-Lunsford

Vice President, Publisher: Tim Moore
Associate Publisher and Director of Marketing: Amy Neidlinger
Executive Editor: Jeanne Glasser
Operations Specialist: Jodi Kemper
Marketing Manager: Megan Graue
Cover Designer: Chuti Prasertsith
Managing Editor: Kristy Hart
Project Editor: Elaine Wiley
Copy Editor: Karen Annett
Proofreader: Sarah Kearns
Senior Indexer: Cheryl Lenser
Senior Compositor: Gloria Schurick
Manufacturing Buyer: Dan Uhrig

Publishing as FT Press
Upper Saddle River, New Jersey 07458

FT Press offers excellent discounts on this book when ordered in quantity for bulk purchases or special sales. For more information, please contact U.S. Corporate and Government Sales, 1-800-382-3419, corpsales@pearsontechgroup.com. For sales outside the U.S., please contact International Sales at international@pearsoned.com.

Company and product names mentioned herein are the trademarks or registered trademarks of their respective owners.

Printed in the United States of America

First Printing June 2013

ISBN-10: 0-133-15880-2
ISBN-13: 978-0-133-15880-9

Pearson Education LTD.
Pearson Education Australia PTY, Limited.
Pearson Education Singapore, Pte. Ltd.
Pearson Education Asia, Ltd.
Pearson Education Canada, Ltd.
Pearson Educación de Mexico, S.A. de C.V.
Pearson Education—Japan
Pearson Education Malaysia, Pte. Ltd.

Library of Congress Cataloging-in-Publication Data

Faulkner, Michael L.
  Power verbs for managers and executives : hundreds of verbs and phrases to communicate more dynamically and effectively / Michael Lawrence Faulkner.
     pages cm
  ISBN 978-0-13-315880-9 (pbk. : alk. paper)
  1. Communication in organizations. 2. Communication in management. 3. Business communication.
4. Interpersonal communication. I. Title.
  HD30.3.F3843 2013
  658.001'4—dc23

To all my colleagues at DeVry, Inc., DeVry University, and Keller Graduate School of Management who have willingly and unselfishly shared their experiences, backgrounds, knowledge, and understanding of the authentic concepts of leadership and management.

Contents

Foreword

Americans who have spent time in or near the center of power in the industrial, political, social, or academic sectors of society have developed an intrinsic sense of the pivotal importance of vocabulary to catalyze an idea and transform the thinking of an individual, engender a new sense of identity of a work group, transform the mission of a large business enterprise, or even stimulate a sense of purpose and destiny of an entire society.

Dr. Faulkner's extensive experience base in the industrial and academic sectors uniquely positions him to offer a singularly insightful and valuable perspective on "power verbs," sharing previously undisclosed usage techniques and powerful concatenations of verbs that have the "weight" to transform and empower new ideas and catalyze a renewed sense of purpose and commitment and potentially even transform the life of the user. Dr. Faulkner characterizes these power verbs as "verbs that are emotionally edgy, powerfully positioned, with a kick, punch, and pizzazz."

Dr. Faulkner puts power verbs into a practical framework that focuses on the usage and dynamics of thoughtfully structured verbs that can generate real energy and power. It is an interesting, entertaining, and generally fun-to-read book with the serious potential to transform a person's career!

The motivation for this new book is centered only on the use of power verbs rather than developing a work on language skills. Dr. Faulkner compellingly develops the significance of language as having the power to shape the thinking of others—and he highlights the importance of what people really hear rather than the exactness of what is spoken. He sensitizes the reader about the power of words to do well or harm—it all depends on the synthesis of power verbs and the dynamism of the speaker. Most impressively, Dr. Faulkner explains how specific characterizations of power verbs and the use of imagery can significantly alter the mind-set and mood of the listener.

This refreshing and novel approach to language is entertaining, interesting, and exceedingly practical for anyone wanting to expand his or her sense of contribution to nearly any aspect of human endeavor. It is a "can't miss" opportunity to be nourished in the reading of this important and novel body of work!

Eric J. Addeo, Ph.D., Chair: Networking and Communications Department, College of Engineering and Information Sciences, DeVry University

Acknowledgments

Many people assisted with this book in many ways. Much of this help was a family affair. My wife, Jo-Ann, lent her love, patience, support, and advice. My son, Kenny, provided ideas for format when I was at a dead end. My grandsons, Andrew and Alex, looked up some words, and my daughter, Michelle, did yeoman's work, editing, writing content, working on style, and offering advice.

About the Author

Dr. Michael Lawrence Faulkner is the author of six books. He is a professor at the Keller Graduate School of Management at DeVry University. He is a former U.S. Marine, who spent 30 years in a variety of leadership and executive management positions with Fortune 500 firms and major nonprofit trade associations, as well as helping run the family business before beginning his second career in academics. Michael is a member of MENSA, a Rotary International Fellow, the Keller Master Teacher Award, and holds a Silver Certification by the Toastmaster's International. In addition to his Ph.D., Michael has earned two master's degrees, one from NYU and an MBA from NYIT.

Michelle Faulkner-Lunsford is a 2001 graduate of Middle Tennessee State University where she majored in English and minored in Writing. Mrs. Lunsford spent 10+ years in the world of advertising and marketing as an Account Manager and Director of Marketing and New Business Development, managing multi-million dollar accounts from male enhancement medications to beer ads. In 2011, Michelle left the corporate world for the opportunity to raise her daughter.

Introduction

"Words mean more than what is set down on paper. It takes the human voice to infuse them with shades of deeper meaning."

—Maya Angelou

There is little doubt that communication is one of man's most important tools. We use the tool (speaking, listening, graphic expression, and writing) to make sense of our world; to interact with other people; to network; and to express our feelings, moods, and intent. Communications, particularly our words, affect who and what we are as a species. How we use words has a major impact on the kind of world we create for ourselves and others. The roles of leaders, managers, and executives has not changed much since man became civilized but the mythologies—the way we carry out the roles—has changed.

There is a quotation attributed to Plutarch, although there are no sources that can trace it to him, which goes, "When Cicero spoke, people said, 'How well Cicero speaks!' But, when Demosthenes spoke, they said, 'Let us march against Phillip.'" The point here is that when leaders speak, it is usually, but not always, to persuade. Sometimes the purpose is to inform, but as Rudyard Kipling said, "Words are the most powerful drug used by mankind" so whenever we speak, we are using a powerful human tool. Thomas Fuller may have said it best, "When the heart is afire, some sparks will fly out of the mouth." This book will give you some sparks.

This book is not intended to teach specific skills of leadership, management, or even public speaking, oration, rhetoric, or how to deliver a good presentation. You will not learn detailed skills of visualization, or in-depth channeling of your message. You will not learn details of tone, cadence, pitch, or resonance. You will not learn the details of nonverbal body language such as hand and arm gestures. However, it is a book that will introduce these concepts (and hopefully you will explore them further on your own).

It is a book that can help make you a better leader, manager, or supervisor by helping you become a more powerful, more effective communicator. It can do this because it will help you choose the most powerful verbs—the spark of sentences—powerful verbs that will resonate deeply with people, powerful verbs that people will react to and remember.

I am referring to the power verbs that are the flame that makes phrases and sentences that will ignite peoples' passions, the power verbs that kindle, illuminate purpose, and make people want to take action…to march on Phillip.

Michael Faulkner

1

The Technology and Power of Language

Why a book on verbs, you may be asking? Not just verbs, but "power verbs." There are a couple of reasons. First, there are already more books on language skills and specifically verbs than you can imagine, so the world does not need another one of those books. Second, it would not be much fun to write or read another boring language skills book (not that all the other books on verbs are boring). But, if they were so interesting, wouldn't there be a movie or a music video of one of these books by now? Lastly, this isn't a book about the old standby verbs. Everyone knows the 16 basic English language verbs: *be*, *do*, *have*, *come*, *go*, *see*, *seem*, *give*, *take*, *keep*, *make*, *put*, *send*, *say*, *let*, and *get*. We won't spend much time of these.

Power verbs, on the other hand, are verbs that are emotionally edgy, powerfully positioned, with a kick, punch, and pizzazz. There will be more on these gregarious verbs later.

There are hundreds of books, guidebooks, blogs, and other ways for people to learn about how to use verbs and grammar. However, we wrote this book because in our combined half century of experience in leading, teaching, managing, mentoring, coaching, and marketing (and, oh yes, parenting), we learned one fundamental truth: It's the combination of the chosen word(s) and the power of the way they are delivered—the rhythm—that makes the greatest difference in how people receive and react to words. We also realized that using power verbs adds color, flavor, spark, enhanced rhythm, and kick to our written words as well, such as poems, plays, and other writing. We have noticed that many writers and speakers hang safely to bland "verbs of being." Just as a reminder, verbs of being are forms of the infinitive *to be*—*am*, *are*, *is*, *was*, *were*, *be*, *being*, *been*, *have*, *had*, *might*, *may*, *must*, *could*, *can*, *would*, *will*, *should*, and *shall*. No one has to tell you these tend to be stylistically passive, stiff, somewhat bland, dull, and pedantic—somewhat boring, but safe. Of course, sometimes these verbs of being are necessary and that is when they should be used—when necessary.

LET'S TAKE A MOMENT AND THINK ABOUT LANGUAGE

"Words are the counters of wise men, and the money of fools."
—Thomas Hobbes

One of the peculiar characteristics of our culture is how we deal with communicating with one another. Communication is perhaps the most important human function in which we engage and we don't do it very well and aren't trained very well. Because we don't trust our instincts driven by our amygdala (which some refer to as our animal brain) as much as we should, we have trouble really absorbing the nonverbal human communications adequately.

Think about all our acculturation that teaches us to deny our amygdala-driven instincts (e.g., "We'll cross that bridge when we come to it," "Don't judge a book by its cover," "Don't jump to conclusions," "Look before you leap," "Act in haste, repent at your leisure," "We should have a committee meeting to talk it over first"). In spite of the knowledge of how much communication is transferred by nonverbal cues, there is very little education and training in our schools to improve human nonverbal perception.

We know from empirical research that an overwhelming amount of human communications (as much as 97%) is conveyed by nonverbal cues. These nonverbal cues are what some people refer to as body language. Much of this body language is found in various facial expressions. Research has shown that in spite of wide cultural differences in language and cultural norms, there are eight universal facial nonverbal expressions recognized throughout the world. Dr. Paul Ekman spent years studying facial cues and discovered 190 muscles in the nose and eye region of humans; many of these muscles respond involuntary and are keys to determine whether a person is telling the truth or lying. Some of these muscle movements are so subtle that only a trained expert can detect movement. However, most people "feel" these by their amygdala, the almond-shaped portion of their brain or what some refer to as the animal or reptile brain. Long before humans developed our thinking brain—the cerebral cortex—our amygdala functioned and provided the fight-or-flight emotion. Fortunately for our species, we chose flight early on in a hostile environment where we were outgunned by bigger, faster, and fiercer predators. We were low on the food chain but had the advantage of having the amygdala, which allowed our species to survive and evolve.

For the 3% of human communication that is conveyed by language, we generally don't listen as effectively as we could and our educational system often fails students and society with minimal communication skills (writing and speaking skills). When you consider that communication is how we express almost every desire, need, emotion, feeling, want, expectation, demand, and frustration to other humans, it is surprising and disappointing that lower forms of life do a better job of communicating.

We know that man communicated with other men for thousands of years prior to the invention of human language. Long before human verbal language, people found mates, raised families, hunted together, joined in early tribal communities, and selected leaders, but there was virtually no innovation, hardly any art or crafts, no real trade or commerce, and a very short life span. Then came language and everything changed.

This book is by no means an attempt to explain any particular theory of human development, but merely an extremely simplified explanation of how language may have developed for the purposes of positioning language as an important component of your culture.

Kevin Kelly wrote a book in 2010 entitled *What Technology Wants*. In this provocative book, Kelly introduced a brand-new view of technology in which he suggests that technology is not just hardwired metal and chips, but a living, natural system whose origin goes back to the big bang.

My intention is not to review the book. However, I would recommend it be read by every manager, supervisor, boss, mentor, coach, influencer, instigator, team leader, team member, entrepreneur, capitalist, investor, futurist, investor, provocateur, teacher, professor, minister, government employee, politician, or new parent.

One point of Kelly's book to which I will refer is the point he makes with regard to the technology of language. However, to get to that point, it is necessary to cover some human history, so stay with me for a little while.

We know humans developed language about 50,000 years ago. There are theories that language developed slowly and other theories that it developed more or less spontaneously. For our discussion, it doesn't matter how language developed—it only matters that human language developed about 50,000 years ago. Kelly traces the development of human language to the behavior of humans. By tracing the behavior of the human species, we can follow Kelly's argument that language followed certain human behavior patterns.

At some point about 2.5 million years ago, the human brain grew larger and we began to use more refined tools than our ape line. Archaeological evidence shows the growth of human brains and simple stone tools. At this point, the first migration began out of Africa for two human species—Neanderthal to Europe and Homo erectus to Asia—sapiens remained in Africa. It is important to note all three species had the same brain size and same rough tools. Over the next 50 million years, all three species developed at about the same pace (none with language skills). All three species hunted with simple tools, developed crude art, had children, lived relatively short lives, did not bury their dead, and the population of these groups remained unchanged. This was the Mesolithic Period.

Then around 50,000 years ago, something radically different changed, something radical happened, something very radically different occurred. The sapiens in Africa suddenly underwent significant genetic changes. The sapiens became full of ideas and innovations and developed the desire to innovate, move, and explore new worlds. They spread out of Africa in what is known as the second migration and in 40,000 years had settled in every corner of the earth.

In a fraction of 1 percent of the time it took for the first migration to take place and for the first wave to settle in one spot, the sapiens covered the world. Not only did the sapiens have the desire to move, but they were also full of innovation. They developed fishhooks, fishnets, variable size spears and bows and arrows, sewing, and hearth stoves; they buried their dead; and they created sophisticated art and jewelry. Sapiens developed trade, pottery, and animal traps and built garbage pits. In the process of mastering all these innovative things, they overwhelmed their Neanderthal and Homo erectus brothers, leaving sapiens the only human species on the planet.

The question we have to ask is what caused the radical change in sapiens? How did it occur? It can be argued that there was a point mutation or a rewiring of the brain was the cause. We are not proposing a cause, only stating the fact that there was an outcome that something radically changed, that something happened, that something very different occurred 50,000 years ago, and that radical change was language occurred and radically changed mankind forever.

WHAT IS THE SPECIAL SIGNIFICANCE OF LANGUAGE?

Language accelerates learning; it speeds up innovation by permitting communication and coordination. A new idea can be spread quickly if someone can explain it and communicate it to others before they have to discover it themselves.

Taking the new technology one step further, language gave sapiens and us autogeneration, which is the ability of the mind to question itself. It is a mirror that reveals to the mind what the mind is thinking, allowing self-awareness and self-reference, and language explains the innovations and ideas that have formed in the mind. Without language, we could not access the bank of thoughts and ideas. We could not tell stories, interpret case studies, or compare things; we could not consciously create.

We use language, verbal and nonverbal, to make sense of our world. We use it to interact, confirm, beg, act, command, inquire, network, court, teach, coach, and entertain. A few verbal and nonverbal messages can influence us, can change our minds, can cause us to do something different, or can change our position or vote. Words affect who we are. Without words, we would be isolated. Language and its nuances are uniquely human.

Language is something we learn completely by audio cues—by listening. We do this because human brains are hardwired—genetically prewired to learn language by listening as an infant. It is interesting that we are not even consciously aware we are cognitively learning. Before we had the ability to speak words, others could understand us. Our species survived and advanced, making other members understand with nonverbal cues. For millions of years, children communicated to their mothers that they were hungry. Men communicated to women and women to men that they were interested in them as partners. Hunters collaborated on big animal kills long before a word was spoken; man even showed another how to start and keep a fire going long before there were words for such things. Anthropologists believe the spoken word appeared on the scene around 50,000 BC—a long time to use grunts and pointing and body language.

The special significance of language as a great idea lies in the fact that it is related to all other great ideas insofar as ideas and thoughts are expressed to other persons, for the most part, in words, in speech, in language.

In Plato's dialogues, he used Socrates as a character and he spoke of people continually, calling attention to the slippery nature of words and how sometimes words conceal thoughts as well as express them. In more modern times, philosophers like Hobbes and Locke wrote about the abuse of words and how language should be used.

Today, we sort of view language as an enemy, a barrier to communication, a tyranny of words. There is even a debate over whether communications and speech are the same thing.

THE POWER OF WORDS

"The great use of words is to hide our thoughts."
—*Voltaire*

As Dr. Frank Luntz says, "It's not what you say. It's what people hear" (Luntz 2007, xi). The meaning of this is the audience will translate your message through a prism of their own biases, interests, knowledge, awareness, feelings, attention span, and many other interpretative filters.

Once you have spoken words, they are no longer yours. Other people will translate them, evaluate them, and measure them. Choose your words, make them appropriate for the situation, and be aware of the power of words. Poorly chosen words or speech used for personal, hubris, or evil can impact self-esteem, destroy morale, kill enthusiasm, inflame bias, incite hatred, lower expectations, hold people back, and even make people physically or mentally ill. Inappropriate words can make work and home toxic, abusive environments. There are many empirical studies showing that people who live and/or work in toxic environments suffer more colds, more cases of flu, more heart attacks, more depression, more of almost all chronic disorders, physical and emotional, than people who report living and/or working in happy, enjoyable, caring environments.

The old parental advice, "Sticks and stones can break your bones, but words can never hurt you," was simply bad advice. However, well-chosen words or speech for the benefit of good or hope for others can motivate or inspire others to greater feats and deeds. They can offer hope; create vision; impact thinking beliefs and behavior of others; and alter results of strategy, plans, objectives, and people's lives.

Peggy Noonan, the national syndicated columnist, knows a thing or two about words and how they impact us. She wrote recently about the advice Clare Boothe Luce once gave the newly inaugurated U.S. President John F. Kennedy. Ms. Luce was truly a remarkable woman. Her career spanned seven decades and nearly as many professional interests—journalism, politics, theatre, diplomacy, and intelligence.

According to Ms. Noonan, the sentence idea comes from a story Clare Boothe Luce told about a conversation she had in 1962 in the White House with her old friend John F. Kennedy. She said she told him that "a great man is one sentence." His leadership can be so well summed up in a single sentence that you don't have to hear his name to know who's being talked about. "He preserved the union and freed the slaves" or "He lifted us out of a great depression and helped to win a World War." You didn't have to be told "Lincoln" or "FDR."

She wondered what Kennedy's sentence would be. She was telling him to concentrate, to know the great themes and demands of his time, and focus on them. It was good advice. History has imperatives, and sometimes they are clear. Sometimes they are met, and sometimes not. When they're clear and met, you get quite a sentence (*The Wall Street Journal* 2009).

Let's look at a more contemporary example: the historic 2012 presidential debates. These debates may have more significance than previous ones because of the words chosen by the candidates, their rhythm, and their physical, nonverbal cues. A big part of communicating successfully depends on how well we negotiate the paradox of how the vast majority of human communication is conducted.

We know that more than 97% of human communication involves non-verbal cues (body language). To have a successful presentation, speech, or presidential debate performance, we must compose a sophisticated but seamless message, uniting our words in the proper rhythm, and use the corresponding nonverbal cues. If the words chosen don't match the nonverbal cues or vice versa, the audience will be confused and the message will be diminished or, worse, ignored.

In the world of movies, theater, art, and entertainment, words have a dramatic impact. In a recent *Wall Street Journal* edition, a special report entitled "What's In a Name?" discussed a number of box office successes that might have had a different result if their original titles had not been changed. For example, the Bogart classic *Casablanca* had an original title of *Everybody Comes to Ricks*. The Julia Roberts/Richard Gere blockbuster *Pretty Woman* had an original title of *$3,000*. The successful *G.I. Jane* was supposed to be released as *In Defense of Honor*. The world might not have ever remembered Diane Keaton and Woody Allen in *Anhedonia*, which was fortunately changed to *Annie Hall* (*Wall Street Journal* 2012).

Words have the power to affect both the physical and emotional health of people to whom we speak, for better or for worse. Words used to influence are inspiring, uplifting, and challenging. They encourage, motivate, and persuade; they can be visionary; they can change people's lives for the better. Verbal communication is a powerful human instrument and we must learn to use it properly. We need to not only learn to think about speaking in new ways, but also learn to think about language and human nature, psychology, and sociology.

Throughout history, there have been many examples of memorable quotes to demonstrate how what is said is just as important as how it was said. For example, when Lyndon B. Johnson was stumping for political office, he was debating an opponent and was asked the difference between himself and the opposing candidate. He famously replied, "He matriculated and I never matriculated."

Some of the most famous speeches made by Abraham Lincoln are memorable not just for the message, but also for the fact that he condensed an enormous amount of information into them. It was not only the power of his words, but also his cadence that made the impact of the speeches more powerful. His second inaugural speech was only 700 words and the Gettysburg Address was just under three minutes.

The power of words can actually harm others. Power verbs express an action that is to be taken or that has been taken. When used correctly, a powerful verb has the power to impact your life whether you are going into battle, running for president, or simply interviewing for a job. Researchers have observed that when students are given standardized tests and told the tests are "intelligence exams," the average scores are from 10% to 20% lower than when the same exam is given to similar students and told it is "just an exam."

We know that words create impressions, ideas, images, concepts, and facsimiles. Therefore, the words that we hear and read influence how we think and consequently how we behave. This means there is a correlation between the words we select and use and the results that occur.

Using powerful verbal imagery helps people to imagine vivid images and allows people to figuratively and literally see concepts being mentioned. This was first discovered in the early twentieth century and was initially known as the Perky effect and later called visual simulation. Individuals can project abstract thoughts. Almost everyone does this from time to time, but we refer to it as daydreaming. When a person daydreams, he is completely awake and his eyes are wide open, yet he imagines being somewhere else, doing something else.

Visual simulation impacts what people hear and how fast they respond. A cognitive psychologist, Rolf Zwann, has done a lot of research on the topic of what impact in terms of visual simulation is there when objects are in different orientations and shapes and people are asked to describe the objects, particularly if the people are prompted with words or sentences with the object beforehand. The results indicate people respond faster because what they see and hear were mentally simulated beforehand (Bergen 2012, 95). Many studies have confirmed that people construct visual simulations of objects they hear or read about.

People construct shape and orientation simulation. Studies show that when people listened, they more often looked at the set of objects that fit with the meaning of the verb, even before they heard the name of the relevant object. People make predictions about what the rest of the sentence will contain as soon as words that they have already heard start to constrain what could reasonably follow. People start to cobble their understanding of the sentence incrementally (Bergen 2012, 125).

Grammar helps get the visual simulation going by pulling together all the pieces contributed by the words in the correct configuration. People will more easily and clearly understand and comprehend your meaning if you have structured your sentence correctly. One particular form is transitive sentences. It is one that has a transfer of possession meaning. They start with a noun or noun phrases, are followed by a verb, and then have one or two noun phrases. The following is an example:

The outgoing CEO **kicked the problem down the road** to the new CEO.

If we use the intended transfer definition, the transitive describes an intended transfer of an object to a recipient, and, naturally, the recipient must be capable of receiving something (Bergen 2012, 106).

Words we use and the impact they have can even be impacted by our background and other influences. Consider the words *buy* and *invest.* If you are selling life insurance, you want the customer to buy, but in your mind, the purchase is a long-term investment. The premiums will be invested, the face value of the policy will grow, there will eventually be loan value, and the investment will appreciate beyond the purchase price.

However, the customer thinks in terms of buying and how much it costs. The issue comes full circle again if the customer does buy and if he or she wants the insurance company to make good investments.

Nan Russell, writing for *Career Know-How*, introduces this word choice: problem or challenge. Would you rather your boss see your mistake as a problem or a challenge? Is it just semantics? Problems are things that are fixed; challenges are met. Different words evoke a set of different emotions and different feelings. People usually have a much more positive feeling about "meeting a challenge" than "fixing a problem."

There is information about the medicinal benefits of power verbs as well as a warning about the power of words which, if used inappropriately, can actually cause individuals to become ill.

"In the study, published in *Pain*, researchers used functional magnetic resonance tomography (fMRI) to examine how 16 healthy people processed words associated with experiencing pain. The brain scans revealed which parts of the brain were activated in response to hearing the words.

In the first experiment, researchers asked the participants to imagine situations that corresponded with words associated with pain—such as 'excruciating,' 'paralyzing,' and 'grueling'—as well as negative but non-pain associated words such as 'dirty' and 'disgusting' and neutral and positive words. In the second experiment, the participants read the same words but were distracted by a brainteaser.

The results showed that in both cases there was a clear response in the brain's pain-processing centers with the words associated with pain, but there was no such activity pattern in response to the other words. Researchers say preserving painful experiences as memories in the brain may have been an evolutionary response to allow humans to avoid painful situations that might be dangerous." (http://www.webmd.com/pain-management/news/20100402/words-really-do-hurt)

Using Words in Special Ways

Words are used to paint pictures. Public speakers, teachers, radio broadcasters, and people who have an audience listening to a voice as their primary medium for communication paint pictures with words.

Weave in Beautiful Words

What words make you feel warm and happy? Sure, it's different for all of us, but there are some words with universal appeal (at least in English). The British Council, which oversees education of the English language, conducted a study of the "Most Beautiful Words in the English Language."

40,000 people participated in the study. The top ten words were the following:

1. Mother
2. Passion
3. Smile
4. Love
5. Eternity
6. Fantastic
7. Destiny
8. Freedom
9. Liberty
10. Tranquility

In our culture, there appears to be a growing trend of taking words that are nouns and converting them into verbs. *Verbed* (a word that has been used by many in the social media blogosphere to signify that so many nouns have become verbs in our everyday language) has made its way into the mainstream and is used in everyday language.

THE IMPACT OF POWER VERBS

People, especially the millennial generation (those born after 1977), don't talk much on the phone anymore; they text each other. Although texting is fine for quick, impersonal communications, it should never be substituted for professional communication. This phenomenon of taking nouns and turning them into verbs means that the English language is constantly evolving and changing, and therefore style manuals are outdated before they even hit the shelves, which is why this book is not a style manual.

This book does not attempt to identify these urbane, hip, or chic fad words. Instead, a number of nouns that are now action verbs have been included in this compilation because in today's business culture, the commonly accepted practice is to include particular noun/verbs in the vernacular. Examples of these nouns that have also become accepted action verbs include the following:

Noun	Action Verb
Silo	Siloed
E-mail	E-mailed
Spam	Spammed
Message	Messaged

The impact of action verbs and how they are woven into our collective conscience is evident in the names that advertisers use for their products. For everyday items, we associate those products with action verbs. For example, the **Accord** car model, **Act** mouthwash, **Agree** shampoo, **Allure** ski product, **Ban** deodorant, **Budget** Rent A Car, **Converse** sneakers, **Dodge** cars, **Eclipse** exercise machine, **Endeavor** spaceship, **Edge** shaving cream, **Equal** sugar substitute, **Escalade** Cadillac, **Excel** software, **Glamour** magazine, **Gleem** toothpaste, **Google** the company, **Intuit** software, **Kindle** e-reader, **Marvel** comics, **Pilot** pens, **Pledge** cleaner, **Pioneer** sound systems, **Puff** tissues, **Quip** the precursor to the fax machine, **Raid** bug killer, **Shuffle** iPod product, **Spam**, **Target** retail store, and **Vanish** home-cleaning product. There are many more…these are just a few examples.

Over the course of time, the inconsistency of English grammar has made it increasingly difficult for nonnative speakers to learn English and even difficult for those who speak English as a first language to speak correctly. Some rules and styles are antiquated and not enforced. As a result, we have become lazy and are losing the war on poor grammar. English is a minefield of rules, and while I can assure you that this book is not a style manual, it goes without saying that if you were to follow all of the rules, then you would have to spend a lifetime studying them, you would end up speaking a language that a normal person would not understand, and, finally, you would be a complete bore.

As with any rule, there are also exceptions, counterexceptions, special rules, do's and don'ts, and other confusing rules. There are over 60 different rules and variations of rules for verbs alone. Once you have learned the rules, you still have to follow exceptions. For example, consider the word *lightning* used as a verb. We say it is "thundering and lightning all night." In this case, it is the only exception to the rule that *ing* can be added to the base verb to produce the -ing form. We do not say or write it as "thundering and lightninging all night," nor do we say or write it as "thundered and lightning all night"; in another exception to the rules, we say "we relayed a message" but "we relaid a carpet" (Crystal 1995, 205).

For all my former English teachers, professors, and the dedicated writers of the grammar books on linguistic style and theory who will wonder why there is nothing in this book about active and passive voice, conjugation, copulas, indicative, imperative, subjunctive mood, gradability and comparison, person and number usage, verbal dueling, lexical, linking verbs, modal, primary, axillary, serial, deflective and transitive or intransitive usage, that is your job. This guide can be thought of as a road map to help individuals toward success in everyday communications. It is that simple!

There is no attempt to excuse people from their responsibility and duty to learn the language correctly. However, there is a time and place for everything. Noam Chomsky, perhaps the most influential figure in the theoretical linguistics of the English language in recent times, conceived the goal of linguistics (all the rules, principles, and regulations) as a description of the mental grammar of native speakers.

Chomsky perceives linguistics to be the system of all these rules to those that characterize the mental structure that underlies our ability to speak and understand the language. Furthermore, Chomsky hypothesizes that humans have an innate language ability that enables children to acquire a mental grammar quickly when they are exposed to a particular language.

It's pretty amazing to think that a child learns an entire language by listening and some nonverbal cues. By the age of five, a person has about 70% of their lifetime vocabulary and linguistic rules learned by listening and observation.

Chomsky (and this is the last reference to a theorist or an intellectual, I promise) draws a distinction between competence in a language and performance in a language. Competence is the underlying knowledge of the theory and applications, whereas performance is the actual use made of that knowledge. This book doesn't assume anything; it provides a performance tool for one part of the language—POWER VERBS.

2

The Connection Between Communications and Success in Leadership and Management

"Volatility of words is carelessness in actions; words are the wings of actions."

—*Lavater*

There are two factors for which there are mountains of empirical evidence that overwhelmingly account for the success of individuals in any field. Those two factors are the verbal and networking skills of the successful people.

Common sense and simple observation can be your laboratory. Just look at most of the people you know or people you have worked for. Furthermore, look at the people who ran or owned the organizations and firms for which you, or people you know, have worked. Think about the people who owned and ran the vendor firms and organizations that serviced and supplied the firms and organizations for which you, or people you know, have worked. If you think about it, what is it that most of these people have in common?

The vast majority of these people have big vocabularies and extensive networks. Consequently, that is probably a primary reason why many are successful and they are the managers, leaders, and owners of businesses and organizations as well as civic and social leaders. The common denominator of most successful people in a cross section of fields isn't education, family, money, race, or gender…It's what they know and who they know!

It has long been known that successful executives do not have large, useful vocabularies merely because of their positions. That would be an incorrect correlation and not a proper explanation of cause and effect. In fact, it is the opposite that is true. Successful business executives (as well as successful people in other fields) are successful because they are helped tremendously to advance by their skills in vocabulary—and networking (Funk and Lewis 1942, 3).

Leadership is not something achieved by birthright or tenure but rather something that is gained by followers acclaiming someone as their leader. This is a consequence of the leader's behavior, actions, work, effort, results, intentions, plans, world view, responses, what they practice, and mostly what they do and say in every moment of every opportunity.

The 80/20 principle (Parato's law) is in practice for leaders. Twenty percent of what a leader does is technique and process (i.e., tools, methodology) and 80% is actions (i.e., behavior, communications).

It has been said before: It isn't what you say that matters but how you say it that really counts. Dr. Frank Luntz takes it a step further and claims it isn't what you say that counts—it's what people hear. The issue is you have to choose your words! In addition, you have to time the right words and give the right words the necessary emphasis by the correct supporting body language so the receiver fully grasps what is being said and has no pause or hesitation in understanding your meaning (Luntz, 2007).

This guide is all about power verbs and how they can help you be a much more effective communicator and by extension a more successful consultant, coach, and mentor.

Verbs are the catalysts of sentences. Power verbs bring sentences to life. More to the point, the right power verbs bring conversations, meetings, speeches, directives, résumés, memos, speeches, presentations, networking contacts, sales plans, marketing plans, business and branding plans, and sales proposals to life. Frankly, the right power verbs can put a pop into all interpersonal communications.

The definitive source for the English language, the *Oxford English Dictionary*, states it this way: "It is a simple truth that in most sentences you should express action through verbs just as you do when you speak. Yet in so many sentences the verbs are smothered; all their vitality trapped beneath heavy noun phrases based on the verbs themselves" (Oxford English Dictionary, 1991).

A successful leader, manager, or supervisor will make use of the power of human communication to give expressive life to his or her strategies, operational plans, directives, proposals, ideas, and positions. Human communications is, of course, a combination of nonverbal cues (body language) and the actual words spoken. Even the words that are chosen to be spoken by successful leaders, managers, and executives are frequently invigorated and fortified with linguistic enhancement, such as metaphors, similes, figures of speech, and other vigorous uses of imagery, including hyperbole.

Sometimes the words are combined in rhythmic and symbolic phrasing called alliteration, repetition, antithesis, and parallelism. Successful leaders, managers, and supervisors are generally considered to be good communicators or at least it is recognized that communication skills are necessary for them to succeed. These people can enhance their positions with their staff, direct reports, stakeholders, upper-level management, vendors, media, and others with greater communication skills, including the use of stories, citing references, using quotations, or using figures of speech with two very, very important caveats. Whatever is used has to be fresh and it has to be apropos. Tired metaphors, idioms, similes, figures of speech, old stories, and lame references are worse than none at all. More important, using an inappropriate phrase, figure of speech, metaphor, simile, or a poor analogy can hamper communications.

For those readers who are old enough to remember, recall when live radio entertainment included speakers who had to sell the listeners on the plot or story by painting verbal pictures with words. Today, we still have the need to create vivid imagery in our daily communications with what we say and how we say it. Furthermore, we have one more issue: We are dealing with a more attention-conflicted audience. So, we add a third need: We have to be aware of the fact that it is not always what we say that matters, or even how we say it, but now we have to deal with what it is that people hear.

There are so many filtering biases, prejudices, attention sappers, and diversions that many people simply do not hear what has been said; instead, they hear only what they want or need to hear. We cannot always control this phenomenon, nor do we want to, but we need to be aware of this dynamic.

VERB FORMS

We say that verbs are a part of speech that describes an action or occurrence or indicates a state of being. Most of the time (there we go with those nasty grammar rules and their confounding exceptions), it makes more sense to define a verb by what it does than by what it is. By doing this, verbs can serve as either a noun or a verb, and the same verb can play a number of different roles depending on how it's used.

Put simply, verbs move our sentences along in a variety of ways. Power verbs really make the sentence jump.

Speaking of jumping…there are more forms than we will want to cover here, so let's jump to just the ones we want to cover.

Progressive Forms

The Present Progressive Tense—Verbs Showing ONGOING ACTION

The present progressive tense is one form that describes an action that is ongoing and one that is happening at the same moment for which the action is being spoken about or written about.

To form this tense, use **am/is/are** with the verb form ending in **-ing**.

Examples:

I **am meeting** with the others tomorrow. [present progressive ongoing action—using am + -ing]

The project management team **is examining** the stakeholder's proposal. [present progressive ongoing action—using is + -ing]

The team members **are researching** ideation and other options. [present progressive ongoing action—using are + -ing]

She **is** happy.

Use the present tense to describe something that is true regardless of time.

Past Progressive Tense—Verbs Showing SIMULTANEOUS ACTION

The past progressive tense is one that describes an action that was happening when another action occurred. To form this tense, use **was/were** with the verb form ending in **-ing**.

Examples:

The new project team **was presenting** its recent findings when the power went out. [past progressive on simultaneous action—using was + -ing]

Four team members **were meeting** with the sponsor when the news broke about the award. [past progressive on simultaneous action—using were + -ing]

Future Progressive Tense—Verbs Showing FUTURE ACTION

The future progressive tense is one that describes an action that is ongoing or continuous and one that will take place in the future. This tense is formed by using the verbs **will be** or **shall be** with the verb form ending in **-ing**.

Examples:

Only one team member **will be presenting** during the annual meeting in June. [future progressive on future action—using will be + -ing]

The clock **is** ticking. [future progressive on future action—using is + -ing]

The band **is** playing. [future progressive on future action—using is + -ing]

The clock **ticks**.

The band **plays**.

When the progressive form is not used for continuing events, a dramatic style effect can be produced.

Present Perfect Progressive—Verbs Showing PAST ACTION, CONTINUOUS ACTION, POSSIBLY ONGOING ACTION

The present perfect progressive tense is one that describes an action that began in the past, continues in the present, and may continue into the future. To form this tense, use **has/have been** and the present participle of the verb (the verb form ending in **-ing**).

Example:

The project sponsor **has been considering** an increase in the budget.

Past Perfect Progressive—Verbs Showing PAST ACTION, ONGOING ACTION COMPLETED BEFORE SOME OTHER PAST ACTION

The past perfect progressive tense describes a past, ongoing action that was completed before some other past action. This tense is formed by using **had been** and the present perfect of the verb (the verb form ending in **-ing**).

Example:

Before the budget increase, the project team **had been participating** in many sponsor meetings.

Future Perfect Progressive—Verbs Showing ONGOING ACTION OCCURRING BEFORE SOME SPECIFIED TIME

The future perfect progressive tense describes a future, ongoing action that will occur before some specified future time. This tense is formed by using **will have been** and the present participle of the verb (the verb form ending in **-ing**).

Example:

By the next fiscal year, the new product development project team **will have been researching** and **proposing** more than 60 new product categories.

Lastly, we need to mention transitive and intransitive verbs.

An intransitive verb has two characteristics. First, it is an *action verb,* expressing a doable activity like *arrive, go, lie, sneeze, sit, die,* and so on. Second, unlike a *transitive verb,* it will not have a *direct object* receiving the action.

Here are some examples of intransitive verbs:

Huffing and puffing, we **arrived** at the church with only seconds to spare. [**Arrived** = intransitive verb]

Jorge **went** to the campus café for a bowl of hot chicken noodle soup. [**Went** = intransitive verb]

To escape the midday heat, the dogs **lie** in the shade under our trees. [**Lie** = intransitive verb]

Around fresh ground pepper, Sheryl **sneezes** with violence. [**Sneezes** = intransitive verb]

In the early morning, mom **sits** on the front porch to admire her beautiful flowers. [**Sits** = intransitive verb]

Flipped on its back, the roach that Dee dosed with pest repellent **dies** under the stove. [**Dies** = intransitive verb]

Sorry, Ms. Finney (seventh-grade English teacher), I know you would want me to talk about transitive and intransitive verbs, lexical and auxiliary verbs, compound verbs, copulas, prepositional phrases, gerunds, participles, adverbs, tense, aspect, mood, model and nonmodel verbs, subjects, objects, complements, modifiers, and so on, but I promised this would not be a style manual.

3

How to Use This Book

If you have a presentation or a speech to give, there are basic rules of the road for every presentation. The following are the fundamental rules for any presentation, in addition to including power verbs. You will find different rules in other sources on how to use verbs in your sentences, but these rules are summarized from 35 years of personal experience and research:

1. Know to whom you are speaking. You have to know who will be listening to you. Who are the people, and what is their education, work history, and social and behavioral backgrounds?

2. Prepare, prepare, prepare. What you say and how you say it are both important elements. As a coach, mentor, leader, manager, or executive, your position gives you power, prestige, and elevated authority. People look up to you.

3. People read your body language and especially your nonverbal cues before your words. They begin to interpret the meaning of what you are saying before you are finished, so your nonverbal clues and language should connect with the thoughts and ideas you want to get expressed.

4. Select tone, style, pitch, rate, and time that is appropriate.

5. From the following lists, carefully select powerful verbs that add punch to your sentences.

In this book, power verbs are arranged alphabetically. You still have to put the rest of your sentences together using good grammar, style, syntax, and tense, but the power, muscle, clout, and sway of your sentences and phrases will come from your power verbs.

As previously stated in Chapter 2, it is the responsibility of managers and executives of organizations to use words in a way that makes the organization's mission and vision clear to the stakeholders. Then the managers and executives must set the goals and objectives using words that drive the organization forward.

LEADERSHIP STYLES

There are literally dozens and dozens of leadership styles that have been written about, discussed, taught, and bantered about. Without giving credence to one or another, one taxonomy has been selected for this book. It was adapted from *The Wall Street Journal Essential Guide to Management* by Alan Murray, published by HarperBusiness. In the book *Primal Leadership*, Daniel Goleman, who popularized the notion of "Emotional Intelligence," describes six different styles of leadership. The most effective leaders can move among these styles, adopting the one that meets the needs of the moment. They can all become part of the leader's repertoire.

In the book, leadership is discussed as something that is less about the needs of the leader, and more about the needs of the people and the organization being led. Leadership styles are not something to be tried on like so many suits, to see which fits. Rather, they should be adapted to the particular demands of the situation, the particular requirements of the people involved, and the particular challenges facing the organization. The six styles identified in *Primal Leadership* are included as a taxonomy to provide readers with a context to view and use the power verbs in this book.

VISIONARY

This style is most appropriate when an organization needs a new direction. Its goal is to move people toward a new set of shared dreams. "Visionary leaders articulate where a group is going, but not how it will get there—setting people free to innovate, experiment, take calculated risks," wrote Mr. Goleman and his coauthors.

COACHING

This one-on-one style focuses on developing individuals, showing them how to improve their performance, and helping to connect their goals to the goals of the organization. Coaching works best, Mr. Goleman writes, "with employees who show initiative and want more professional development." But it can backfire if it's perceived as "micromanaging" an employee and undermines his or her self-confidence.

AFFILIATIVE

This style emphasizes the importance of teamwork and creates harmony in a group by connecting people to each other. Mr. Goleman argues this approach is particularly valuable "when trying to heighten team harmony, increase morale, improve communication or repair broken trust in an organization." But he warns against using it alone because its emphasis on group praise can allow poor performance to go uncorrected. "Employees may perceive," he writes, "that mediocrity is tolerated."

DEMOCRATIC

This style draws on people's knowledge and skills and creates a group commitment to the resulting goals. It works best when the direction the organization should take is unclear, and the leader needs to tap the collective wisdom of the group. Mr. Goleman warns that this consensus-building approach can be disastrous in times of crisis, when urgent events demand quick decisions.

COMMANDING

This is a classic model of "military" style leadership—probably the most often used, but the least often effective. Because it rarely involves praise and frequently employs criticism, it undercuts morale and job satisfaction. Mr. Goleman argues it is only effective in a crisis, when an urgent turnaround is needed. Even the modern military has come to recognize its limited usefulness.

The more than 450 power verbs in this book are listed in straight alphabetical order and the six leadership categories of Posner are just a way to demonstrate how the power verbs can be used by any leaders using any leadership style under any circumstance in any condition.

In most cases, the power verbs have examples of the specific word in actual use. These examples include the power verb used in sentences, in famous speeches, in quotations, and in newspaper and magazine articles. Some power verbs have a list of words that collocate or have a tendency to be found to be grouped or chunked with that power verb.

ADDITIONAL SUPPORT FOR YOU

To give readers an additional element of support, I have included a selection from Dr. Frank Luntz's list of the twenty-eight words that work for the twenty-first century (from his book *Words that Work: It's Not What You Say, It's What People Hear*):

1. Consequences: n. The phenomenon that follows and is caused by some previous phenomenon.

2. Impact: n. A forceful consequence; causes listeners to assume they will see and feel a measurable difference. It is no longer good enough to speak about potential solutions or best effort; people want results.

   Impact: v. To have an effect upon; causes listeners to assume they will see and feel a measurable difference. It is no longer good enough to speak about potential solutions or best effort; people want results.

3. Diplomacy: n. Subtle, skillful, peaceful, nondramatic solution to problems. People are tired of drama, anxiety, and tension; they want leadership in diplomacy.

4. Dialogue: n. Dialogue is the discussion of diplomatic issues.

5. Reliability: n. The quality of being dependable in a way that was expected or better.

6. Mission: n. An authentic and genuine purpose.

7. Commitment: n. Dedication to what one promised.

In addition to these aids, where possible and appropriate, examples of using the power verb in more vivid language phrasing and form are included. These include the following:

- **Alliteration**—The repetition of the consonant sound of close or adjoining words. An example of alliteration is "Step forward, Tin Man. You dare to come to me for a heart, do you? You **c**linking, **c**lanking, **c**lattering **c**ollection of **c**aliginous junk…And you, Scarecrow, have the effrontery to ask for a **b**rain! You **b**illowing **b**ale of **b**ovine fodder!"—delivered by Frank "Wizard of Oz" Morgan (from the movie *The Wizard of Oz*).

- **Antithesis**—The juxtaposition of contrasting ideas frequently in parallel structure. Examples might include "Ask not what your country can do for you, ask what you can do for your country" (John F. Kennedy) or "All men dream, but not equally. Those who dream by night in the dusty recesses of their minds, wake in the day to find that it was vanity: but the dreamers of the day are dangerous men, for they may act on their dreams with open eyes, to make them possible" (T. E. Lawrence).

- **Metaphor**—An implicit comparison between things that are essentially different yet have something in common. It is different from the simile because the metaphor does not contain words such as *like* or *as*. Examples of metaphors might include the following: The same sun warms rich and poor; "great managers manage by chess, good managers manage by checkers" (Marcus Buckinghame); "life is a journey, travel it well" (United Airlines); or "life is a zoo in a jungle" (Peter De Vries).

- **Parallelism**—A pair or series of related words, phrases, or sentences. An example of parallelism might include "We <u>defeated</u> communism. We <u>defeated</u> fascism. We <u>defeated</u> them on the field of battle, and we <u>defeated</u> them on the field of ideas" (Colin Powell).

- **Repetition**—Repeating the same word or set of words at the beginning or end of successive sentences, phrases, or clauses. Repetition usually results in parallelism and builds a strong cadence in the speaker's delivery. Examples of repetition are "We will not tire, we will not falter, and we will not fail" (George W. Bush). "The ever important murmur, dramatize it, dramatize it!" (Henry James, American expatriate writer, 1843–1916).

- **Similes**—An explicit comparison between things that are essentially different yet have something in common and always includes word such as *like* or *as*. Examples of similes might include *busy as a bee*, *hungry as a tiger*, or *light as a feather*. It is important to note that overuse of similes creates clichés and diminishes the vivid impression you were trying to create.

- **Vivid Imagery** —The use of vivid, figurative, expressive, or evocative language to represent themes, objects, actions, or ideas.

Here are some examples from the book:

ACHIEVE

(1) accomplish; attain; complete; conclude; do; finish; get; reach; perform; pull off; realize

(2) succeed in doing something

Word Used in Sentence(s)

(1), (2) "The results you <u>achieve</u> will be in direct proportion to the effort you apply."

—Denis Waitley

Word Used with Rhythm and Imagery

- **Alliteration**—If you help others **a**ccomplish their goals and **a**ttain their objectives, you will **achieve** your dreams.

- **Parallelism**—"Some people are born mediocre, some people <u>achieve</u> mediocrity, and some people have mediocrity thrust upon them" (Joseph Heller).

- **Repetition**—If you want to <u>achieve</u>, you have to rise early; if you want to <u>achieve</u>, you have to work hard every day; if you want to <u>achieve</u>, you have to accomplish something every day before you go to sleep.

ATTACK

(1) approach; assail; attempt to launch an assault; blast; fire; flank; onrush; onset; set upon; snipe

(2) to set to work on; take the initiative and go on the offensive

Word Used with Rhythm and Imagery

- **Alliteration**—"Men rise from one **a**mbition to another: first, they seek to secure themselves **a**gainst **attack**, **a**nd then they **attack** others" (Niccolo Machiavelli, Italian writer and statesman, Florentine patriot, author of *The Prince*, 1469–1527).

- **Antithesis**—"Invincibility lies in the defense; the possibility of victory in the *attack*" (Sun Tzu, Chinese general and author, 500 BC).

- **Metaphor**—"Yesterday, December 7th, 1941—a date which will live in infamy—the United States of America was suddenly and deliberately attacked by naval and air forces of the Empire of Japan" (President Franklin Roosevelt, Pearl Harbor address to the nation, Washington, D.C., 12/08/1941).

- **Repetition**—"Nobody ever defended anything successfully, there is only attack and attack and attack some more" (General George S. Patton, American general in World War I and II, 1885–1945).

- **Repetition**—"Yesterday, the Japanese government also launched an attack against Malaya.

  Last night, Japanese forces attacked Hong Kong.

  Last night, Japanese forces attacked Guam.

  Last night, Japanese forces attacked the Philippine Islands.

  Last night, the Japanese attacked Wake Island.

  And this morning, the Japanese attacked Midway Island" (President Franklin Roosevelt, Pearl Harbor address to the nation, Washington, D.C., 12/08/1941).

- **Simile**—Attack *as* viciously as a lioness attacking a gazelle in search of a meal for her cubs.

The list of power verbs that follow are displayed in alphabetical order. The list includes the power verb, several synonyms, an abbreviated definition, examples of the power verb used in sentences and quotes, and for many power verbs, words that the verbs collocates with.

4

Power Verbs for Managers and Executives

ABANDON

(1) abdicate; abjure; break off; cast aside; cede; cop out; desert; discard; drop; eliminate; forfeit; forgo; forsake; give over; give up; halt in progress; jettison; leave; not continue; quit; relinquish; renounce; surrender; throw over; yield; waive; walk out

(2) ease; lightheartedness; natural spontaneity; unrestraint; cast aside

(3) give in to emotion

Word Used in Sentence(s)

(1) We had to <u>abandon</u> plans to produce in China when the quality issues could not be resolved.

(1) "Once you start a working on something, don't be afraid of failure and don't <u>abandon</u> it. People who work sincerely are the happiest."

—Chanakya, Indian politician, strategist, and writer
(350 BC–275 BC)

Word Used with Rhythm and Imagery

- **Antithesis**—"Hope never abandons you; you <u>abandon</u> it" (George Weinberg, American psychologist, writer, and activist).
- **Vivid imagery**—"When you have faults, do not fear to abandon them" (Confucius, philosopher and political theorist, 551 BC–479 BC).

ABASH

(1)   to make ashamed; to embarrass

Word Used in Sentence(s)

(1) Ronnie felt <u>abashed</u> by her failure to remember all the names of the members of the executive committee of the board of directors.

Word Used with Rhythm and Imagery

- **Vivid imagery**—"<u>Abash'd</u> the Devil stood, And felt how awful goodness is, and saw Virtue in her shape how lovely" (John Milton, English poet, historian, and scholar, 1608–1674).

ABATE

(1)   die away; reduce; put an end to; slack; subside

Word Used in Sentence(s)

(1) Businesses are sometimes given tax <u>abatement</u> in return for building or expanding in economic depressed communities.

(1) "The decision to restrict gasoline sales was a departure for Mayor Michael Bloomberg and Gov. Andrew Cuomo, who had said last week that anticipated fuel shortages would have <u>abated</u> by now."

—York, Michael Howard. 2012. Gas Rationing Put in Place in New York. *Wall Street Journal*, November 19.

Word Used with Rhythm and Imagery

- **Parallelism**—"We should every night call ourselves to an account: what infirmity have I mastered to-day? what passions opposed? what temptation resisted? what virtue acquired? Our vices will <u>abate</u> of themselves if they be brought every day to the shrift" (Seneca, Roman philosopher, mid-1st century AD).

ABDICATE

(1)   to step down from a position of power or responsibility

Word Used in Sentence(s)

(1) I will ask Jon to <u>abdicate</u> his role as board chairman.

(1) If you cannot function as head of the new products development team, then you must <u>abdicate</u>.

Word Used with Rhythm and Imagery

- **Antithesis**—"Power <u>abdicates</u> only under the stress of counter-power" (Martin Buber, German Jewish biblical translator, philosopher, and interpreter, 1878–1965).

ABDUCE

(1) to advance evidence for; allege; cite

(2) to abduct; draw away

Word Used in Sentence(s)

(1) "If we <u>abduce</u> the eye unto either corner, the object will not duplicate."

—Sir Thomas Browne. English author (1605–1682)

(1) The project management team must <u>abduce</u> reasons for the cost overruns when there was no indication at the last stage gate of any such overage.

ABERRATE

(1) go astray; to diverge or deviate from the straight path; diverge from the expected

Word Used in Sentence(s)

(1) The CEO <u>aberrated</u> from being a perfect gentlemen.

ABET

(1) advocate; approve; assist; back; back up; encourage; espouse; foment; help incite; put up to; sanction; support; urge (especially in wrongdoing)

Word Used in Sentence(s)

(1) Although Jon had not benefited in the insider trading, he left himself open to charges of <u>abetting</u> the perpetrators by his association with them.

(1) "No state should be allowed to profess partnership with the global coalition against terror, while continuing to aid, <u>abet</u> and sponsor terrorism."

—Atal Bihari Vajpayee, Indian politician, former prime minister of India (1924–)

(1) "At first I wasn't sure that I had the talent, but I did know I had a fear of failure, and that fear compelled me to fight off anything that might <u>abet</u> it."

—Gordon Parks, American photographer, musician, writer (1912–2006)

(1) "The Court then agreed that the statute identifies the corporation as the "person" which may be found guilty of the misdemeanor of mis-branding or adulterating drugs. To reach corporate officers and man-agers, the Court relied on the historic conception of a misdemeanor under which any person aiding or assisting in the commission of a mis-demeanor is also guilty of the misdemeanor. Applying this principal, the Court found that while the statute technically implicated only the corpo-ration for the misdeed, 'All persons who aid and <u>abet</u> its commission are equally guilty.' Thus, the offense is committed by all who have a respon-sible share in the furtherance of the transaction that the statute outlaws. The Dotterweich case set the stage for United States v. Park, in which the president of Acme Markets, a food distributor, was charged with violat-ing section 301 of the FFDCA. Park was tried and convicted for failing to prevent exposure of food in his company's warehouse to rodent contamination."

—Darmody, Stephen. 1993. The Oil Pollution Act's Criminal Penalties: On a Collision Course with the Law of the Sea. *Boston College Environmental Affairs Law Review* 21 (1): 89.

ABORT

(1) abandon; call off; call a halt to; end; halt; stop progress of something

(2) cancel; terminate before completion

(3) interfere with the development

Word Used in Sentence(s)

(1) The drilling project using pressurized water drilling will have to be <u>aborted</u> due to the severe drought.

ABRIDGE

(1) abbreviate; condense; shorten; truncate; reduce the length of

Word Used in Sentence(s)

(1) <u>Abridge</u> provided that Congress shall make no law abridging the freedom of speech or of the press.

—U.S. Constitution, First Amendment

Word Used with Rhythm and Imagery

- **Antithesis**—"The use of the head abridges the labor of the hands" (Henry Ward Beecher, liberal U.S. congregational minister, 1813–1887).

Collocates to: immunities, law, privileges, rights

ABROGATE

(1) abolish; get rid of; negate; nullify by authority; repeal

Word Used in Sentence(s)

(1) *"[On love:] I have no respect for anyone who says they've given up, or that they're not looking or that they're tired. That is to abrogate one's responsibility as a human being."*

—Harlan Ellison, American writer (1934–)

(1) He should not abrogate that responsibility which is inherent to the chairman of the board.

Collocates to: contracts, rights, states, laws, treaties

ABSORB

(1) assimilate; acquire; attract; consume; digest; endure; engulf; fascinate; imbibe; insure; sustain; soak up; take in; use up

(2) to draw into oneself; grasp; realize; recognize; take in; understand

(3) to become captivated, interested, engaged, or preoccupied in; fascinated

Word Used in Sentence(s)

(1) "Smart is an elusive concept. There's a certain sharpness, an ability to absorb new facts. To ask an insightful question. To relate to domains that may not seem connected at first. A certain creativity that allows people to be effective."

—Bill Gates, American business magnate and philanthropist (1955–)

(1) Overhead costs have absorbed all our profits for the year.

(1) The acquiring firm will be absorbing our losses.

Word Used with Rhythm and Imagery

- **Metaphor**—"Unless a serpent devour a serpent it will not become a dragon. Unless one power <u>absorb</u> another, it will not become great" (Proverb).

<u>Collocates to:</u> able, body, costs, heat, energy, impact, light, moisten, shock, water

ABSTAIN

(1)   deny; desist; do without; give up; go without; refrain; refuse to partake; sit on the fence; withhold; withdraw

Word Used in Sentence(s)

(1) "As a general rule, I <u>abstain</u> from reading reports of attacks upon myself, wishing not to be provoked by that to which I cannot properly offer an answer."

—Abraham Lincoln, 16th president of the United States (1809–1865)

(1) "The people are the best guardians of their own rights and it is the duty of their executive to <u>abstain</u> from interfering in or thwarting the sacred exercise of the lawmaking functions of their government."

—William Henry Harrison, 9th president of the United States (1773–1841)

(1) "The companies that tried to keep pace with the telecommunications mergers in the first half of the first decade of the 21st century by launching mergers of their own not only failed to usurp the leader Ericsson but also found themselves under by the only player that <u>abstained</u> from the M&A frenzy: the Chinese company Huawei."

—Keil, Thomas, and Tomi Laamanen. 2011. When Rivals Merge, Think Before You Follow Suit, Idea Watch. *Harvard Business Review* (December): 25.

Word Used with Rhythm and Imagery

- **Vivid imagery**—"All philosophy lies in two words: Sustain and <u>Abstain</u>" (Epictetus, Greek philosopher, AD 55–c.135).

<u>Collocates to:</u> alcohol, food, intentions, marriage, relations, sex, vote

ABJURE

(1)   profess to abandon; renounce under oath; repudiate; swear off something formally or informally

Word Used in Sentence(s)

(1) Let me abjure you of any further action that could be construed as harassment of the fired employee.

Word Used with Rhythm and Imagery

- **Vivid imagery**—"I have from an early age abjured the use of all meat, and the time will come when men such as I will look upon the murder of animals as they now look upon the murder of men" (Leonardo DaVinci, Italian Renaissance polymath: painter, sculptor, architect, musician, 1452–1519).

Collocates to: allegiance, forced, renounced, sort, test

ABNEGATE

(1)   deny oneself; renounce; relinquish; self-deny; surrender

Word Used in Sentence(s)

(1) "Scientists, being people of cognitive complexity, must start making their own decisions as to whether what they're doing adds to human happiness or detracts from it, and not abnegate moral responsibility."

—Weldon, Fay. 1992. A "Profile" of the Creator, OUTLOOK. *Washington Post*, July 19.

Collocates to: moral, responsibility, serve, otherwise

ABOMINATE

(1)   abhor; dislike strongly; loathe

Word Used in Sentence(s)

(1) "A dissenting minority feels free only when it can impose its will on the majority: what it abominates most is the dissent of the majority."

—Eric Hoffer, American moral and social philosopher (1902–1983)

Collocates to: demons, loathe, respectable

ABSQUATULATE

(1) abscond; bolt; decamp; depart in a hurry; flee; levant; leave; make off with; run off; take flight

Word Used in Sentence(s)

(1) In the early days of fire insurance, the insurance companies also ran firehouses and would sometimes show up at a fire and if the burning home wasn't a policyholder, the fire brigade would try to sell a policy. If the policy couldn't be sold, in many instances the fire brigade would <u>absquatulate</u> leaving the building to burn.

ACCEDE

(1) agree to; allow; approach; ascend; attain; come to; comply; conform; consent; enter upon; give assent; grant; succeed to; take over

<u>Word Used in Sentence(s)</u>

(1) The union leaders eventually <u>acceded</u> to the demands of the management committee.

(1) "I am not willing to be drawn further into the toils. I cannot <u>accede</u> to the acceptance of gifts upon terms which take the education policy of the university out of the hands of the Trustees and Faculty and permit it to be determined by those who give money."

—Woodrow Wilson, 28th president of the United States (1826–1924)

<u>Collocates to: demands, requests, treaty, refused, wishes</u>

ACCELERATE

(1) gather speed; go faster; hasten; hurry; increase speed; move increasingly quicker; pick up speed; pick up the pace; step up

(2) happen or develop faster; progress faster

Word Used in Sentence(s)

(1) "The rush shows the extent to which wrangling in Washington over deficit reduction already is affecting the way taxpayers are spending their money. In addition to rethinking their charitable giving, some taxpayers are <u>accelerating</u> large medical expenses, selling appreciated stock and even prepaying mortgages."

—Saunders, Laura, and Hanna Karp. 2012. Fiscal Talks Spur Charitable Giving. *Wall Street Journal*, December 7.

(1) "The concept of teaming helps individuals acquire knowledge, skills, and networks. And it lets companies accelerate *the delivery of current products of services while responding to new opportunities."*

—Edmondson, Amy C. 2012. Teamwork on the Fly, Spotlight. *Harvard Business Review* (April): 74.

ACCENTUATE

(1) accent; emphasize; draw attention; heighten intensify; make more noticeable; play up; prominence; stress something

Word Used in Sentence(s)

(1) "Delete the negative; Accentuate *the positive!"*

—Donna Karan, American fashion designer (1948–)

(1) "A science is said to be useful if its development tends to accentuate *the existing inequities in the distribution of wealth, or more directly promotes the destruction of human life."*

—Godfrey Harold Hardy, English mathematician (1877–1947)

Collocates to: differences, opportunities, positives, shapes

ACCLIMATE

(1) accommodate; acclimatize; adapt; acculturate; accustom yourself; adjust; become accustomed to a new environment or situation; familiarize; get use to

Word Used in Sentence(s)

(1) A job change may require the individual to acclimate *himself to a completely different environment.*

(1) Businesses that offer returnships for workers returning to work after extended periods out of the workforce should create similar opportunities for veterans, which would help them acclimate *to the civilian workforce.*

ACCOMPLISH

(1) achieve; attain; bring about; carry out; cause to happen; complete; do; gain; get done; finish; fulfill; make happen; make possible; produce; pull off; reach; realize; undertake

Word Used in Sentence(s)

(1) "Success is not measured by what you <u>accomplish</u>, but by the opposition you have encountered, and the courage with which you have maintained the struggle against overwhelming odds."

—Orison Swett Marden, American spiritual author (1850–1924)

(1) "Chance can allow you to <u>accomplish</u> a goal every once in a while, but consistent achievement happens only if you love what you are doing."

—Bart Conner, American Olympic gymnast (1958–)

<u>Collocates to: goals, job, mission, objectives strategy, tactics, task, work</u>

ACHIEVE

(1) accomplish; attain; complete; conclude; do; finish; get; reach; perform; pull off; realize

(2) succeed in doing something

Word Used in Sentence(s)

(1) "The results you <u>achieve</u> will be in direct proportion to the effort you apply."

—Denis Waitley, American motivational speaker and author (1933–)

(1) "That some <u>achieve</u> great success, is proof to all that others can <u>achieve</u> it as well."

—Abraham Lincoln, 16th president of the United States (1809–1865)

(1) "Organizations do well when the people in them work hard to <u>achieve</u> high performance, as individuals and as members of teams."

—Schermerhorn, John, Richard Osborn, Mary UHL-Bien, and James Hunt. 2012. *Organizational Behavior*. 12th ed. New York: John Wiley & Sons, Inc., 4.

Word Used with Rhythm and Imagery

- **Vivid imagery**—"First, have a definite, clear practical ideal; a goal, an objective. Second, have the necessary means to <u>achieve</u> your ends; wisdom, money, materials, and methods. Third, adjust all your means to that end" (Aristotle, Ancient Greek philosopher, scientist, and physician, 384 BC–322 BC).

<u>Collocates to: able, goals, help, objectives, results, necessary, order, success</u>

ACQUIESCE

(1) accept meekly; agree without dissent; assent; comply passively

Word Used in Sentence(s)

(1) "No man can sit down and withhold his hands from the warfare against wrong and get peace from his <u>acquiescence</u>."

—Woodrow Wilson, 28th president of the United States (1856–1924)

Word Used with Rhythm and Imagery

- **Vivid imagery**—"Men <u>acquiesce</u> in a thousand things, once righteously and boldly done, to which, if proposed to them in advance, they might find endless objections" (Robert Dale Owen, American politician, 1801–1877).

<u>Collocates to: choice, compelled, council, demands, forced, must, refused, quietly</u>

ACQUIRE

(1) attain; buy; come to possess; earn; gain; get; hold; obtain; purchase; receive

Word Used in Sentence(s)

(1) "A true friend is the greatest of all blessings, and that which we take the least care of all to <u>acquire</u>."

—Francois de La Rochefoucauld, French author (1630–1680)

(1) "Men <u>acquire</u> a particular quality by constantly acting in a particular way."

—Aristotle, Ancient Greek philosopher and polymath (384 BC–322 BC)

(1) "The drive to acquire is most easily satisfied by an organization's reward system—how effectively it discriminates between good and poor performances, ties rewards to performance, and gives the best people opportunities for advancement."

—Nohria, Nitin, Boris Groysberg, and Linda-Eling Lee. 2008. Employee Motivation a Powerful New Tool, Honing Your Competitive Edge. *Harvard Business Review* (July/August): 81.

Word Used with Rhythm and Imagery

- **Antithesis**—"The more I read, the more I meditate; and the more I acquire, the more I am enabled to affirm that I know nothing" (Voltaire, French philosopher and writer, 1694–1778).

- **Antithesis**—"Nobody can acquire honor by doing what is wrong" (Thomas Jefferson, American founding father, third president of the United States, 1743–1826).

- **Metaphor**—"Work and acquire, and thou hast chained the wheel of Chance" (Ralph Waldo Emerson, American poet, lecturer, and essayist, 1803–1882).

Collocates to: ability, able, information, land, knowledge, necessary, students, skills

ACTUATE

(1)   activate; arouse to action; motivate; put into motion; trigger; start

Word Used in Sentence(s)

(1) A great leader can begin to actuate a new movement just with his or her vision.

(2) Senator Rubio's speech actuated the Congress to finally act on the bill.

ADAPT

(1)   acclimate; accommodate; adjust; change; conform; fashion; fit; get use to; make suitable; reconcile; square; suit; tailor

(2)   make fit often by modification

(3)   to cause something to change for the better

Word Used in Sentence(s)

(1) *"Since there are no similar models to study, economists say it is impossible to predict what is likely to happen to South Africa's economy. Some predict that the bigger corporations will be able to* <u>adapt</u> *to a decline in the labor pool. Most are already in the process of shedding employees as they mechanize, computerize and in general try to become more competitive."*

—Daly, Suzanne. 1998. A Post-Apartheid Agony: AIDS on the March. *New York Times*, July 23.

(1) *"*<u>Adapt</u> *yourself to the things among which your lot has been cast and love sincerely the fellow creatures with whom destiny has ordained that you shall live."*

—Marcus Aurelius, Roman emperor (AD 121–AD 180)

Word Used with Rhythm and Imagery

- **Antithesis**—"Reasonable people <u>adapt</u> themselves to the world. Unreasonable people attempt to <u>adapt</u> the world to themselves. All progress, therefore, depends on unreasonable people" (George Bernard Shaw, Irish playwright and a cofounder of the London School of Economics, 1896–1950).

- **Simile**—"The wise <u>adapt</u> themselves to circumstances, as water molds itself to the pitcher" (Chinese proverb).

Collocates to: ability, able, change, conditions, environment, must, quickly

ADDUCE

(1)   allege; cite or bring forth as evidence; proof

Word Used in Sentence(s)

(1) Let me <u>adduce</u> *the following reasons for recommending the merger.*

(1) "In an effort to defend against a hate crime charge, some defendants may try to prove their lack of prejudice by introducing evidence of non-racist speech, memberships, and activities. How could a judge rule such evidence irrelevant? If the defendant is permitted to <u>adduce</u> *such*

evidence, however, the prosecutor will almost certainly be allowed to introduce rebuttal evidence of the defendant's racism."

—Jacobs, James B. 1993. Should Hate Be a Crime? *Public Interest* Fall (113): 3–14.

Collocates to: can, evidence, might, link

ADOPT

(1) to choose; take formally and put into practice; take up and practice or use

Word Used in Sentence(s)

(1) "Netflix, Inc. said Monday its board <u>adopted</u> an anti-takeover plan intended to block activist investor Carl Icahn from expanding his nearly 10% stake in the streaming video and DVD mail company."

—Bennsinger, Greg. Poison Pill at Netflix, Corporate News. *Wall Street Journal*, November 6.

(1) "I shall try to correct errors when shown to be errors, and I shall <u>adopt</u> new views so fast as they shall appear to be true views."

—Abraham Lincoln, 16th president of the United States (1809–1865)

Word Used with Rhythm and Imagery

- **Simile**—"We cannot expect that all nations will <u>adopt</u> like systems, for conformity is the jailer of freedom and the enemy of growth" (John Fitzgerald Kennedy, 35th president of the United States, 1917–1963).

ADJUST

(1) accommodate; alter; amend; attune; bend; change; correct; fine-tune; fix; modify; pacify; rectify; regulate; resolve; settle; tune up; tweak

Word Used in Sentence(s)

(1) "I can't change the direction of the wind, but I can <u>adjust</u> my sails to always reach my destination."

—Jimmy Dean, American country music singer, television host, actor, and businessman (1928–2010)

(1) "There are things I can't force. I must <u>adjust</u>. There are times when the greatest change needed is a change of my viewpoint."

—Denis Diderot, French philosopher (1713–1784)

(1) "The problem is this. The spread of markets outpaces the ability of societies and their political systems to <u>adjust</u> to them, let alone to guide the course they take."

—Kofi Annan, Ghanaian diplomat, seventh secretary-general of the United Nations

<u>Collocates to: compensate, ideas, models, standards, themes, work</u>

ADMINISTER

control; deal out; direct; dispense; furnish a benefit; give out; govern; hand out; manage; mete out; order; run; supervise; oversee a process

Word Used in Sentence(s)

(1) "A pure democracy is a society consisting of a small number of citizens, who assemble and <u>administer</u> the government in person."

—James Madison, fourth president of the United States (1751–1836)

Word Used with Rhythm and Imagery

- **Simile**—"It is as useless to argue with those who have renounced the use of reason as to <u>administer</u> medication to the dead" (Thomas Jefferson, American founding father, third president of the United States, 1743–1826).

<u>Collocates to: contracts, exams, plans, policies, programs, projects, tests</u>

ADULTERATE

(1) contaminate; make impure

Word Used in Sentence(s)

"Some importers are <u>adulterating</u> tequila, and they're doing great damage to our image, said Jose Luis Gonzalez, president of the Tequila Regulatory Council, which governs the industry. The vast majority of imported mixto is by established companies like Cuervo and Sauza, and we have no doubt that their product is genuine. But some of the others <u>adulterate</u> it and even use silly, offensive brand names that make Mexico look ridiculous."

—Collier, Robert. 1997. Tequila Temptation. *San Francisco Chronicle*, November 19.

Word Used with Rhythm and Imagery

- **Simile**—"The test of friendship is assistance in adversity, and that too, unconditional assistance. Co-operation which needs consideration is a commercial contract and not friendship. Conditional co-operation is like <u>adulterated</u> cement which does not bind" (Mohandas Gandhi, Indian, preeminent leader of Indian nationalism in British-ruled, 1869–1948).

ADUMBRATE

(1)   foreshadow; disclose in part; give a general description of something but not the details; prefigure; obscure; overshadow; predict; presage; summary

Word Used in Sentence(s)

(1) The global political troubles <u>adumbrated</u> an eventual worldwide economic recession.

(1) It is never good for a manager to <u>adumbrate</u> news of a partial layoff to just a few employees.

ADVANCE

(1)   enhance; develop; go or move forward; move to a forward position; press forward; proceed; progress

(2)   improve; rise in status

(3)   loan money

Word Used in Sentence(s)

(1) "DreamWorks has been <u>advancing</u> efforts to increase its intellectual-property base, especially through the Classic Media Acquisition, and identify ways to translate its characters into merchandising opportunities."

—Orden, Erica. 2012. How to Train Your Branding, Media. *Wall Street Journal*, December 10.

AFFECT

(1)   change; concern; have an effect on; impact; impinge on; impress; influence; move; shape; strike; sway; touch

(2)   distress; disturb; move; touch; upset

(3)   assume; fake; imitate; pretend or have; put on

Word Used in Sentence(s)

*(1) How various countries attract or discourage import and export oper-
ations <u>affect</u> the way American firms structure their global operations.*

*(1) "Being fit matters...New research suggests that a few extra pounds
or a slightly larger waistline <u>affects</u> an executive's perceived leadership
ability as well as stamina on the job."*

—Kwoh, Leslie. 2013. Marketing. *Wall Street Journal*, January 16.

<u>Collocates to: adversely, does, factor, how, negatively, performance, positive</u>

AIR OUT

(1) bring out in the open

Word Used in Sentence(s)

*(1) There is only one way to prevent simmering employee conflicts from
creating greater problems and that is to <u>air out</u> the issues, bring them out
in the open and discuss them.*

ALLEVIATE

(1) assuage; ease; facilitate; improve; lighten; lessen; to relieve; make bear-
able

Word Used in Sentence(s)

*(1) "The new technologies that we see coming will have major benefits
that will greatly <u>alleviate</u> human suffering."*

—Ralph Merkle, American, inventor of cryptographic hashing, and more
recently a researcher and speaker on molecular nanotechnology (1952–)

Word Used with Rhythm and Imagery

- **Metaphor**—"We have discovered that the scheme of 'outlawing war'
  has made war more like an outlaw without making it less frequent and
  that to banish the knight does not <u>alleviate</u> the suffering of the peasant"
  (C. S. Lewis, British scholar and novelist, 1898–1963).

<u>Collocates to: concerns, pain, poverty, some, suffering</u>

ALIGN

(1) adjust; be or come into adjustment; being into proper or desirable coordination; correlate

(2) place in line so as to arrange in a particular order

Word Used in Sentence(s)

(1) As I consider this position, I want to be sure I am <u>aligned</u> with the values and culture of the organization.

(2) The firm's objectives and goals must be <u>aligned</u>.

(1) "Institutional logic should be <u>aligned</u> with economic logic but need not be subordinate to it. For example, all companies require capital to carry out business activities and sustain themselves. However, at great companies profit is not the sole end; rather, it is a way of ensuring that returns will continue."

—Kanter, Rosabeth. 2011. How Great Companies Think Differently. *Harvard Business Review* (November): 68.

(1) "Parallels between ancient leaders and modern executives will never <u>align</u> perfectly, but there is definite value in making the comparisons. Ancient leaders obviously operated under different conditions and lacked many advantages that modern-day CEOs take for granted, but they ran their empires by utilizing similar styles of leadership."

—Forbes, Steve, and John Prevas. 2009. *Power Ambition Glory*. New York: Crown Business Press, 10.

ALLAY

(1) alleviate; calm; dispel; put to rest; relief; subside

Word Used in Sentence(s)

(1) "But some advertising and media experts said that explaining the technology behind the ads might not <u>allay</u> the fears of many consumers who worry about being tracked or who simply fear that someone they share a computer with will see what items they have browsed."

—Rossman, Jim. 2010. *DallasNews.com*, August.

(1) "Defending the truth is not something one does out of a sense of duty or to <u>allay</u> guilt complexes, but is a reward in itself."

—Simone de Beauvoir, French writer, intellectual, existentialist philosopher, political activist, feminist (1908–1986)

(1) "In order to <u>allay</u> the concerns of recalcitrant Republicans, GOP leaders in the House said Tuesday that had split the $60.4 billion package into two parts and removed roughly $400 million in spending some lawmakers thought was unnecessary or unrelated to Hurricane Sandy relief."

—Grossman, Andrew. 2013. Fiscal Cliff's Shadow Stills Sandy Aid Bill. *Wall Street Journal*, January 2.

ALLOCATE

(1) allot; assign; distribute

(2) divide a sum of money or amount of resources

Word Used in Sentence(s)

(1), (2) We will be <u>allocating</u> reserve funds for the project.

(1), (2) I will <u>allocate</u> an annual budget toward the direct costs of the group's work.

(1), (2) "Ironically, managing a law firm's own resources is one of the biggest challenges for lawyers in managing a client's work. 'It was so hard for firms to realize that they had to <u>allocate</u> money among different practice departments,' Roster says. For example, due to a shift in anticipated workload, 'They had to decide how to <u>allocate</u> more money one year to their labor department than their tax department…. That is something clients have to do all the time.'"

—Schachner Chanen, Jill. 1997. Constructing Team Spirit. *ABA Journal* (August) 83 (8): 58.

Collocates to: available, budgets, capital, cash, energy, limited, money, resources

ALLUDE

(1) assume others know something; casually refer; covertly mention; make passing reference to; refer indirectly

Word Used in Sentence(s)

(1) I <u>alluded</u> to the merger during the press conference.

Collocates to: character, fact, images, thus, tradition

ALTER

(1)   adjust; amend; use to change; change; make an alteration; modify; rework; revise; very

Word Used in Sentence(s)

"As I grew to understand the business, it became clear to me that it was fundamentally broken. To fix it, I needed to dramatically <u>alter</u> the company's culture."

—Grossman, Mindy. 2011. HSN's CEO on Fixing the Shopping Networks Culture. *Harvard Business Review* (December): 44.

AMALGAMATE

(1)   blend into a coherent single unit; combine or unite two or more units

Word Used in Sentence(s)

(1) The respective boards of directors voted to <u>amalgamate</u> the firms immediately.

<u>Collocates to: business units, into, cells, several, slough, soil, particles, nations</u>

AMELIORATE

(1)   improve; make better or more tolerable; put right; upgrade

Word Used in Sentence(s)

(1) Phillip <u>ameliorated</u> the issues in the business plan prior to the meeting with the investors.

<u>Collocates to: conditions, economic, effects, effort, help, might, situation, social, problems</u>

AMPLIFY

(1)   augment; elevate; enlarge; expand; increase; intensify; magnify

(2)   add details to; clarify; develop; elaborate on; go into details

Word Used in Sentence(s)

(1) "Cross selling generates marketing expenses; second, cross-buying, <u>amplifies</u> costs by extending undesirable behavior to a greater number of products or services."

—Shah, Denish, and V. Kumar. 2012. The Dark Side of Cross-Selling, Idea Watch. *Harvard Business Review* (December): 22.

ANALYZE

(1) consider; dissect; evaluate; examine in great detail; explore; inspect; investigate; probe; question; scrutinize; study closely

Word Used in Sentence(s)

(1) Would you <u>analyze</u> the data from the study and make recommendations based upon your analysis?

(1) "You are a product of your environment. So choose the environment that will best develop you toward your objective. <u>Analyze</u> your life in terms of its environment. Are the things around you helping you toward success—or are they holding you back?"

—W. Clement Stone, American author (1902–2002)

(1) "We are not won by arguments that we can <u>analyze</u> but by the tone and temper, by the manner which is the man himself."

—Samuel Butler, English novelist, essayist, and critic (1835–1902)

(1) "The research shows that in almost every case, a bigger opportunity lies in improving your performance in the industry you're in, by fixing your strategy and strengthening the capabilities that create value for customers and separate you from your competitors. This conclusion was reached after <u>analyzing</u> shareholder returns for 6,138 companies in 65 industries worldwide from 2001 to 2011."

—Hirsh, Evan, and Kasturi Rangan. 2013. The Grass Isn't Greener, Idea Watch. *Harvard Business Review* (January/February): 23.

<u>Collocates to: ability, collect, data, evaluate, identify, information, results, sample, situation, used</u>

ANODYNE

(1) capable of showing comfort; eliminating pain

(2) not likely to offend

Word Used in Sentence(s)

> *(1) Illusion is an <u>anodyne</u>, bred by the gap between wish and reality."*

—Herman Wouk, American author (1915–)

ANTICIPATE

(1) await; be hopeful for; expect; discussion or treatment; to foresee and deal with in advance; give advance thought; look forward to; wait for; think likely

Word Used in Sentence(s)

> *(1) We need to <u>anticipate</u> our customer's concerns and be prepared with the proper response.*

> *(1) If we <u>anticipate</u> the potential risk factors, we can build into the budget a more defensible contingency.*

> *(1) "Research shows that morning people get better grades in school, which get them into better colleges, which then lead to better job opportunities. Morning people also <u>anticipate</u> problems and try to minimize them."*

—Randler, Christopher. 2012. The Early Bird Really Does Get the Worm, Defend Your Research. *Harvard Business Review* (July/August): 30.

APPEAL

(1) ask; call for; demand; petition for; request; urge

(2) attract; charm; draw; fascinate; grab; interest; please; pull; tempt

Word Used in Sentence(s)

> *(1) "If I am trying to persuade others, I first have to understand their position, which means I have to listen to them. I have to <u>appeal</u> to their values, which means I have to show them respect. I have to find the best*

argument for my position, which means I have to think about my values in the context of their concerns."

—Jenkins, John. 2013. Persuasion as the Cure for Incivility. *Wall Street Journal*, January 9.

APPORTION

(1)   allot; assign; to divide and give out parts or shares according to a plan

APPRAISE

(1)   assess; consider; evaluate; determine worth; indicate value of; judge; review; weigh up

Word Used in Sentence(s)

(1) "You Yourself created the counterfeit and the genuine. You Yourself appraise all people. You appraise the true, and place them in Your Treasury; You consign the false to wander in delusion."

—Sri Guru Granth Sahib, the holy book of sikhs

APPRISE

(1)   cause to be aware; inform; notify; tell

Word Used in Sentence(s)

(1) I want to appraise you of the situation with regard to merger talks.

Collocates to: development, progress, public, readers, thought

APPROVE

(1)   accept; agree to; attest; back up; command; commend; endorse; favor; praise; ratify; sanction; support
(2)   allow; authorize; consent; grant; pass; sanction

Word Used in Sentence(s)

(1) "They that approve a private opinion, call it opinion; but they that dislike it, heresy; and yet heresy signifies no more than private opinion."

—Thomas Hobbes, English philosopher (1588–1679)

(2) "Fools admire, but men of sense approve."

—Alexander Pope, English poet (1688–1744)

ARRANGE

(1) array; authorize; catalogue; classify; fix; order; organize; position; set up, sort; stage

(2) make plans for something to be done

Word Used in Sentence(s)

(1) "A shrewd man has to <u>arrange</u> his interests in order of importance and deal with them one by one; but often our greed upsets this order and makes us run after so many things at once that through over-anxiety to obtain the trivial, we miss the most important."

—François de la Rochefoucauld, French classical author (1613–1680)

Collocates to: alphabetically, ascending, carefully, chronologically, descending, haphazardly, hierarchically, symmetrically

ARTICULATE

(1) convey; enunciate; express thoughts, ideas, or feelings coherently; utter intelligible pronounce; put into words; say; speech; speak clearly; utter

Word Used in Sentence(s)

(1) "For the past 30 years, a group of social scientists around the world—from pioneers like Edward Deci and Richard Ryan, at the University of Rochester, to a new generation of scholars such as Adam Grant, at Wharton—have <u>articulated</u> a more subtle view of what motivates people in a variety of settings, including work."

—Pink, Daniel. 2012. A Radical Prescription for Sales. *Harvard Business Review* (July/August): 77.

"Leaders <u>articulate</u> a lucid sense of purpose, create effective leadership teams, prioritize, and sequence their initiatives carefully, redesign organizational structures to make good execution easier, and most importantly, integrate these tactics into one coherent strategy."

—Wheeler, Steven, Walter McFarland, and Art Kleiner. 2007. A Blueprint for Strategic Leadership. *Strategy+Business* Winter (49): 46.

ASCERTAIN

(1) determine; discover; establish; find out; learn; realize; uncover

(2) to find out with certainty

Word Used in Sentence(s)

(1) A manager can <u>ascertain</u> the cause of many problems by careful observation.

Collocates to: able, extent, difficult, order, study, try, whether

ASSEMBLE

(1) accumulate; amass; bring together; collect in one place; draw together; gather; get together; join; mass; meet; muster

Word Used in Sentence(s)

(1) "The next step was to <u>assemble</u> the right talent around me."

—Grossman, Mindy. 2011. HSN's CEO on Fixing the Shopping Networks Culture. *Harvard Business Review* (December): 44.

(1) "When you approach a problem, strip yourself of preconceived opinions and prejudice, <u>assemble</u> and learn the facts of the situation, make the decision which seems to you to be the most honest, and then stick to it."

—Chester Bowles, American diplomat and politician (1901–1986)

ASSESS
(1)   impose; estimate; judge; value
(2)   to estimate the value, cost, benefit, or worth of

Word Used in Sentence(s)

(1), (2) In order to <u>assess</u> the pros and cons of this merger, we will need to assemble an ad hoc intradepartmental team.

(1), (2) "A mid-career transition is a great opportunity for a leader to help an employee <u>assess</u> her current interest areas and identify areas of satisfaction as well as development opportunities. In addition, a leader can look at burnout areas and determine if there are opportunities to rekindle that interest."

—Karkau, Betty. 2011. Stopping the Mid-Career Crisis. *Harvard Business Review* (September): 24.

Collocates to: ability, designed, difficulty, effects, situation, student, study, items, impact, order, used, whether

ASSEVERATE

(1) assert or declare earnestly or solemnly

Word Used in Sentence(s)

(1) Let me asseverate that I'll greatly appreciate your help as we launch the new strategic plan.

ASSIMILATE

(1) absorb; accommodate; incorporate; standardize

Word Used in Sentence(s)

(1) "True ideas are those that we can assimilate, validate, corroborate, and verify. False ideas are those that we cannot."

—William James, American philosopher and psychologist (1842–1910)

(1) "Nothing is more revolting than the majority; for it consists of few vigorous predecessors, of knaves who accommodate themselves, of weak people who assimilate themselves, and the mass that toddles after them without knowing in the least what it wants."

—Johann Wolfgang von Goethe, German playwright, poet, novelist, and dramatist (1749–1832)

(1) "It's important for companies to gather insights form former outsiders who have assimilated successfully; managers who have grown up in an organization often don't realize they even have a culture."

—Watkins, Michael. 2007. Help Newly Hired Executives Adapt Quickly, Corporate Culture. *Harvard Business Review* (June): 26.

ASSIST

(1) abet; aid; back; befriend; collaborate; facilitate; help with; promote; support; sustain

Word Used in Sentence(s)

(1) "There is no more noble occupation in the world than to assist another human being—to help someone succeed."

—Alan Loy McGinnis, American, author, Christian psychotherapist (1933–2005)

Collocates to: effort, design, goals, program, resources

ASSUAGE

(1) appease; ease the pain; make less severe; satisfy; soothe; mitigate; mollify; pacify

Word Used in Sentence(s)

(1) I've never know any trouble than an hour's reading didn't <u>assuage</u>.

—Arthur Schopenhauer, German philosopher (1788–1860)

ATTAIN

(1) accomplish; acquire; achieve; arrive at; conquer; gain; manage; make; obtain; procure; reach; realize

Word Used in Sentence(s)

(1) "Desire is the key to motivation, but it's determination and commitment to an unrelenting pursuit of your goal—a commitment to excellence—that will enable you to <u>attain</u> the success you seek."

—Mario Andretti, American racecar driver (1940–)

(1) "The highest activity a human being can <u>attain</u> is learning for understanding, because to understand is to be free."

—Baruch Spinoza, Dutch philosopher (1632–1677)

(1) "While progress has been made in many firms, more work clearly needs to be done. Even among the best and brightest managers, gender equality has yet to be <u>attained</u>."

—Carter, Nancy, and Christine Silva. 2010. Women in Management: Delusions of Progress, Idea Watch. *Harvard Business Review* (March): 21.

ATTENUATE

(1) cause to decrease the amount of value, power, amount; spread thin; lighten amount

<u>Collocates to: ability, can, effect, may, stress</u>

ATTUNE

(1) accustom to; adjust; bring into accord with someone or something; regulate; standardize

Word Used in Sentence(s)

(1) "Kantor makes the case that being <u>attuned</u> to the signals of a conversational system—an approach he calls "structural dynamics"—is the first step toward becoming a far more prescient and effective leader."

—Art Kliener, Building the Skills of Insight. *Strategy + Business*, http://www.strategy-business.com/article/00154?gko=d4421&cid= TL20130117&utm_campaign=TL20130117 (accessed January 17, 2013).

AUGMENT

(1)   add to; increase; make bigger or better or stronger

Word Used in Sentence(s)

(1) We plan to <u>augment</u> the company security with an outside vendor.

(1) "The traditional product life cycle has created a kind of tunnel vision for marketers. Typically they layer new product benefits on top of old ones in an endless struggle to differentiate... Over time the <u>augmented</u> product becomes the expected product."

—Moon, Youngme. 2005. Break Free from the Product Life Cycle. *Harvard Business Review* (May): 88.

Word Used with Rhythm and Imagery

* **Parallelism**—"There are two ways of being happy: We must either diminish our wants or <u>augment</u> our means—either may do—the result is the same and it is for each man to decide for himself and to do that which happens to be easier" (Benjamin Franklin, American statesman, scientist, philosopher, printer, writer, and inventor, 1706–1790).

Collocates to: ability, data, current, design, income, replace

AUGUR

(1)   betoken; bode; divine; forebode; foreshadow; foretell; portend; predict

Word Used in Sentence(s)

(1) "These readings <u>augur</u> well in the very near term for supportive bond price action. We, however, still look for core inflation to tick up modestly and for overall labor market conditions to improve gradually."

—Chris Sullivan

Collocates to: does, future, might, not, poorly, well

AUTHORIZE

(1)   accredit; commission; empower; enable; entitle; license; grant; qualify

Word Used in Sentence(s)

(1) "So great moreover is the regard of the law for private property, that it will not authorize the least violation of it; no, not even for the general good of the whole community."

—William Blackstone, English jurist (1723–1780)

(1) Only a vice president can authorize an expenditure that has not been budgeted.

AVER

(1)   affirm; assert the truthfulness of something; avow; claim; declare; maintain; profess; state; swear

Word Used in Sentence(s)

(1) Some philosophers aver that both moral blame and legal responsibility should be based on prior behavior.

AVOW

(1)   admit; claim on; declare boldly

Word Used in Sentence(s)

(1) I avow never to let the company be taken over by outside interests.

Collocates to: both, should, many, others

BACK DOWN

(1)   back off; bow out; give up; pull out; retreat from a position; surrender

Word Used in Sentence(s)

(1) "Don't back down just to keep the peace. Standing up for your beliefs builds self-confidence and self-esteem."

—Oprah Winfrey, American television personality, actress, and producer (1954–)

(1) "You are a coward when you even seem to have <u>backed down</u> from a thing you openly set out to do."

—Mark Twain, American humorist, writer, and lecturer (1835–1910)

Word Used with Rhythm and Imagery

- **Antithesis**—"Officials tend to <u>back down</u> when the people get their backs up" (Unknown).

BACK OUT

(1) abandon; back pedal; back off; bail out; cancel or renege on an arrangement; leave; pull back; retreat

Word Used in Sentence(s)

(1) "When in doubt, <u>back out</u> on a technicality."

—Walter Shapiro, American columnist

BALANCE

(1) assess; collate; calculate; compare; consider; evaluate; even out; equalize; keep upright; offset; settle; square; stabilize; stay poised; steady; tally; total; weigh; weight up

Word Used in Sentence(s)

(1) Managing a global enterprise requires a CEO who is adept at <u>balancing</u> many interests.

(1) Managers need to <u>balance</u> their approach in handling worker disputes.

BE ARGUS-EYED

(1) In Greek mythology, Argus was a giant with one hundred eyes each looking in a different direction. Argus was employed by the goddess Hera as a watchman to guard the nymph Io. Zeus had Argus killed by Hermes so he could pursue his passion love Io.

(2) having keen eyes; keenly watchful for danger; sleepless; vigilant; watchful; wary; wide awake

Word Used in Sentence(s)

(1) Corporate espionage costs firms billions of dollars, so it is impera-tive that all employees be Argus-eyed and report any suspicious activity.

BELABOR

(1)   to go over and over again; to ply diligently; repeat; to work carefully upon.

Word Used in Sentence(s)

(1) "I wish more people would belabor the obvious, and more often."

—Ibn Warraq, Why I Am Not a Muslim

(1) I feel like we are wasting time if we belabor the same points already covered in previous negations.

Collocates to: need, not, obvious, point, want

BELIE

(1)   disprove; to give false impression or to contradict

Word Used in Sentence(s)

(1) The small, unassuming building belied the global Internet business that was taking place inside.

(1) "Man is a creature of hope and invention, both of which belie the idea that things cannot be changed."

—Tom Clancy, American novelist

Word Used with Rhythm and Imagery

- **Repetition**—"Our very hopes belied our fears, / Our fears our hopes belied - / We thought her dying when she slept, / And sleeping when she died!" (Thomas Hood, English poet and humorist, 1799–1845).

Collocates to: fact, image, notion, numbers, seem, words

BENCHMARK

(1)   assessment of something so it can be compared; make a measurement that becomes a standard; to make a comparison of performance or effectiveness

Word Used in Sentence(s)

(1) "My parents' generation's <u>benchmark</u> was simple: Fat Equals Bad."

—Arabella Weir, British comedian, actress, and writer (1957–)

(1) "A Chinese animation studio is already using an early commercial version of the software to increase the quality of its television productions, and Zhou is collaborating with the Frankfurt-based gaming studio Crytek—maker of the popular Crysis series of games, which are often used to <u>benchmark</u> the graphics performance of PCs—to improve the realism of its products."

—Anonymous. 2011. THE NEXT GENERATION OF TECHNOLOGY: 35 Innovators Under 35. *Technology Review* (September/October).

(1) "This <u>benchmarking</u> process realigns the job positions with the most-up-to-date strategic business initiatives."

—Hayashi, Shawn Kent. 2012. *Conversations for Creating Star Performers.* New York: McGraw Hill, 19.

(1) "After brainstorming and formalizing our instincts, we commissioned a consulting firm to provide us with competitor <u>benchmarketing</u>. Our instincts confirmed, we clearly saw the way forward; We would reinforce our Burberry heritage, our Brutishness, by emphasizing and growing our core luxury products, innovating them and keeping them at the heart of everything we do."

—Ahrendts, Angele. 2013. Turning an Aging British Icon into a Global Luxury Brand, How I Did It. *Harvard Business Review* (January/February): 41.

BESMIRCH

(1) charge falsely or with malicious intent; smear so as to make dirty or stained; sully

Word Used in Sentence(s)

(1) Because of the ubiquity of social media, it is much easier to <u>besmirch</u> someone and not be held accountable.

Word Used with Rhythm and Imagery

- **Metaphors**—"Men are nicotine-soaked, beer-besmirched, whiskey-greased, red-eyed devils" (Carry Nation, American temperance activist).

Collocates to: anything, man, name, otherwise, reputation, would

BESTRIDE SOMETHING LIKE A COLOSSUS

(1)   to be a giant in some endeavor, field; to be preeminent

Word Used with Rhythm and Imagery

- **Simile**—"Why man, he doth bestride the narrow world like a Colossus, and we petty men walk under his huge legs and peep about to find ourselves dishonorable graves" (William Shakespeare, English poet and playwright [1564–1516], Julius Caesar, I.ii.135-8).

BET THE FARM/RANCH

(1)   count on something/someone; to risk everything you have because you are certain of something

Word Used in Sentence(s)

(1)   "I wouldn't bet the farm on it, but I'd bet the main house. I wouldn't even bet the outhouse on Mondale."

—Richard Nixon, 37th president of the United States (1937–1994)

(1)   TV networks are obviously willing to bet the ranch on special sports events—they paid millions to broadcast the Olympics.

(1)   No matter how confident you are in the future, you should never bet the farm on one idea.

BIFURCATE

(1)   biramous; branch; divide; fork; prong; split into two groups or branches

Word Used in Sentence(s)

(1)   "Labor also has started to bifurcate, as minimum-wage workers have begun to see their interests as distinct from—and often opposed to—those of relatively well-paid unionized workers in industry and the public sector."

—Armijo, Leslie Elliott. 1996. Inflation and Insouciance: The Peculiar Brazilian Game. *Latin American Research Review* 31 (3): 7.

BLANDISH

(1)   coax; cajole; influence with gentle flattery

(2)   flourish or shake menacingly

Word Used in Sentence(s)

(1) A leader most likely would not attempt to <u>blandish</u> a follower into accepting his point of view but rather resort to the use of influence.

(2) When Susan stood and <u>blandished</u> the bylaws, everyone knew the executive session was going to be a long one.

BLAZE

(1)   brilliant; flash; glare; rush; speed around

Word Used in Sentence(s)

(1) The new product was announced with a <u>blaze</u> of adverting and promotions.

Word Used with Rhythm and Imagery

- **Antithesis**—"When beggars die there are no comets seen; but the heavens themselves blaze forth the death of princes" (William Shakespeare, English dramatist, playwright, and poet, 1564–1616).

- **Metaphor**—"I would rather be ashes than dust! I would rather that my spark should burn out in a brilliant blaze than it should be stifled by dry-rot. I would rather be a superb meteor, every atom of me in magnificent glow, than a sleepy and permanent planet. The function of man is to live, not to exist. I shall not waste my days trying to prolong them. I shall use my time" (Jack London, American short-story writer and novelist, 1876–1916).

- **Metaphor**—"The <u>blaze</u> of reputation cannot be blown out, but it often dies in the socket; a very few names may be considered as perpetual lamps that shine unconsumed" (Samuel Johnson, English poet, critic, and writer, 1709–1784).

BLOW HOT / COLD

(1)   to show interest then disinterest; enthusiasm then lack of enthusiasm

Word Used in Sentence(s)

(1) "People's feelings turn cool and warm; the ways of the world run hot and cold."

—Unknown

Word Used with Rhythm and Imagery

- **Vivid imagery**—"Like to the time o' th' year between the <u>extremes Of hot and cold</u>, he was nor sad nor merry" (Shakespeare, English dramatist, playwright, and poet, 1564–1616).

BLOW SOMEONE'S DOORS OFF

(1) surpass; utterly defeat someone

BLUE SKY

(1) visionary thinking; out-of-the-box strategic, long-range thinking

Word Used in Sentence(s)

(1) I want the senior management team to meet in retreat to <u>blue sky</u> ideas for where this company needs to be in twenty years.

BOOST

(1) advance; build up; encourage; enhance; further; heighten; improve; increase; make better; motivate; promote; strengthen; support; uplift

Word Used in Sentence(s)

(1) "When Laura Esserman, MD became the director of the Carol Franc Buck Brest Care Center in 1997, she hoped to <u>boost</u> the institution's prominence and patience throughput by delivering integrated care in on attractive setting."

—Pfeffer, Jeffrey. 2010. Power Play. *Harvard Business Review* (July/August): 85.

(1) "Outstanding leaders go out of their way to <u>boost</u> the self-esteem of their personnel. If people believe in themselves, it's amazing what they can accomplish."

—Sam Walton, American retail executive and founder of Wal-Mart Stores, Inc. (1918–1992)

BOOTSTRAP

(1) initiative; manage without assistance; succeed with few resources

Word Used in Sentence(s)

(1) Many new product initiatives move forward by bootstrapping meth-ods until stakeholders see the value.

(1) Bootstrapping until investors began to see the potential is common for new firms.

(1) "Many entrepreneurs will attest to the value of bootstrapping: launching ventures with modest personal funds. From this perspective, Ross Perot, who started EDS with $1,000 and turned it into a multimil-lion dollar enterprise remains the rule, not the exception."

—Bhide, Amar. 1988. *Bootstrap Finance, The Art of Start Ups. Harvard Business Review on Entrepreneurship*. Boston: HBR Press, 152.

BOWDLERIZE

(1) censor; to clean up a document by deleting or changing offensive words or passages; to expurgate

Word Used in Sentence(s)

(1) "'The job of second-in-command wasn't worth a warm bucket of spit' is what John Garner Nance, FDR's first Vice-President was sup-posed to have said. But this was before hot microphones and newspaper-men were kind enough to bowdlerize it for him."

—Mark Hemingway. Mar. 28, 2010. "Biden is a Bad @&%* Vice President." *Washington Examiner*.

BRAINSTORM

(1) come up with; dream up; devise; free generation of ideas; strategic think-ing; think

Word Used in Sentence(s)

(1) Don had his people brainstorm to keep them on track and produce enough ideas with which to work.

BREAKTHROUGH

(1) unexpected gain or improvement

(2) new idea

Word Used in Sentence(s)

(1) "There is the assumption that an industry that seems superior today will remain so. There are always some industries that seem superior today and will remain so. There are always some industries in a 'hot' part of the growth cycle because of a <u>breakthrough</u> innovation, favorable regulation, or some other advantage."

(1) "New businesses with the potential to deliver <u>breakthrough</u> growth for established companies face stiff headwinds well after launch…limits to innovation have less to do with technology or creativity than organizational agility."

—Gaovondarajan, Vijay, and Chris Trimbla. 2005. Building Breakthrough Businesses Within Established Organizations. *Harvard Business Review* (May): 58.

BRIDGE

(1) connect; cross over; hook up; join

Word Used in Sentence(s)

(1) "A traditional project management approach would not work for the proposed project. Success depended on <u>bridging</u> dramatically different national, organizational, and occupational cultures to collaborate in fluid groupings that emerged and dissolved in response to needs that were identified as the work progressed."

—Edmondson, Amy C. 2012. Teamwork on the Fly, Spotlight. *Harvard Business Review* (April): 74.

BROACH

(1) bring up something; mention or suggest a topic

Word Used in Sentence(s)

(1) "The essays as a whole reflect the influence of anthropological concepts as well as studies conducted since the early 1980s by cultural historians of Europe and the United States (such as Lynn Hunt's work on

the French Revolution). They <u>broach</u> a wide range of topics: popular religious celebrations, the delightful subject of street songs and dance, work and labor conditions, the notion of public space and its use, educational reform, civic festivals, and village bands."

—Murray, Pamela. 1997. Diverse Approaches to Nineteenth-Century Mexican History. *Latin American Research Review* 32 (3): 187.

BUILD

(1) assemble; construct; erect; fabricate; join together; make; manufacture; put together; put up

(2) encourage; foster; grow

Word Used in Sentence(s)

(1) "The TAD covering Atlantic Station has poured nearly $330 million in bonds to transform a former steel mill into one of the city's biggest retail attractions. The money helped <u>build</u> office towers, retail developments, housing units and the posh Twelve Hotel, as well as the roads and infrastructure that help link the complex to the rest of Atlanta."

—Bluestein, Greg. 2012. Uneven Results for Tax Districts. *Atlanta Journal Constitution, NEWS*, June 13.

Word Used with Rhythm and Imagery

- **Alliteration**—(1) "Law firms seeking to **b**ecome international **b**ehemoths are chasing cross-**b**order mergers to **build b**rands with thousands of lawyers from **B**oston to **B**eijing and **b**eyond" (Smith, Jennifer. 2012. With CROSS-Border Mergers, Law Firms Enter Arms Race, MarketPlace. *Wall Street Journal*, December 10).

- **Antithesis**—(1),(2) "To build may have to be the slow and laborious task of years. To destroy can be the thoughtless act of a single day" (Winston Churchill, British orator, author, and prime minister, 1874–1965).

- **Antithesis**—(1),(2) "I don't <u>build</u> in order to have clients. I have clients in order to <u>build</u>" (Ayn Rand, American writer and novelist, 1905–1982).

BURBLE

(1) babble on; to speak a length

Word Used in Sentence(s)

(1) The most significant improvement in the sound was the elimination of the low <u>burble</u> you always get with lv disks.

BURGEON

(1) blossom; to expand; flourish; grow; spout

Word Used in Sentence(s)

(1) "If the debate continues to burgeon in this way, between the state and the 'governing institutions' of organized labor and organized capital, the net result may be the gradual emergence of a new, cross-disciplinary historical political economy, richer than anything we have had since the nineteenth century."

—Marquand, David. 1991. IX: Big Ends or Little Ends. *History Today* 41 (9): 38–41.

Word Used with Rhythm and Imagery

- **Vivid imagery**—"Only those within whose own consciousness the sun rise and set, the leaves burgeon and wither, can be said to be aware of what living is" (Joseph Wood Krutch, American naturalist and writer, 1893–1970).

BURN ONE'S BOATS

(1) burn one's bridges; choose a killing ground; commit to a course of action; cut oneself off from all means or hope of retreat; go for broke; irreversible course of action; nail one's colors to the mast; to put oneself in a position from which there is no going back

Word Used in Sentence(s)

(1) In 310 BC, Agathocles of Syracuse sailed his army to Carthage and <u>burned his boats</u> so his soldiers knew that the price of failure would be their death.

BURNISH

(1) brighten; cause to glow; gloss; make lustrous or shiny; to polish or shine

Word Used in Sentence(s)

(1) "Radio Sawa is hardly the first government-funded use of popular culture to <u>burnish</u> America's image. During the cold war, Voice of America radio beamed jazz into the Soviet bloc."

—Bayles, Martha. 2008. The Return of Cultural Diplomacy. *Newsweek*, December 31.

Word Used with Rhythm and Imagery

- **Vivid imagery**—"In the Spring a livelier iris changes on the <u>burnish'd</u> dove; in the Spring an yon man's fancy turns to thoughts of love" (Alfred, Lord Tennyson English poet, 1809–1892).

Collocates to: brand, credentials, image, opportunity, reputation; surface

BUTTRESS

(1) back; give added strength

Word Used in Sentence(s)

(1) An architect should live as little in cities as a painter. Send him to our hills, and let him study there what nature understands by a <u>buttress</u>, and what by a dome."

—Gore Vidal, American novelist and essayist (1925–)

CACHINNATE

(1) to laugh loudly or inappropriately

CAJOLE

(1) blandish; coax; coheres; entice; flatter; inveigle; persuade; push; soft-soap; sweet talk; threaten; wheedle

Word Used in Sentence(s)

(1) I did not want to head the task force but was <u>cajoled</u> into the role by the members.

(1) "Christians are to be taught that the pope would and should wish to give of his own money, even though he had to sell the basilica of St. Peter, to many of those from whom certain hawkers of indulgences <u>cajole</u> money."

—Martin Luther, German priest and scholar (1483–1546)

CALIBRATE

(1) to determine, rectify, or mark the graduations *especially* to measure against a standard

Word Used in Sentence(s)

(1) "Almost one in five American men between the ages of 25 and 54 doesn't have a job. Fiscal and monetary policy should be <u>calibrated</u> to get more of them working before that permanently unemployable."

—Wessel, David. 2012. Long-Term Economic To-Do List. *Wall Street Journal Capital*, November 8.

(1) American secondary and collegiate education needs to be <u>calibrated</u> more toward providing students with educations that prepare them for knowledge-based work, which is what the American industry needs now.

Collocates to: analyze, careful, data, difficult, model, properly, used

CALL THE SHOT

(1) to direct the outcome of an activity or affair; to predict the outcome of something

Word Used in Sentence(s)

(1) I've waited years for the opportunity to run an operation, to <u>call the shots</u>.

(1) "At the outset when Robert Eaton was named as CEO replacing Lee Iacocca at General Motors he informed key staffers that he believed in participatory management, not consensus management. The message was that Eaton would be <u>calling the shots</u>."

—DuBrin, Andrew. 1998. *Leadership Research Findings, Practice, and Skills*. Boston: Houghton Mifflin Company, 13.

CAPITALIZE

(1) benefit from; draw advantage from; exploit; get the most of; make the most of; profit or take advantage of

(2) fund; supply capital for

Word Used in Sentence(s)

(1) "Expect the best. Prepare for the worst. Capitalize on what comes."

—Zig Ziglar, American author, salesman, and motivational speaker (1906–2012)

(1) "What you have, what your are—your looks, your personality, your way of thinking—is unique. No one in the world is like you. So capitalize on it."

—Jack Lord, American television, film, and Broadway actor (1920–1998)

(1) "We're looking to have the ability to come in and be able to capitalize on the marketing in order to grow the top-line. We basically leverage what has worked with our other successful acquisitions—investment in marketing, retention and student services.

—John Larson, American, U.S. Representative (1948–)

(1) "He poured resources in R&D and capitalized on two of the company's exceptional capabilities—rapid innovation using deep customer insights, and flexible manufacturing."

—Hirsh, Evan, and Kasturi Rangan. The Grass Isn't Greener, Idea Watch. *Harvard Business Review* (January/February): 23.

CAPITULATE

(1) accede; give away; give in; give up; submit; surrender; yield

Word Used in Sentence(s)

(1) The union bargaining team was forced to capitulate on the pension issue.

(1) "I will be conquered; I will not capitulate."

—Samuel Johnson, English poet, critic, and writer (1709–1784)

(1) Today, successful selling should produce a win-win outcome not one in which the buyer feels like they had to capitulate.

CARE

(1) anxious for; be concerned for; have interest in; prefer or wish for; worry

(2) aid; act on; be in charge of; deal with; dispose of; handle; manage

Word Used in Sentence(s)

> *"Life is short, don't waste time worrying about what people think of you. Hold on to the ones that <u>care</u>, in the end they will be the only ones there."*

—Unknown

Word Used with Rhythm and Imagery

- **Vivid imagery**—"Whatever words we utter should be chosen with <u>care</u> for people will hear them and be influenced by them for good or ill" (Buddha, spiritual teacher from the Indian subcontinent, on whose teachings Buddhism was founded).

CAREEN

(1) lurch; lean; sway; swerve; tip to one side

Word Used in Sentence(s)

> *(1) A career should seem like a trip on a well-mapped route, not a car <u>careening</u> out of control.*

CASTIGATE

(1) correct; criticize; chasten; chastise; emend; punish; rebuke; reprimand

Word Used in Sentence(s)

> *(1) Sometimes the political left will <u>castigate</u> the fundamentals of the free market concept.*

> *(1) "You are quick to <u>castigate</u> those who dare to heap verbal or visual abuse upon liberals and the socialistic programs The Chronicle's editorial policies endorse, but fail to acknowledge the one-sided news reporting and total unfairness in maligning 3.4 million NRA members, 60 to 100 million American gun owners, and most members of Congress, as something less than loyal Americans and patriotic citizens."*

—Letters to the editor, Editorial. 1995. *San Francisco Chronicle*, May 17.

CATALOG

(1) arrange; classify; list; put together; register

Word Used in Sentence(s)

(1) "Mr. Beranke <u>cataloged</u> the reasons why the past few lousy years might have lingering effects: So many workers have been sidelined for so long they may never go back to work. Business investment declined sharply during the recession, leaving firms and workers less to work with, and individuals, businesses and investors may be so shaken that they will take fewer risks that produce efficiencies, new companies and new ways of doing things."

—Wessel, David. 2013. Checking the Economy's Pulse, Agenda 2013: US. *Wall Street Journal*, January 2.

CATAPULT

(1) fling; hurl; hurtle; throw with great force; project; propel; shoot; sling; sling shot; thrust suddenly; throw; toss

Word Used in Sentence(s)

(1) "Mr. Petrosian—whose father names him Tigran after a former chess champion with the same surname—is one of a legion of top chess players that have <u>catapulted</u> the poor nation of three million into world beaters on the 64-square board."

—Parkinson, Joe. 2012. Winning Move: Chess Reigns as Kingly Pursuit in Armenia. *Wall Street Journal*, December 4.

(1) "Some authors have what amounts to a metaphysical approach. They admit to inspiration. Sudden and unaccountable urgencies to write <u>catapult</u> them out of sleep and bed. For myself, I have never awakened to jot down an idea that was acceptable the following morning."

—Fanny Hurst, American novelist (1889–1968)

(1) "The initiative, known as a middle college high school, is patterned after similar programs in California, Texas and New York. It is the first of its kind in Maryland. 'The idea behind the program is to <u>catapult</u> a young person forward, providing them not just with access but with skills on how to be successful,' said Cecilia Cunningham, the executive director of the New York-based Middle College National Consortium."

—Wiggins, Ovetta. 2012. Doubling Up on Education, Metro. *Chicago Sun-Times*, June 14.

(1) "By positioning—or repositioning—their products in unexpected ways, companies can change how customers mentally categorize them. As a result, companies can rescue products foundering in the maturity stage of the product life cycle and return them to the growth phase. And they can <u>catapult</u> new products forward into the growth phase, leapfrogging obstacles that could slow consumers' acceptance."

—Moon, Youngme. 2005. Break Free from the Product Life Cycle. *Harvard Business Review* (May): 88.

CATCH FIRE

(1) to become remarkably successful

(2) to burn; ignite

Word Used with Rhythm and Imagery

- **Metaphor**—(1) "<u>Catch</u> on <u>fire</u> with enthusiasm and people will come for miles to watch you burn" (John Wesley, English evangelist, 1703–1791).

- **Metaphor**—(2) "For it is your business, when the wall next door <u>catches fire</u>" (Horace, Ancient Roman poet, 65 BC–8 BC).

CATCH THE WAVE

(1) to seize an opportunity; take advantage of trend

Word Used in Sentence(s)

(1) Many businesses will try to <u>catch the wave</u> with social media.

(1) A business strategy is a well-thought-out plan, not 'let's <u>catch the wave</u>' of the next hot industry cycle.

CAVIL

(1) raise petty and irritating objections

Word Used in Sentence(s)

(1) "Bluster, sputter, question, <u>cavil</u>; but be sure your argument be intricate enough to confound the court."

—William Wycherley, English dramatist of the Restoration period (1640–1715)

CHAFE

(1)   to irritate or annoy; fret

Word Used in Sentence(s)

(1)   "One more substantive issues, CIA agency officers sometimes <u>chafed</u> under what they saw was Mr. Petraeus's more controlling style."

—Nicholas, Peter. 2012. CIA Chief Struggled to Deflect Criticism of Agency, US News. *Wall Street Journal*, November 15.

(1)   "When entrepreneurs begin to create an entity to carry out their ideas, they often face a crippling and seemingly arbitrary question: whether to be a for-profit or a nonprofit. A growing number of entrepreneurs <u>chafe</u> under those classifications."

—Sabeti, Heerad. 2011. The For-Benefit Enterprise. *Harvard Business Review* (November): 98.

CHANNEL

(1)   course; conduit; control; direct; feed; path; route

(2)   concentrate; focus

Word Used in Sentence(s)

(1)   "Afghanistan this week plans to ask during President Hamid Karzia's Washington visit for more US assistance to be <u>channeled</u> directly in government coffers, the country's top finance official said."

—Hodge, Nathan. 2013. Kabul to Seek More Control Over US Aid, World News. *Wall Street Journal*, January 7.

CHALLENGE

(1)   brave; call into question; confront; contest; competition; dare; defy; question; test; throw down the gauntlet

Word Used in Sentence(s)

(1)   "Accept the <u>challenges</u> so that you may feel the exhilaration of victory."

—General George Patton, American general WWI and WWII (1885–1945)

(1) "The greatest <u>challenge</u> to any thinker is stating the problem in a way that will allow a solution."

—Bertrand Russell, English logician and philosopher (1872–1970)

CHALLENGE THE PROCESS/STATUS QUO

(1) call into question; question the existing processes, rules, standards, or regulations

Word Used in Sentence(s)

(1) <u>Challenging the status quo</u> as a leadership behavior requires some finesse on the leader's part. The leaders must strike a balance between challenging respectfully and being a team player.

(1) Research shows that individuals will risk <u>challenging the status quo</u> only when two conditions are met: (1) They have a high-quality relationship with their leader, and (2) They know it's their job to bring up new ideas.

CHAMPION

(1) advocate; back; be a winner; campaign for; crusade for; excel; fight for; stand up for; support; uphold

Word Used in Sentence(s)

(1) "We cannot be both the world's leading <u>champion</u> of peace and the world's leading supplier of the weapons of war."

—Jimmy Carter, 39th president of the United States (1924–)

(1) "<u>Champion</u> the right to be yourself; dare to be different and to set your own pattern; live your own life and follow your own star."

—Wilfred Peterson, American author (1900–1995)

(1) <u>Championing</u> the new compensation plan made Sharon a popular choice for the sales VP.

<u>Collocates to: approaches, causes, freedom, ideas, issues, reforms, values</u>

CHANNEL

(1)   course; conduit; concentrate; control; convey; direct; feed; focus; path; route

Word Used in Sentence(s)

(1) "A strong man and a waterfall always <u>channel</u> their own path."

—Chinese Proverb

(1) "Goals help you <u>channel</u> your energy into action."

—Les Brown, American author, entrepreneur, and motivational speaker

(1) "Marketing and Finance have a famously fractious relationship, with each accusing the other of failing to understand how to create value. That tension may seem to be dysfunctional, but when <u>channeled</u> right, it can actually be productive."

—*Harvard Business Review* (June, 2007): 25.

CHOOSE

(1)   decide; elect; indicate; pick; point out; prefer; select; take; want; wish

Word Used in Sentence(s)

(1) "Leaders are people who use influence to create change, they have followers because other people see value of their ideas or suggestions and <u>choose</u> to go along or align with them."

—Schermerhorn, John, Richard Osborn, Mary UHL-Bien, and James Hunt. 2012. *Organizational Behavior*. 12th ed. New York: John Wiley & Sons, Inc., 4.

(1) "Every act of will is an act of self-limitation. To desire action is to desire limitation. In that sense, every act is an act of self-sacrifice. When you <u>choose</u> anything, you reject everything else."

—G. K. Chesterton , English-born Gabonese critic, essayist, novelist, and poet (1874–1936)

(1) "Every human has four endowments—self awareness, conscience, independent will and creative imagination. These give us the ultimate human freedom... The power to <u>choose</u>, to respond, to change."

—Stephen R. Covey, American writer of business books

CIRCLE THE DRAIN

(1) to be failing: going down the tubes/drain

Word Used in Sentence(s)

(1) "Participating on a highly visible project management team with a C-level manager on the team is an invitation to <u>circle the drain</u> with your career; it's a no-win proposition.

CIRCUMSCRIBE

(1) boundary line; confine; define limit; delineate; demarcate; draw a line around; mark out; restrict

Word Used in Sentence(s)

(1) "George Bush will join John Quincy Adams as the only other son of a president to win the White House. He also joins Adams as one of only four men who won the job despite losing the popular vote. Bush also plunges head-on into political uncertainty that could <u>circumscribe</u> his success."

—Sherman, Mark, Ken Herman, and Cox Washington Bureau. 2000. "Now the Work Begins: President-Elect Bush Faces Big Building Job with Little Time, News. *Atlanta Journal Constitution*, December 14.

<u>Collocates to: activities, boundaries, social, power, tenure, trying</u>

CIRCUMVENT

(1) evade; frustrate; get around

Word Used in Sentence(s)

(1) By <u>circumventing</u> the executive committee, the CEO knew he was taking a huge career risk.

CLUSTER

(1) agglomerate; assemble; bunch up; crowd together; constellate; flock; forgather; form; gather together or grow in bunches; meet

Word Used in Sentence(s)

(1) *"Sometime soon, in some location on Planet Earth, an assortment of companies, research institutions, entrepreneurs, and scientists will* <u>*cluster*</u> *together in an industrial egosystem. Their goal: to exploit the rapid discoveries about the human genome…"*

—Ghadar, Fariborz, John Sviokla, and Dietrich Stephan. 2012. Why Life Science Needs Its Own Silicone Valley, Idea Watch. *Harvard Business Review* (July/August): 25.

(1) *"The Image is more than an idea. It is a vortex or* <u>*cluster*</u> *of fused ideas and is endowed with energy."*

—Ezra Pound, American editor, poet, translator, and critic (1885–1972)

COACH

(1)   direct; drill; guide instruct; mentor; prepare; show; teach; train; tutor

Word Used in Sentence(s)

(1) *"One of the main responsibilities of a mentor is* <u>*coach*</u> *the protégé through the nuances of a new task or give a challenging assignment intended to stretch a protégé beyond his or her comfort zone."*

—Johnson, W. Brad, and Charles R. Ridley. 2004. *The Elements of Mentoring.* New York: Palgrave Macmillan, 4.

(1) *"Although hiring managers typically put premium on analysts' quantitative skills, outstanding* <u>*coaching*</u> *skills are more valuable. Instead of simply answering questions as they arise, people-oriented data experts can provide informal ongoing training to employees in departments outside their own increasing the organization's overall insight IQ."*

—Shah, Shvetank, Andrew Horne, and Jamie Capella. 2012. Good Data Won't Guarantee Good Decisions, Idea Watch. *Harvard Business Review* (April): 24.

COALESCE

(1)   blend; combine; come together; fuse; merge; grow into a single whole; unite

Word Used in Sentence(s)

(1) "After a certain high level of technical skill is achieved, science and art tend to <u>coalesce</u> in esthetics, plasticity, and form. The greatest scientists are always artists as well."

—Albert Einstein, American, theoretical physicist (1879–1955)

(1) Bob was able to <u>coalesce</u> more than 100 diverse stakeholders into an effective, efficient company asset.

COAX

(1) cajole; charm; entice; inveigle; lure; persuade somebody gently; sweet talk; tempt; urge gently; wheedle; win over

Word Used in Sentence(s)

(1) "A few progressive companies have been able to <u>coax</u> better performance from their teams by treating their sales force like a portfolio of investments that require different levels and kinds of attention."

—Steenburgh, Thomas, and Michael Ahearne. 2012. Motivating Salespeople: What Really Works. *Harvard Business Review* (July/August): 71.

(1) "Happiness is like a cat. If you try to <u>coax</u> it or call it, it will avoid you. It will never come. But if you pay no attention to it and go about your business, you'll find it rubbing up against your legs and jumping into your lap."

—William Bennett, American author and politician (1943–)

COLLABORATE

(1) act as a team; join forces; team up; work with others to achieve common goals; work in partnership

Word Used in Sentence(s)

(1) "EMCF's ability to <u>collaborate</u> with industry peers created substantial benefits for society and set an example for others—notably the Obama administration, which found the pilot and inspiration for its Social Innovation Fund…"

—Tierney, Thomas. 2011. Collaborating for the Common Good. *Harvard Business Review* (July/August): 38.

(1) "A traditional project management approach would not work for the proposed project. Success depended on bridging dramatically different national, organizational, and occupational cultures to <u>collaborate</u> in fluid groupings that emerged and dissolved in response to needs that were identified as the work progressed."

—Edmondson, Amy C. 2012. Teamwork on the Fly, Spotlight. *Harvard Business Review* (April): 74.

(1) In today's global economy many businesses must practice co-opition which is <u>collaboration</u> with not only intra departmental groups but also vendors, suppliers, stakeholders, NGOs, and, in some cases, competitors.

COMBINE

(1)   amalgamate; blend; coalesce; come together; fuse; join; intermix; merge; mingle; mix; unite

Word Used in Sentence(s)

(1) "On October 25, 2005, the Swedish telecommunications equipment maker Erickson announced the acquisition of key parts of Marconi's telecom business—thus starting a wave of deals that would reshape the global industry. Many competitors responded to the news by initiating similar moves. Alcatel and Lucent merged in 2006; Nokia and Siemens <u>combined</u> their telecom equipment units the following year."

—Keil, Thomas, and Tomi Laamanen. 2011. When Rivals Merge, Think Before You Follow Suit, Idea Watch. *Harvard Business Review* (December): 25.

(1) "What has once happened, will invariably happen again, when the same circumstances which <u>combined</u> to produce it, shall again <u>combine</u> in the same way."

—Abraham Lincoln, 16th president of the United States (1809–1865)

COMMAND

(1)   to be in authority; to have at one's disposal; be in charge; control over; dominate; give orders; master of; rule

Word Used in Sentence(s)

(1) *"Companies <u>command</u> enormous resources that influence the world for better or worse and their strategies shape the lives of employees, partners, and consumers on whom them depend."*

—Kanter, Rosabeth. 2011. How Great Companies Think Differently. *Harvard Business Review* (November): 68.

Collocates to: chain, center, central, control, post, structure, under

COMMUNICATE

(1) be in touch; be in verbal contact; call; connect; converse; convey; correspond; e-mail; impart; interconnect; publish; reveal; share; speak; talk; text; transmit information, thoughts or feelings; join; wire; write

Word Used in Sentence(s)

(1) *"Great companies have three sets of stakeholders: customers, employees, and shareholders—in order of importance…the board should <u>communicate</u> that formula to the shareholders so they understand the greater good that the company represents."*

—Horst, Gary. 2012. Business Advisor, CEOs Need a NEW Set of Beliefs. *HBR Blog*, September 21.

(1) *"Ninety percent of leadership is the ability to <u>communicate</u> something people want."*

—Dianne Feinstein, American senator (1933–)

(1) *"Start with good people, lay out the rules, <u>communicate</u> with your employees, motivate them and reward them. If you do all those things effectively, you can't miss."*

—Lee Iacocca, American, business executive

(1) *"Mayor Bill Akers of Seaside Height, NJ now removed from the whirlwind of Hurricane Sandy's ferocity, and with the benefit of hindsight, the major says he has his regrets. He could, he says, have stopped by one of the shelters to speak to residents personally. He would have <u>communicated</u> information sooner."*

— *Star Ledger.* 2012. Dan Goldberg Responses to Sandy: From Great to Galling, In Perspective, Middlesex Edition, November 11.

Collocates to: able, ability, effectively, information, language, ways

COMPRISE

(1)   comprehend; consist of; constitute; compose; include; make up

Word Used in Sentence(s)

(1) "Self-professed conservatives <u>comprise</u> about 40% to 45% of the electorate."

—Paul Weyrich, American conservative political activist and commentator (1942–2008)

(1) "Remember, that of all the elements that <u>comprise</u> a human being, the most important, the most essential, the one that will sustain, transcend, overcome and vanquish obstacles is—Spirit!"

—Buddy Ebsen, American character, actor, and dancer (1908–2003)

CONCATENATE

(1)   integrate; linked together; unite or join in a series or chain

CONCEIVE

(1)   create; envisage; imagine; invent original idea; understand; picture; visualize

(2)   elaborate; begin life; dream; form; make up

Word Used in Sentence(s)

(1) "Four score and seven years ago our fathers brought forth on this continent a nation, <u>conceived</u> and dedicated to the proposition that all men are created equal."

—Abraham Lincoln, 16th president of the United States (1809–1865)

CONCENTRATE

(1)   direct one's attention; draw together; make central

Word Used in Sentence(s)

(1) "Research conducted in the auto industry shows that when people see a detailed prototype, something odd happens: they <u>concentrate</u> on the prototype's form and function, forgetting to attend to any remaining

ambiguities about the problem the product is meant to solve or the obstacles in the way.

—Leonardi, Paul. 2011. Early Prototypes Can Hurt a Team's Creativity, Innovations. *Harvard Business Review* (December): 28.

CONFORM

(1)   go along with; comply; follow actions of others

Word Used in Sentence(s)

(1) "This is the very devilish thing about foreign affairs: they are foreign and will not always <u>conform</u> to our whim."

—James Reston Scottish, journalist (1909–1995)

Word Used with Rhythm and Imagery

- **Metaphor**—"A man's faults all conform to his type of mind. Observe his faults and you may know his virtues" (Chinese proverb).

CONNECT

(1)   associate; attach; combine; fasten; join; interrelate; link; relate; tie; unite

Word Used in Sentence(s)

(1) "Self-discipline is an act of cultivation. It requires you to <u>connect</u> today's actions to tomorrow's results. There's a season for sowing a season for reaping. Self-discipline helps you know which is which."

—Gary Ryan Blair, American motivational speaker and author

(1) "We cannot live only for ourselves. A thousand fibers <u>connect</u> us with our fellow men; and among those fibers, as sympathetic threads, our actions run as causes, and they come back to us as effects."

—Herman Melville, American short-story writer, novelist, and poet (1819–1891)

(1) "Creativity is just <u>connecting</u> things. When you ask creative people how they did something, they feel a little guilty because they didn't really do it, they just saw something. It seemed obvious to them after a while. That's because they were able to <u>connect</u> experiences they've had and synthesize new things."

—Steve Jobs, American entrepreneur, cofounder, chairman, and CEO of Apple, Inc. (1955–2011)

Word Used with Rhythm and Imagery

- **Repetition**—"Learn fast, fail fast, correct fast, and <u>connect</u> fast" (Linda Chandler, American businesswoman, executive, and entrepreneur).

CONSERVE

(1) avoid waste; be careful with; go easy on; husband; keep something from damage, harm or loss; preserve; protect; save; safeguard; support; maintain; use sparingly so not to exhaust

(2) bottle; can; put up; store

Word Used in Sentence(s)

(1) The firm's new energy policy will <u>conserve</u> more than 50 thousand megawatts of electrical power per month.

(1) "The U.S. Department of Defense took an unprecedented step on May 15, 2007, blocking troop access to MySpace, YouTube, and other popular Websites. The official reason was to <u>conserve</u> bandwidth."

—Fritzon, Art, Lloyd Howell, and Dov Zakheim. 2000. Military of Millennials. *Strategy +Business* Winter (9): 18.

Word Used with Rhythm and Imagery

- **Parallelism**—"In the end we will <u>conserve</u> only what we love. We will love only what we understand. We will understand only what we are taught" (Baba Dioum, Senegalese environmentalist and poet).

<u>Collocates to: biodiversity, cash, effort, electricity, energy, fuel, heat, help, resources, power, species, water</u>

CONSIDER

(1) bear in mind; believe; care about; cogitate; contemplate; chew over; deliberate; deem; judge; ponder; regard as; reflect or mull over; ruminate; study; take into account; think; weigh

Word Used in Sentence(s)

(1) "You must <u>consider</u> the bottom line, but make it integrity before profits."

—Denis Waitley, American motivational speaker and author (1933–)

(1) "The greatest difficulty is that men do not think enough of them-selves, do not <u>consider</u> what it is that they are sacrificing when they fol-low in a herd, or when they cater for their establishment."

—Ralph Waldo Emerson, American poet, lecturer, and essayist (1803–1882)

CONNOTE

(1) of facts; imply meaning or ideas beyond the explicit; involve as a condition or accompaniment; suggest

Word Used in Sentence(s)

(1) "Freedom is not worth having if it does not <u>connote</u> freedom to err. It passes my comprehension how human beings, be they ever so experi-enced and able, can delight in depriving other human beings of that pre-cious right."

—Mohandas Gandhi, Indian philosopher (1869–1948)

CONQUER

(1) capture; confound; defeat; dominate; master something difficult; over-come; overpower; overthrow; seize by force; subjugate; surmount; take; take control; triumph; win victory; vanquish

(2) win someone's love or affection

Word Used in Sentence(s)

(1) "It is more important for a leader to <u>conquer</u> himself than to <u>con-quer</u> others."

—Aristotle, Ancient Greek philosopher and polymath (384 BC–322 BC)

CONSTITUTE

(1) build; compose; comprise; consist of; enact; establish; form; found; habit; habits; make; make up; physique; set up

Word Used in Sentence(s)

(1) "Bad planning on your part does not constitute an emergency on my part."

—Unknown

(1) "Force does not constitute right... obedience is due only to legitimate powers."

—Jean-Jacques Rousseau, French philosopher and writer (1712–1778)

Word Used with Rhythm and Imagery

- **Metaphor**—"Books <u>constitute</u> capital. A library book lasts as long as a house, for hundreds of years. It is not, then, an article of mere consumption but fairly of capital, and often in the case of professional men, setting out in life, it is their only capital" (Thomas Jefferson, American founding father, third president of the United States, 1743–1826).

CONSOLIDATE

(1) bring together; strengthen; merge; unite

Word Used in Sentence(s)

(1) If we <u>consolidate</u> the two departments, it will make our operations far more efficient.

(1) "Unlike Alexander, Julius Caesar stepped back from conquest to <u>consolidate</u> his holdings and undertake a radical reform of Roman government and society.

—Forbes, Steve, and John Prevas. 2009. *Power Ambition Glory*. New York: Crown Business Press, 8.

CONTRADISTINGUISH

(1) contrast; to differentiate by means of contrasting or opposing qualities; reveal differences; show disparity

Word Used in Sentence(s)

(1) These are our complex ideas of soul and body, as <u>contradistinguished</u>.

—John Locke, English philosopher and physician (1632–1704)

CONSTRUCT

(1) assemble; build; contrive; create; devise; draw to specifications; erect; form; make; put up; raise

(2) blueprint; compose; create; form; piece together; structure

Word Used in Sentence(s)

(1) <u>*Constructing*</u> *prototypes gives the customers a chance to make changes and have new models back the same day.*

(1) *"We* <u>*construct*</u> *a narrative for ourselves, and that's the thread that we follow from one day to the next. People who disintegrate as personalities are the ones who lose that thread."*

—Paul Auster, American author (1947–)

(1) *"Consequently I rejoice, having to* <u>*construct*</u> *something upon which to rejoice."*

—T. S. Elliot, American-born, publisher, playwright, literary and social critic (1888–1965)

CONTEMPORIZE

(1)   bring up to date; modernize; make contemporary

CONTEND

(1)   argue that something is true; assert; declare; insist; maintain; state

(2)   cope; deal with; fight with; oppose; struggle with

Word Used in Sentence(s)

(1) *"A universal theory of leadership* <u>*contends*</u> *that certain personal characteristics and skills contribute to leadership effectiveness in many situations."*

—DuBrin, Andrew. 1998. *Leadership Research Findings, Practice, and Skills.* Boston: Houghton Mifflin Company, 48.

(2) *"Never* <u>*contend*</u> *with a man who has nothing to lose."*

—Baltasar Gracian, Spanish philosopher and writer (1601–1658)

CONTRAVENE

(1)   conflict; deny; inflict; infringe; go against

Word Used in Sentence(s)

(1) "Sometimes it leads me even to hesitate whether I am strictly correct in my idea that all men are born to equal rights, for their conduct seems to me to <u>contravene</u> *the doctrine."*

—Benjamin F. Wade, American lawyer and United States senator (1800–1878)

(1) "Yates has denied wrongdoing and said that, with the benefit of hindsight, he would have reopened an inquiry into electronic eavesdropping of voicemail messages. After the hearing, Rupert Murdoch sent News International staff an email saying that the company has taken responsibility, and that the allegations 'directly <u>contravene</u> *our codes of conduct and do not reflect the actions and beliefs of our many employees.'"*

—Dodds, Paisley. 2011. Murdoch Rejects Blame for Hack Scandal at Hearing. Associated Press, International News, July 20.

CONTROL

(1)   be in charge of; be in command; direct; dominate; govern; have influence or power over; manage; organize; oversee; rule; run

Word Used in Sentence(s)

(1) "<u>Controlling</u> *is one of the four functions of management—ensuring that things go well by monitoring performance and taking corrective action as necessary."*

—Schermerhorn, John, Richard Osborn, Mary UHL-Bien, and James Hunt. 2012. *Organizational Behavior*. 12th ed. New York: John Wiley & Sons, Inc., 4.

CONJURE

(1)   adjure; arouse; bid; bring up; call forth; conspire; entreat; evoke; invoke; press; put forward; raise; stir; summon

Word Used in Sentence(s)

(1) *"Nothing is more memorable than a smell. One scent can be unexpected, momentary and fleeting, yet <u>conjure</u> up a childhood summer beside a lake in the mountains..."*

—Diane Ackerman, American writer (1948–)

Word Used with Rhythm and Imagery

- **Vivid imagery**—"No one who, like me, <u>conjures</u> up the most evil of those half-tamed demons that inhabit the human beast, and seeks to wrestle with them, can expect to come through the struggle unscathed" (Sigmund Freud, Austrian neurologist who became known as the founding father of psychoanalysis, 1856–1939).

CONVEY

(1) channel; communicate; conduct; express; impart; lead; make known; pass; put into words

(2) bring; carry; fetch; get; move; take from one place to another; transfer

Word Used in Sentence(s)

(1) *"Advertising doesn't create a product advantage. It can only <u>convey</u> it."*

—William Bernbach, American advertising executive (1911–1982)

Word Used with Rhythm and Imagery

- **Metaphor**—"Wealth, in even the most improbable cases, manages to <u>convey</u> the aspect of intelligence" (John Kenneth Galbraith, Canadian-American economist, 1908–2006).

CONVOKE

(1) assemble; call together; convene; summon to a meeting

Word Used in Sentence(s)

(1) The minority shareholders wanted to <u>convoke</u> a full ownership meeting to discuss the tenure offer.

(1) *"On Dec. 1, in direct defiance of Mr. Yeltsin, Mr. Khasbulatov will <u>convoke</u> a full Congress of Peoples' Deputies at which the President's*

powers to rule by decree and to name a government will be severely and possibly fatally challenged."

—Editors. 1992. Power of Russian Parliament's Leader Is Becoming Vexing Issue for Yeltsin. *New York Times*, November 25.

CORROBORATE

(1)   back up; confirm

Word Used in Sentence(s)

(1) I was able to <u>corroborate</u> Ken's account of the incident.

(1) "True ideas are those that we can assimilate, validate, <u>corroborate</u>, and verify. False ideas are those that we cannot."

—William James, American philosopher and psychologist (1842–1910)

COOPERATE

(1)   accommodate; aid; band; comply; conjoin; collaborate; to liaise; do what is asked or required; play the game; unite; to work or act together to achieve a common goal

Word Used in Sentence(s)

(1) "The Internet works because a lot of people <u>cooperate</u> to do things together."

—Jon Postel, American computer scientist (1943–1998)

(1) "Only strength can <u>cooperate</u>. Weakness can only beg."

—Dwight D. Eisenhower, 34th president of the United States, Supreme Allied Commander in WWII (1890–1969)

(1) "Leadership is based on inspiration, not domination; on <u>cooperation</u>, not intimidation."

—William Arthur Ward, American scholar, author, editor, pastor, and teacher

Word Used with Rhythm and Imagery

- **Antithesis**—"Only strength can <u>cooperate</u>. Weakness can only beg" (Dwight D. Eisenhower, 34th president of the United States, Supreme Commander of allied forces in WWII, 1890–1969).

<u>Collocates to: agreed, authorities, fully, investigation, police, refused, willing</u>

COORDINATE

(1) align, bring together; combine; direct; harmonize; manage; match up; organize; synchronize; work together

Word Used in Sentence(s)

(1) I want to see marketing and sales <u>*coordinate*</u> *their efforts much better.*

(1) "Of all the things I have done, the most vital is <u>*coordinating*</u> *the talents of those who work for us and pointing them towards a certain goal."*

—Walt Disney, American film producer, director, screenwriter, voice actor, animator, entrepreneur, entertainer, international icon (1901–1965)

(1) "My experience in government is that when things are non-controversial and beautifully <u>*coordinated*</u>*, there is not much going on."*

—John F. Kennedy, 35th president of the United States (1917–1963)

(1) "For Hayek, market institutions are epistemic devices—means whereby information that is scattered about society and known in its totality by no one can be used by all by being embodied in prices. It is from this conception of the role of markets that Hayek derives his most powerful argument for the impossibility of successful central planning. Even if the planners are wholly disinterested, they will be unable to collect centrally the information—often ephemeral and local, and sometimes embodied in traditional skills and entrepreneurial perceptions—that they would need to allocate resources and <u>*coordinate*</u> *activities effectively. Hayek's insight here is truly profound. He grasps that the problem that central-planning institutions cannot solve is not (as his mentor, Ludwig von Mises, supposed) merely a problem of calculation but rather a problem of knowledge. Because the planner cannot know relative costs and scarcities, the planned economy will in fact be chaotic and vastly wasteful. This is the real explanation for the poverty of all socialist and command economies. Their poverty does not flow from the cultural traditions."*

—Grey, John. 1992. The Road from Serfdom. *The National Review* 44 (8): 32–37.

<u>Collocates to: activates, agencies, aid, help, efforts, federal, international, response</u>

COUNSEL

(1) advise; deliberate; inform

Word Used in Sentence(s)

(1) "Counsel and conservation are a secondary education, which improve all the virtue, and correct all the vice of the first, and nature itself."

—Unknown

(1) "The big corporations should also actively counsel the smaller companies about the best practices and standards."

—de Rothschild, Lynn Forester, and Adam Posen. 2013. How Capitalism Can Repair Its Bruised Image, Opinion. *Wall Street Journal,* January 2.

COUNT

(1) add up; calculate; count up; number crunch; tally; total; tote

(2) consider; deep; hold; regard; view

Word Used in Sentence(s)

(1) "Organization charts and fancy titles count for next to nothing."

—Colin Powell, chairman of the U.S. Joint Chiefs of Staff, U.S. secretary of state (1937–)

Word Used with Rhythm and Imagery

- **Anaphoric**—"Many of the things you can count, don't count. Many of the things you can't count, really count" (Albert Einstein, German-born American physicist, 1879–1955).

- **Metaphor**—"We live in deeds, not years: In thoughts not breaths; In feelings, not in figures on a dial. We should count time by heart throbs. He most lives Who thinks most, feels the noblest, acts the best" (Aristotle, Ancient Greek philosopher, scientist, and physician, 384 BC–322 BC).

COUNTER

(1) act in advance or in response; meet or return; offer in response; to retaliate or respond

Word Used in Sentence(s)

(1) "The M&A domino effect occurs in industry after industry. It has played out over the past decade in pharmaceuticals, automotive manu-facturing and financial services. When a major rival executes a headline-making merger, companies often feel under attack...But is <u>countering</u> with your own M&A always the smartest move?"

—Keil, Thomas, and Tomi Laamanen. 2011. When Rivals Merge, Think Before You Follow Suit, Idea Watch. *Harvard Business Review* (December): 25.

COUNTERMAND

(1)   to officially cancel a previous order

Word Used in Sentence(s)

(1) As the national organization president, I have to <u>countermand</u> changes proposed by local clubs that violate national bylaws.

COZEN

(1)   beguile; to cheat; deceive; defraud; flimflam; trick

Word Used in Sentence(s)

(1) "Dalmar wasn't just any man. He was a devil! He'd managed to <u>cozen</u> every member of her household, every servant, every employee, till he had them all eating out of his hand."

—Thornton, Elizabeth. 1990. *The Worldly Widow*. New York: Zebra Books.

CREATE

(1)   bring about; build; cause to come into being; compose; design; give rise to; produce

Word Used in Sentence(s)

(1) It is imperative to our mission that we <u>create</u> new products.

(1) Hanna <u>created</u> the new brochure for the sales team.

(1) "We want to get better at designing and developing products. That requires a real self-awareness as a team, and that's an extremely important part of the culture we want to <u>create</u> here."

—Hann, Christopher. 2012. The Masters. *Entrepreneur* (March): 58.

Word Used with Rhythm and Imagery

- **Antithesis**—"In the sky, there is no distinction of east and west; people <u>create</u> distinctions out of their own minds and then believe them to be true" (Buddha, spiritual teacher from the Indian subcontinent, on whose teachings Buddhism was founded).
- **Parallelism**—"If you don't <u>create</u> change, change will <u>create</u> you" (Unknown).

CROSS THE RUBICON

(1) decision that cannot be reversed; die is cast; no turning back; pass a point of no return; take the plunge

Word Used with Rhythm and Imagery

- **Vivid imagery**—"A great statesman <u>crosses the Rubicon</u> without considering the depth of the river. Once he or she declares to cross it they must face any challenges and risks during the journey. Fretting on the shore won't make the dangers go away" (Chang Dal-Joong, Korea Joong ang Daily).

CROWD FUND

(1) the collective effort of individuals who network and pool their money, usually via the Internet, to underpin a project or business venture

Word Used in Sentence(s)

(1) The concept of <u>crowd funding</u> encompasses an inclusive nonauthoritarian management and provides a clear illustration of the benefit of involving people as stakeholders, rather than positioning people as reluctant customers or obstacles to be confronted and overcome by management.

CULTIVATE

(1) civilize; develop; domesticate; educate; encourage; foster; help; nurture; promote; refine; school; support; tame

(2) to tend to; till; work on

Word Used in Sentence(s)

(1),(2) One must learn to <u>cultivate</u> personal contacts in order to build a successful personal network.

(1), (2) "So how does a business leader go about <u>cultivating</u> a winning culture?...Interviews with academics and entrepreneurs yield some universal themes."

—Haan, Christopher. 2012. The Masters. *Entrepreneur* (March): 56.

(1), (2) "How do tactically strong leaders learn to develop a strategic mind set? By <u>cultivating</u> three skills: level shifting, pattern recognition, and mental stimulation."

—Watson, Michael. 2012. How Managers Become Leaders. *Harvard Business Review* (June): 68.

Word Used with Rhythm and Imagery

- **Antithesis**—(1) "Who provides the opportunity to <u>cultivate</u> patience? Not our friends. Our enemies give us the most crucial chances to grow" (Tenzin Gyatso, the 14th Dalai Lama, 1935–).

- **Metaphor**—(2) "One is wise to <u>cultivate</u> the tree that bears fruit in our soul" (Henry David Thoreau, American essayist, poet, and philosopher, 1817–1862).

CURTAIL

(1) clip; curb; cut back; cut short; decrease; hold back; inhibit; limit, pare down; restrain, restrict, rein in; shorten, trim

Word Used in Sentence(s)

(1) We were forced to <u>curtail</u> the grand opening celebration due to power failure.

(2) "The budget should be balanced. Public debt should be reduced. The arrogance of officialdom should be tempered, and assistance to foreign lands should be <u>curtailed</u>, lest Rome become bankrupt."

—Marcus Tullius Cicero, Ancient Roman lawyer, writer, scholar, orator, and statesman (106 BC–43 BC)

DAUNT

(1) cow; make fearful; intimidate; scare; to suppress the courage of; overwhelm

Word Used in Sentence(s)

(1) The goals presented by the executive committee were <u>daunting</u>.

Word Used with Rhythm and Imagery

- **Metaphor**—"Do not doubt a woman's power to aid; no toil can <u>daunt</u> a pure affection" (Silius Italicus, Roman council and poet, ca. 28–ca. 103).

<u>Collocates to: did, does, even may, others, would</u>

DEAL WITH

(1) contend; cope; handle; manage; see to; take action with regard to something; take care of; take in hand

Word Used in Sentence(s)

A manager with have to <u>deal with</u> much more than what is listed on his or her job description.

DECIDE

(1) adopt; agree; conclude; elect; fix on; go for; make a choice or come to conclusion; make up your mind; opt; pick; resolve; select; settle on; take

Word Used in Sentence(s)

(1) "Whatever you do, you need courage. Whatever course you <u>decide</u> upon, there is always someone to tell you that you are wrong. There are always difficulties arising that tempt you to believe your critics are right."

—Ralph Waldo Emerson, American poet, lecturer, and essayist (1803–1882)

(1) "The possibilities are numerous once we <u>decide</u> to act and not react."

—George Bernard Shaw, Irish literary critic, playwright, and essayist (1856–1950)

DECOMPRESS

(1)   lay back; to be relieved of stress; regain equilibrium; relax; unwind

Word Used in Sentence(s)

(1) "Allow yourself time to <u>decompress</u> and process what has happened."

—Unknown

<u>Collocates to: necessary, need, place, time</u>

DEDUCE

(1)   conclude; derive; determine; infer

Word Used in Sentence(s)

(1) "Beyond the obvious facts that he has at some time done manual labor, that he takes snuff, that he is a Freemason, that he has been in China, and that he has done a considerable amount of writing lately, I can <u>deduce</u> nothing else."

—Arthur Conan Doyle, Sr. Scottish writer, creator of the detective Sherlock Holmes (1859–1930)

<u>Collocates to: able, can, effects, possible</u>

DEEM

(1)   assess; hold; judge; regard; take for; view as

Word Used in Sentence(s)

(1) "They <u>deem</u> him the worst enemy who tells them the truth."

—Plato, classical Greek philosopher, mathematician (427 BC–327 BC)

(1) "I <u>deem</u> it the duty of every man to devote a certain portion of his income for charitable purposes; and that it is his further duty to see it so applied as to do the most good of which it is capable."

—Thomas Jefferson, American founding father, third president of the United States (1743–1826)

DEESCALATE

(1)   abate; to decrease in intensity, magnitude; to diminish in size, intensity, or extent; downsize; dwindle; ease; knock down; lessen; lower; reduce

Word Used in Sentence(s)

(1) A leader would move to <u>deescalate</u> the crisis rather than test fate.

(1) "The wives of domestic violence, for their part, are very, very feisty. Once an argument is started, they don't back down. They greet negative statements with negative responses—what psychologists call negative reciprocity. Like their husbands, they don't <u>deescalate</u> an argument if one gets started."

—Editors. 1993. Inside the Heart of Marital Violence. *Psychology Today* 26 (6): 48.

DEFENESTRATE

(1)   to throw out the window

Word Used in Sentence(s)

(1) "I should think that CNN and MSNBC would actually like to have the comfort of knowing that their on-air spouters and sermonizers weren't total hypocrites, and would <u>defenestrate</u> hosts who violate basic standards. But that isn't the world we live in."

—Michael Tomasky, The Guardian

DEFER

(1)   adjourn; bow; delay; give ground; hold off; lay over; postpone; put off; remit; shelve; stay; submit; suspend; stay; table; yield; wait; waive

Word Used in Sentence(s)

(1) "Morgan Stanley Chairman and Chief Executive James Gorman has been a strong proponent of <u>deferred</u> pay, an approach favored by

regulators and risk management experts. Traders are less likely to engage in risky behavior if they know the firm owes them millions of dollars in <u>deferred</u> compensation, according to his argument."

—Lucchetti, Aaron, and Brett Phibin. 2013. "Bankers Get IOUs Instead of Bonus Cash." *Wall Street Journal*, January 16.

DEFUSE

(1) cease or ease danger of menacing situation

Word Used in Sentence(s)

(1) The ability to <u>defuse</u> a potentially tense confrontation is not typically in a manager's job description.

(1) "Every once in a while, you meet someone who really knows how to 'read a room.' This is the individual, usually a seasoned executive leader, who can walk into a tense meeting and sense why two would-be collaborators are butting heads, why a third manager hardly speaks, and why a fourth seems to be protecting some unspoken priority. Then, with a few words, the room-reader can <u>defuse</u> the problem, get people back on track, and move the team to a new level of productivity."

—Art Kliener, Building the Skills of Insight. *Strategy + Business*, http://www.strategy-business.com/article/00154?gko=d4421&cid=TL20130117&utm_campaign=TL20130117 (accessed January 17, 2013).

(1) "The House defused one potential debt crisis Wednesday, while a top Republican set the stage for a broader debate over whether it is possible to actually balance the U.S. budget in coming years."

—Hook, Janet, Corey Boles, and Patrick O'Connor. 2013. Passing DEBT Bill, GOP Pledges End to Deficits, US News. *Wall Street Journal*, January 24.

<u>Collocates to: anger, crisis, criticism, help, potential, situation, tension, trying</u>

DEKE (OUT)

(1) fake; to trick; use decoy

DEIGN

(1)　condescend; lower oneself; unsuitable role for one's position

Word Used in Sentence(s)

(1) She would not <u>deign</u> to discuss the matter in a public forum.

Word Used with Rhythm and Imagery

- **Metaphor**—"<u>Deign</u> on the passing world to turn thine eyes, And pause a while from learning to be wise. There mark what ills the scholar's life assail—Toil, envy, want, the patron, and the jail" (Samuel Johnson, English writer, 1709–1784).

DELEGATE

(1)　assign; appoint; person assigned to represent others; transfer power

Word Used in Sentence(s)

(1) "Based upon studies on the practices of 20 leading multinational corporations we conclude that a heavy reliance on first tier suppliers is dangerous and the <u>delegation</u> has gone too far."

—Choi, Thomas, and Tom Linton. 2011. Don't Let Your Supply Chain Control Your Business. *Harvard Business Review* (December): 113.

(1) "Best practice companies such as Apple, Dell, HP, Honda, IBM, LGE, and Toyota do what we just advise: They have approved vendor lists but never completely relinquish decisions about a product's components and material to top-tier suppliers. They carefully determine which items they should directly source themselves and which they should totally <u>delegate</u>."

—Choi, Thomas, and Tom Linton. 2011. Don't Let Your Supply Chain Control Your Business. *Harvard Business Review* (December): 113.

DELIBERATE

(1)　confer; consider; consult; debate; meditate; mull over; ponder; plan; reflect; think carefully; weigh carefully

Word Used in Sentence(s)

(1) "Take time to <u>deliberate</u>, but when the time for action has arrived, stop thinking and go in."

—Napoleon Bonaparte, French military and political leader (1769–1821)

<u>Collocates to: act, attempt, choice, decision, deliberate, effort, slow, strategy, speed, policy</u>

DELIMIT

(1) bound; circumscribe; define; demarcate; determine; fix boundaries; mark out; restrict; set limits; state clearly

Word Used in Sentence(s)

(1) One of the steps a researcher should take is to <u>delimit</u> the scope of the study.

(1) Speech sounds cannot be understood, <u>delimited</u>, classified and explained except in the light of the tasks which they perform in language."

—Roman Jakobson, Russian linguist and literary theorist (1896–1982)

DELINEATE

(1) describe accurately; determine; draw an outline; identify or indicate by marking with precision; fix boundaries; represent something

Word Used in Sentence(s)

(1) I plan to <u>delineate</u> my ideas regarding the new product in my presentation to executive committee.

(1) "Do you want to know who you are? Don't ask. Act! Action will <u>delineate</u> and define you."

—Thomas Jefferson, American founding father, third president of the United States (1743–1826)

(1) His responsibility was to <u>delineate</u> the scope of internal audits for the board finance committee.

<u>Collocates to: boundary, combinations, limit, sections, scope, used</u>

DELEVERAGE

(1) bring down to a small extent, size, amount, number, etc.; lower degree of intensity; lower the price; reduce the debt of

DEMAND

(1) ask; call for; command; claim; entail; exact; insist; mandate; necessitate; order; petition; require; requisition; stipulate; ultimatum; want

Word Used in Sentence(s)

(1) "Coaching and mentoring <u>demand</u> a multilayered knowledge that mangers don't need to call their own."

—Nigro, Nicholas. 2003. *The Everything Coaching and Mentoring Book*. Avon, MA: Adams Media Corp., 58.

(1) "Power concedes nothing without a <u>demand</u>. It never did and it never will."

—Frederick Douglass, American abolitionist, lecturer, author (1817–1895)

(1) "Great organizations <u>demand</u> a high level of commitment by the people involved."

—Bill Gates, American entrepreneur and founder of Microsoft Co. (1955–)

DEMYSTIFY

(1) clear up; clarify; eliminate or remove mystery; make rational or comprehensible

Word Used in Sentence(s)

(1) "Some teachers who are able to <u>demystify</u> the compositional process by providing sequential instruction in how to compose which helps students capture the spirit."

—Conway, Colleen. 2008. The Implementation of the National Standards in Music Education: Capturing the Spirit of the Standards. *Music Educators Journal* 94 (4): 34–39.

<u>Collocates to: attempts, experience, help, process, research, trying</u>

DENOTE

(1) announce; be a sign or symbol of; designate; indicate; mean; represent; signify; symbolize

(2) allude to; convey; express; imply; in the name of; mean; refer to

Word Used in Sentence(s)

(1) "Accordingly, humanities has come to <u>denote</u> not just poems and stories but all refined art, including painting, music, sculpture, film, and the like. As a result, humanistic now means arty—in other words, refined, cultivated, and effete."

—Hocutt, Max. 1990/1991. Humanities? No. Liberal arts? Yes. *Academic Questions* 4 (1): 59.

(1) "In commercial circles, the term 'Power Center' has come to <u>denote</u> strip malls dominated by large stores with little space for small merchants."

—Morganfield, Robbie. 1995. Faith and Finances; Power Center Seen as Model for Urban Life. *Houston Chronicle*, September 10.

DEPLETE

(1) consume; eat up; exhaust; use up completely; wipe out

Word Used in Sentence(s)

(1) "Time and health are two precious assets that we don't recognize and appreciate until they have been <u>depleted</u>."

—Denis Waitley, American motivational speaker and writer, consultant (1933–)

<u>Collocates to: layer, protocol, resources, substances</u>

DEPRECIATE

(1) lower the value of; disparage; belittle; derogate

Word Used in Sentence(s)

(1) "Today people who hold cash equivalents feel comfortable. They shouldn't. They have opted for a terrible long-term asset, one that pays virtually nothing and is certain to <u>depreciate</u> in value."

—Warren Buffet, American business magnate, investor, and philanthropist (1930–)

Word Used with Rhythm and Imagery

- **Metaphor**—"Those who profess to favor freedom, and yet <u>depreciate</u> agitation, are men who want crops without plowing up the ground" (Frederick Douglass, American social reformer, orator, writer, and statesman, 1818–1895).

DERAIL

(1) interrupt; throw off course

Word Used in Sentence(s)

(1) He managed to <u>derail</u> the proposed merger.

(1) "I put less stock in others' opinions than my own. No one else's opinions could <u>derail</u> me."

—Judd Nelson, American screenwriter and producer (1959–)

DESIGNATE

(1) assign; delegate; design; doom; indicate; intend; point out or specify

Word Used in Sentence(s)

(1) "God is the name by which I <u>designate</u> all things which cross my path violently and recklessly, all things which alter my plans and intentions, and change the course of my life, for better or for worse."

—Carl Gustav Jung, Swiss psychiatrist and psychologist (1875—1961)

DESCRIBE

(1) account; delineate; depict; explain something; to give an account of something by giving details of its characteristics; report; outline

Word Used in Sentence(s)

(1) "When people <u>described</u> their personal best leadership experiences they told of a time when they imagined an exciting, highly attractive future for their organization. They had visions and dreams of what could be."

—Kouzes, James, and Barry Posner. 1995. *The Leadership Challenge.* San Francisco, CA: Jossey-Bass Publishers, 10.

(1) "If you are out to <u>describe</u> the truth, leave elegance to the tailor."

—Albert Einstein, American theoretical physicist (1879–1955)

(1) "In argument similes are like songs in love; they <u>describe</u> much, but prove nothing."

—Franz Kafka, German writer (1883–1924)

DETECT

(1)   ascertain; become aware of; discover; descry; distinguish; expose; find; identify; notice; perceive; reveal; sense; spot; uncover

Word Used in Sentence(s)

(1) Great managers have a skill of quickly <u>detecting</u> the strengths in their people.

(1) "It's hard to <u>detect</u> good luck—it looks so much like something you've earned."

—Frank A. Clark, English author and writer (1943–)

(1) "The Center for Creative Learning staff collected hundreds of peer-performance reviews and health-screening results from CEOs and other senior-level managers. From this data they <u>detected</u> a correlation that a leader's weight may indeed influence perceptions of leaders among subordinates, peers and superiors.

—Kwoh, Leslie. 2013. Marketing. *Wall Street Journal*, January 16.

DETERMINE

(1)   agree to; bound; decide; delimit; delimitate; demarcate; discover; establish; limit; judge; mark out; measure; resolve; settle on
(2)   ascertain; clarify; establish; find out; uncover
(3)   affect; control; govern; influence; mold; shape

Word Used in Sentence(s)

(1) The success of a strategy will be <u>determined</u>, in larger part, by the manager's ability to be flexible in the tactics used.

(1) The results of the research are one factor in whether or not we <u>determine</u> to proceed with the new product.

(1) "Your attitude, not your aptitude, will <u>determine</u> your altitude."

—Zig Zigler, American author, salesman, and motivational speaker (1926–2012)

(1) "Best practice companies such as Apple, Dell, HP, Honda, IBM, LGE, and Toyota do what we just advise: They have approved vendor lists but never completely relinquish decisions about a product's components and material to top-tier suppliers. They carefully <u>determine</u> which items they should directly source themselves and which they should totally delegate."

—Choi, Thomas, and Tom Linton. 2011. Don't Let Your Supply Chain Control Your Business. *Harvard Business Review* (December): 113.

DEVELOP

(1) achieve; advance; build up; evolve; exploit; expand; expound; extend; generate; gain; grow; increase; mature; strengthen; unfold; widen

(2) make known gradually

Word Used in Sentence(s)

(1) Someone will have to <u>develop</u> the software for this project.

(1) A manager's role includes <u>developing</u> his or her people to their fullest potential.

(1) "Smaller scale financial models since have been <u>developed</u>, with more advanced techniques including models called Edo and Sigma."

—Hilenrath, Jon. 2012. Fed's Computer Models Pose Problems, The Outlook. *Wall Street Journal*, December 31.

Collocates to: ability, help, plan, program, relationships, skills, strategies, students, understanding

DEVOLVE

(1) become someone else's obligation; pass on to a deputy or successor; transfer to another

(2) deteriorate

Word Used in Sentence(s)

(1) My desire to <u>devolve</u> authority has nothing to do with a wish to shirk responsibility.

—Dalai Lama, Tibean, high lama in the Gelug or "Yellow Hat" school of Tibetan Buddhism (1935–)

(1) "When a detailed prototype was built, the discussion rapidly <u>devolved</u> into arguments. Everyone kept saying 'why doesn't it have this feature or that feature?' One participant said the haggling went on for years."

—Leonardi, Paul. 2011. Early Prototypes Can Hurt a Team's Creativity, Innovations. *Harvard Business Review* (December): 28.

<u>Collocates to: authority, into, power, responsibility, soon, upon</u>

DEVISE

(1) conceive; concoct; contrive; create; design; develop; formulate; imagine or guess; invent; plan; plot; sot up; think up; work out or create something

Word Used in Sentence(s)

(1) The engineering team should <u>devise</u> the solution for the problem.

(1) "Because Zynga and Yelp and online startups with inherently social products, <u>devising</u> their social strategies is relatively straightforward."

—Pisorski, Mikotaj Jan. 2011. Social Strategies That Work. *Harvard Business Review* (November): 119.

DIAGNOSE

(1) analyze the cause or nature of something; detect; establish; identify a condition; make a diagnosis; spot

Word Used in Sentence(s)

(1) First <u>diagnose</u> the problem and then devise a solution to get the equipment running again.

(1) "In India, the Ministry of Agriculture's watershed management program coordinates NGOs that train government and other NGO staff to evaluate social impacts and <u>diagnose</u> organizational problems."

—Fisher, Julie. 2003. Local and Global: International Governance and Civil Society. *Journal of International Affairs* 57 (1): 19–39.

<u>Collocates to:</u> able, difficult, doctors, treat, problems, used

DIFFERENTIATE

(1) acquire a different and unique character; be a distinctive feature, attribute, or trait; become distinct; become different or specialized by being modified; mark as different; segregate; set apart; separate; tell apart

Word Used in Sentence(s)

(1) "Jack Trout updated his ideas on positioning consumer products with his book, The New Positioning, *co-authored with Steve Rivikin. Trout also began talking about <u>differentiation</u>, in which the focus of the marketing effort is communicating how your product is unique compared to competitive products."*

—Trout, Jack, and Steve Rivikin. 2006. *Differentiate or Die by The Marketing Gurus,* New York: Penguin Books, 1.

DIRECT

(1) address; aim; calculate; conduct; command; engineer; guide; head; immediate; lead; maneuver; orchestrate; send; take aim; target

(2) control the course; guide; point the way; show the way; steer

Word Used in Sentence(s)

(1) <u>Directing</u> is one of the four primary functions of management.

(1) "The results you achieve will be in <u>direct</u> proportion to the effort you apply."

—Denis Waitley, American motivational speaker and author (1933–)

(1) "In essence, if we want to <u>direct</u> our lives, we must take control of our consistent actions. It's not what we do once in a while that shapes our lives, but what we do consistently."

—Anthony Robbins, American advisor to leaders

(1) "Great ambition is the passion of a great character. Those endowed with it may perform very good or very bad acts. All depends on the principals which <u>direct</u> them."

—Napoleon Bonaparte, French general, politician, and emperor (1769–1821)

DISBURSE

(1) distribute; give out; hand out; expend; lay out; pay out

Word Used in Sentence(s)

(1) Our company <u>disburses</u> thousands of dollars in college scholarships every year.

DISCERN

(1) to have insight; see things in a certain way; discriminate; know the difference

Word Used in Sentence(s)

(1) "As far as we can <u>discern</u>, the sole purpose of human existence is to kindle a light in the darkness of mere being."

—Carl Gustav Jung, Swiss psychotherapist and psychiatrist who founded analytical psychology (1875–1961)

Word Used with Rhythm and Imagery

- **Antithesis**—"The first point of wisdom is to <u>discern</u> that which is false; the second, to know that which is true" (Lactantius, North African, early Christian author, 240–320).

DISCOMBOBULATE

(1) disturb; upset; puzzle; perplex

Word Used in Sentence(s)

(1) Too many fancy words will just <u>discombobulate</u> simple people.

(1) The frenzied pace of commodities trading can leave one <u>discombobulated</u>.

DISCOMFIT

(1)   confuse; deject; disconcert; foil; frustrate; mix-up; thwart

Word Used in Sentence(s)

(1)   The protesters can continue to argue but their points will not <u>discomfit</u> me, my mind is made up.

DISCLOSE

(1)   bring into view; communicate; divulge; make known release; reveal; unveil

Word Used in Sentence(s)

(1)   "In Atlanta, Delta, Newell-Rubbermaid, and Equifax have boosted contributions to defined contribution plans such as 401(k)s. Coca-Cola and SunTrust are among companies replacing their traditional pensions with cash-balance plans. # Coca-Cola and SunTrust say the moves aren't pension freezes since they're switching to cash-balance plans, which are also defined-benefit plans. However, in filings with the Securities Exchange Commission, both companies <u>disclose</u> that they have frozen or are freezing portions of their older pension plans."

—Grantham, Russell. 2009. Traditional Pensions All But Retired; Financial Crisis Forces Firms to Freeze Plans, NEWS. *Atlanta Constitution and Journal*, July 5.

<u>Collocates to: companies, declined, details, information, failed, required, status</u>

DISPARAGE

(1)   belittle; criticize; demean; denigrate; deride; laugh at; mock; pour scorn on; ridicule; run down, slight; sneer; vilify

Word Used in Sentence(s)

(1)   "When men are full of envy, they <u>disparage</u> everything, whether it be good or bad."

—Publius Cornelius Tacitus, Roman senator and a historian of the Roman Empire (AD 56–AD 117)

(1) *"But the <u>disparaging</u> of those we love always alienates us from them to some extent. We must not touch our idols; the gilt comes off in our hands."*

—Gustave Flaubert, French writer (1821–1880)

DISSEMINATE

(1) broadcast; circulate; distribute; propagate; publish; spread; scatter

Word Used in Sentence(s)

(1) *"Propaganda has a bad name, but its root meaning is simply to disseminate through a medium, and all writing therefore is propaganda for something. It's a seeding of the self in the consciousness of others."*

—Elizabeth Drew, American political journalist and author (1935–)

(1) *"The actions performed by great souls to spread, promote and disseminate knowledge to every strata of society is a great service to mankind."*

—Sam Veda, American, yogawear designer (1945–)

DISSIPATE

(1) blow; disappear; disintegrate; dissolve; fade; fritter away; thin out; throw away; spread out; waste

Word Used in Sentence(s)

(1) *"Beware of <u>dissipating</u> your powers; strive constantly to concentrate them. Genius thinks it can do whatever it sees others doing, but it is sure to repent every ill-judged outlay."*

—Johann Wolfgang von Goethe, German playwright, poet, novelist, and dramatist (1749–1832)

Word Used with Rhythm and Imagery

- **Metaphor**—"To penetrate and <u>dissipate</u> these clouds of darkness, the general mind must be strengthened by education" (Thomas Jefferson, American founding father, third president of the United States, 1743–1826).

DISSUADE

(1)   advise against; convince to take alternative action; deter; discourage; put off; talk out of

Word Used in Sentence(s)

(1) "The shortness of life cannot <u>dissuade</u> us from its pleasures, nor console us for its pains."

—Marquis de Vauvenargues, French moralist and essayist (1715–1747)

(1) "Cultures contain many cues and inducements to <u>dissuade</u> the individual from approaching ultimate limits, in much the same way that a special warning strip of land around the edge of a baseball field lets a player know that he is about to run into a concrete wall when he is preoccupied with catching the ball. The wider that strip of land and the more sensitive the player is to the changing composition of the ground under his feet as he pursues the ball, the more effective the warning. Romanticizing or lionizing as individualistic those people who disregard social cues and inducements increases the danger of head-on collisions with inherent social limits. Decrying various forms of social disapproval is in effect narrowing the warning strip."

—Thomas Sowell, American writer and economist (1930–)

DISTINGUISH

(1)   tell apart; tell the difference between; stand out

(2)   perform well and receive recognition

Word Used in Sentence(s)

(1) "Without feelings of respect, what is there to <u>distinguish</u> men from beasts?"

—Confucius, Chinese teacher, editor, politician, and philosopher (551 BCE–479 BCE)

(1) "Every man's life ends the same way. It is only the details of how he lived and how he died that <u>distinguish</u> one man from another."

—Ernest Hemingway, American writer (1899–1961)

(1) "Learn to <u>distinguish</u> the difference between errors of knowledge and breaches of morality."

—Ayn Rand, Russian-American novelist, philosopher, playwright, and screenwriter (1905–1982)

DITHER

(1) falter; flap; fuss; hesitate; shiver; shutter; tizzy; wait

Word Used in Sentence(s)

*(1) "Practice easing your way along. Don't get het up or in a **dither**. Do your best; take it as it comes. You can handle anything if you think you can. Just keep your cool and your sense of humor."*

—Smiley Blanton, American psychiatrist and psychoanalyst (1882–1966)

DIVAGATE

(1) digress; diverge; lose clarity; stray; turn aside from the main point; wander off the ranch

Word Used in Sentence(s)

(1) It is important for the speaker to not <u>divagate</u> from the critical point with too many side issues.

DO A ONE-EIGHTY

(1) to turn around and go in the opposite direction; to radically reverse one's decision, ideas, or opinions

Word Used in Sentence(s)

(1) He <u>did a one-eighty</u> in his political beliefs when he grew a little older.

DO YOUR HOMEWORK

(1) be prepared; get ready; be informed

Word Used in Sentence(s)

(1) Shana really <u>did her homework</u> in preparation for the job interview.

DOCUMENT

(1)   account for; detail; give proof; record; verify; write down

Word Used in Sentence(s)

(1)   "Fed officials are well aware of the flaws in the computer models. Chairman Ben Bernanke himself <u>documented</u> the importance of finance fragility in his days as an academic. "

—Hilenrath, Jon. 2012. Fed's Computer Models Pose Problems, The Outlook. *Wall Street Journal*, December 31.

DON'T FLY TOO CLOSE TO THE SUN

(1)   don't get carried away with success; don't become self-centered; don't try to be more than you are; don't become overexuberant

DOUBLE DOWN

(1)   to engage in risky behavior, especially when one is already in a dangerous situation

Word Used in Sentence(s)

(1)   "Voters go to the polls with an unusually clear choice in U.S. economic policy: We can <u>double down</u> on the current approach in hopes that bigger government will create jobs, or we can adopt growth policies that are more market-oriented and less government-centered."

—Malpass, David. 2012. Romney, Obama and the Economic Choice, Opinion. *Wall Street Journal*, November 6.

(1)   "Leading figures on both sides <u>doubled down</u> on their positions in interviews that aired Sunday. They blamed each other for the current standoff, reflecting the talks that House Speaker John Boehner (R,. Ohio) told Fox News Sunday have gone nowhere."

—Paletta, Damiah. 2012. Fiscal Cliff Talks at Stalemate, US News. *Wall Street Journal*, December 3.

DOWN SCOPE

(1)   downsizing a project; reevaluating whether a project should be done; strategic divestiture

Word Used in Sentence(s)

(1) Unlike <u>down scoping</u>, downsizing involves strategically laying off employees during times of economic stress. Such activity is clearly different from <u>down scoping</u>, which centers on refocusing to capture proper strategic control of the firm.

DRAW LINES IN THE SAND

(1) a particular idea or activity will not be supported or accepted; to create or declare an artificial boundary and imply that crossing it will cause trouble

Word Used in Sentence(s)

(1) "House Speaker John Boehner of Ohio in a conference call Wednesday told fellow Republicans to avoid <u>drawing lines in the sand</u>. 'We don't want to box the Whitehouse out.'"

—*Wall Street Journal*, November 9, 2012.

(1) If you have been negotiating in good faith and have been truthful, yet the other side continues to hold on to untenable positions, you may have to <u>draw a line in the sand</u> and be prepared to walk away.

DREAM

(1) to have an image; thoughts or emotions passing through the mind; a vision

Word Used in Sentence(s)

(1) "Do not dwell in the past, do not dream of the future, concentrate the mind on the present moment."

—Buddha, spiritual teacher from the Indian subcontinent, on whose teachings Buddhism was founded

(1) "There are those who look at things the way they are, and ask why... I dream of things that never were, and ask why not?"

—John F. Kennedy, 35th president of the United States (1917–1963)

(1) "This Is No Place to <u>Dream</u> Small"

—Ad headline for NY state in *Wall Street Journal*, December 12, 2012

Word Used with Rhythm and Imagery

- **Antithesis**—"<u>Dream</u> as if you'll live forever, live as if you'll die today" (James Dean, American motion picture actor, 1931–1955).

DRINK FROM THE WATERS OF LETHE

(1) to forget absolutely; have no memory of something; to be in oblivion

Word Used in Sentence(s)

(1) In Virgil's Aeneid, the souls of the dead <u>drank from the waters of the River Lethe</u> to erase the traces of their past lives before they could be born again into new bodies.

DRIVE

(1) ambition; energy; determination to make something occur; force into a particular state or condition; get up and go; initiative; instinct; passion to succeed; provide momentum; move or propel forcefully; steer progress towards

Word Used in Sentence(s)

(1) "We herd sheep, we <u>drive</u> cattle, we lead people. Lead me, follow me, or get out of my way."

—General George S. Patton, American general in World War I and II (1885–1945)

(1) "Enthusiasm releases the <u>drive</u> to carry you over obstacles and adds significance to all you do."

—Norman Vincent Peale, American protestant clergyman and writer (1898–1993)

(1) "Good business leaders create a vision, articulate the vision, passionately own the vision, and relentlessly drive it to completion."

—Jack Welch, American chemical engineer, business executive, and author (1935–)

(1) "We are all <u>driven</u> to acquire goods that bolster our sense of wellbeing. We experience delight when this drive is fulfilled, discontentment when it is thwarted."

—Nohria, Nitin, Boris Groysberg, and Linda-Eling Lee. 2008. Employee Motivation a Powerful New Tool, Honing Your Competitive Edge. *Harvard Business Review* (July/August): 81.

EARMARK

(1) allocate; appropriate; assign; allot; set aside; to set aside or reserve for special purpose

(2) to mark the ears of livestock for special identification

(3) to set a distinctive mark on

Word Used in Sentence(s)

(1) The manager earmarked those funds for a future project.

Collocates to: ban, money, process reform, request, spending

EARN ONE'S WINGS

(1) authorize; certify; check out; cut it; empower; enable; endow; entitle; equip; fill the bill; fit; make it; make the cut; make ready; measure up; pass; pass muster; prepared; prove competency or worth; sanction; score; qualify; to be reliable

Word Used in Sentence(s)

(1) There are too many young people coming out of college today who don't want to earn their wings in the traditional manner as a generalist but rather by specializing in a highly individualized role.

EDUCATE

(1) coach; create by training or teaching; edify; educate; give education to; inform; instruct; mentor; school; teach or refine; tutor

Word Used in Sentence(s)

(1) "Hajj recalls introducing cinnamon rolls to Dubai. 'There are a lot of foreigners there who know what we were about', he says, 'but we had to educate the locals with heavy sampling.'"

—Daley, Jason. 2012. New Market Opportunities. *Entrepreneur* (March).

EDUCE

(1) bring out; develop; elicit; develop; infer

Word Used in Sentence(s)

(1) "In other words, 'apartheid' becomes shorthand for the most egregious instances of systemic and overt racism that necessarily and automatically <u>educe</u> (or should <u>educe</u>) severe international condemnation."

—Editors. 2005. The Ethnicity of Caste. *Anthropological Quarterly* 78 (3): 543–584.

EDIFY

(1) bring out; derive something; develop; draw forth; elicit; enlighten; instruct

Word Used in Sentence(s)

(1) "Wherefore comfort yourselves together, and <u>edify</u> one another, even as also ye do."

—1 Thessalonians 5:11

<u>Collocates to: entertain, heal, inform, mortify, power</u>

EFFECT

(1) accomplish; bring about; to go into operation; make happen

Word Used in Sentence(s)

(1) The strategic plan is now in <u>effect</u>.

—Blaise Pascal, French mathematician, philosopher, and physicist (1623–1662)

Word Used with Rhythm and Imagery

- **Metaphor**—"Cause and <u>effect</u>, means and ends, seed and fruit cannot be severed; for the <u>effect</u> already blooms in the cause, the end preexists in the means, the fruit in the seed" (Ralph Waldo Emerson, American poet, lecturer, and essayist, 1803–1882).

EFFECTUATE

(1)   accomplish; cause to happen; to do

Word Used in Sentence(s)

(1) "...opportunity for all persons in the armed services without regard to race, color, religion or national origin. This policy shall be put into effect as rapidly as possible, having due regard to the time required to effectuate any necessary changes without impairing efficiency..."

—Morris J. MacGregor Jr., Integration of the Armed Forces (1940–1965)

Word Used with Rhythm and Imagery

- **Vivid imagery**—"...when it is such as we have been more accustomed to contemplate This opinion is indeed plausible at the first view, because it may be said that we go half-way to meet that Author, who proposeth to reach an end by means which have an apparent probability to effectuate it; but it will appear upon reflection, that this very circumstance, instead of being serviceable, is in reality detrimental ..." (John Ogilvie, "An Essay on the Lyric Poetry of the Ancients").

Collocates to: able, design, intent, necessary, justice, policy, purpose

ELICIT

(1)   bring out; bring to light; call forth; provoke a reaction; uncover

Word Used in Sentence(s)

(1) "The test of leadership is not to put greatness into humanity, but to elicit it, for the greatness is already there."

—James Buchanan, 15th president of the United States (1791–1868)

(1) "When you make speeches you elicit expectations against which you will be held accountable."

—Bill Bradley, American retired NBA basketball player and senator (1943–)

Collocates to: design, information, likely, questions, response, sympathy

EMANATE

(1)   give off; issue or originate from; ooze; send out; spring from; start; proceed

Word Used in Sentence(s)

(1) The sounds <u>emanating</u> from the board meeting were not comforting.

(1) "Every effort for progress, for enlightenment, for science, for religious, political, and economic liberty, <u>emanates</u> from the minority, and not from the mass."

—Emma Goldman, Lithuanian-born American international anarchist (1869–1940)

Word Used with Rhythm and Imagery

- **Simile**—"Speech <u>emanating</u> from a pure heart and mind of learned men and scholars are naturally pure just like water of a river." (Yajur Veda, one of the four canonical texts of Hinduism, the *Vedas*. By some, it is estimated to have been composed between 1000 and 600 BCE.)

Collocates to: from, light, rays, seem, sound

EMBARK

(1) begin something; board; get on; get started; go ahead

(2) put or take passengers aboard a ship or airplane

(3) begin a journey

Word Used in Sentence(s)

(1) "One company that has <u>embarked</u> on an ambitious program based upon the results of a skills-gap analysis is the division of the United Kingdom's Health Services that serves London."

—Hancock, Bryan, and Dianna Ellsworth. 2013. Redesigning Knowledge Work. *Harvard Business Review* (January/February): 62.

EMBED

(1) implant; insert; place something or place something solidly; set in; set or fix firmly in a surrounding mass to set flowers in the earth

(2) fix in the mind or memory

(3) insert a code, virus, or a routine for monitoring into a software program

(4) assign an observer to a group

Word Used in Sentence(s)

(1) "Business leaders naturally want their company's strategy to be understood and accepted by employees or, as we call it, '<u>embedded</u>.'"

—Calunic, Charles, and Immanuel Hermerck. 2012. How to Help Employees "Get" Strategy, Communications. *Harvard Business Review* (December): 24.

(1) "What accounts for the overwhelming importance of top managers to <u>embeddedness</u>? We believe the explanation is twofold. Senior leaders should have a unique understanding of their company's strategy; there may be no equal substitute when it comes to communicating and discussing it. And their position at the top is powerfully symbolic, giving them more credibility and authority than others have."

—Calunic, Charles, and Immanuel Hermerck. 2012. How to Help Employees "Get" Strategy, Communications. *Harvard Business Review* (December): 24.

(1) "<u>Embedded</u> in the five fundamental practices of exemplary leadership discussed above are behaviors that can serve as the basis for learning to lead. We call these the Ten Commandments of Leadership."

—Kouzes, James, and Barry Posner. 1999. *The Leadership Challenge.* San Francisco, CA: Jossey-Bass Publisher, 17.

EMBODY

(1) exemplify, express, or represent abstract; express; personify; represent; stand for; symbolize

Word Used in Sentence(s)

(1) "Alexander the Great <u>embodies</u> the 'my way or the highway' brand of leadership, something very different than the Xenophon's style. With this approach, you are either an ally or an enemy, there is no middle ground."

—Forbes, Steve, and John Prevas. 2009. *Power Ambition Glory.* New York: Crown Business Press, 6.

(1) "Laws that do not <u>embody</u> public opinion can never be enforced."

—Elbert Hubbard, American editor, publisher, and writer (1856–1915)

(1) "If we want the world to <u>embody</u> our shared values, then we must assume a shared responsibility."

—William Jefferson Clinton, 42nd president of the United States (1946–)

<u>Collocates to: culture, essence, ideals, institutions, principles, spirit, values</u>

EMBRACE

(1) adopt; incorporate; involve; make use of something; support; take on; take up; welcome something

(2) cling to; enfold; hold; hug

Word Used in Sentence(s)

(1) "Large companies, taking a page from start-up strategy, are <u>embracing</u> open innovation and less hierarchical management and are integrating entrepreneurial behaviors with their existing capabilities."

—Anthony, Scott D. 2012. The New Corporate Garage. *Harvard Business Review* (September): 46.

(1) "For some firms, history can be instrumental in transforming cultures that are no longer useful. Cultural change, we know, can be extremely difficult for people to <u>embrace</u>."

—Smith, George D. 2012. Your Company's History as a Leadership Tool. *Harvard Business Review* (December): 47.

EMPOWER

(1) allow; authorize; give authority or power to; sanction

(2) make one stronger and more confident, especially in controlling his or her life and claiming his or her rights

Word Used in Sentence(s)

(1) "I'm slowly becoming a convert to the principle that you can't motivate people to do things, you can only demotivate them. The primary job of the manager is not to <u>empower</u> but to remove obstacles."

—Scott Adams, American cartoonist (1957–)

(1) "As we look ahead into the next century, leaders will be those who empower others."

—Bill Gates, American business magnate and philanthropist, former chief executive and current chairman of Microsoft Co. (1955–)

(1) "Fear does not have any special power unless you empower it by submitting to it."

—Les Brown, American big band leader and composer (1912–2001)

(1) "In most companies, cultural resistance to empowering employees to use technology is system wide."

—Bernoff, Jeff, and Ted Schadler. 2010. Empowered. *Harvard Business Review* (July/August): 95.

Collocates to: America, individuals, people, students, women

EMULATE

(1) compete to successfully imitate; strive to equal, match or better; by means of imitation

Word Used in Sentence(s)

(1) Many foreign companies attempt to emulate American manufacturing but never manage to match the quality.

(1) "What do we lose by another's good fortune? Let us celebrate with them, or strive to emulate them, That should be our desire and determination."

—Sri Sathya Sai Baba, Indian spiritual leader (1926–2011)

(1) "When you see a worthy person, endeavor to emulate him. When you see an unworthy person, then examine your inner self."

—Confucius, Chinese teacher, editor, politician, and philosopher

(1) "Former Deloitte & Touche chairman Michael Cook courageously resigned from a males-only club frequented by his customers when he made a public commitment to the advancement of women. Other firms later emulated Deloitte's women's initiative."

—Kantor, Rosabeth. 2011. Courage in the C-Suite. *Harvard Business Review* (December): 38.

ENABLE

(1) aid; allow; assist; empower; facilitate; permit; render capable or able for some task; make possible; qualify; support

Word Used in Sentence(s)

(1) "The 1648 settlement at Westphalia though setbacks were many and vicious, <u>enabled</u> procedures fostering what eventually would be 'the international community,' a term curled many a lip in the midst of the twentieth-century world wars."

—Hill, Charles. 2012. Notable & Quotable, Opinion. *Wall Street Journal*, December 1.

(1) "Still, creating a system that <u>enables</u> employees to achieve great things—as a group—often comes down to the work of a single leader."

—Hann, Christopher. 2012. The Masters. *Entrepreneur* (March): 58.

(1) "Moral courage <u>enables</u> people to stand up for a principle rather than stand on the sidelines."

—Kantor, Rosabeth. 2011. Courage in the C-Suite. *Harvard Business Review* (December): 38.

(1) "Employees are motivated by jobs that challenge and <u>enable</u> them to grow and learn and they are demoralized by those that seem to be monotonous or lead to a dead end."

—Nohria, Nitin, Boris Groysberg, and Linda-Eling Lee. 2008. Employee Motivation a Powerful New Tool, Honing Your Competitive Edge. *Harvard Business Review* (July/August): 81.

ENABLE OTHERS

(1) develop talents of others; empower others; give authority and responsibility; help others achieve their goals; removing barriers

Word Used in Sentence(s)

(1) If you <u>enable others</u>, you begin a process of enabling yourself.

ENCOURAGE

(1) advance; assist something to occur; boost; further; give hope, confidence, or courage; motivate to take a course of action

Word Used in Sentence(s)

(1) *"Our duty is to* <u>encourage</u> *everyone in his struggle to live up to his own highest idea, and strive at the same time to make the ideal as near as possible to the Truth."*

—Swami Vivekananda, Indian spiritual leader of the Hindu religion (1863–1902)

(1) *"Leaders must* <u>encourage</u> *their organizations to dance to forms of music yet to be heard."*

—Warren G. Bennis, American scholar, organizational consultant, and author (1925–)

(1) *"Our analysis, to our knowledge, the first of its kind, found that firms that indiscriminately* <u>encourage</u> *all their customers to buy more [by cross selling] are making a costly mistake: A significant subset of cross-buyers are highly unprofitable."*

—Shah, Denish, and V. Kumar. The Dark Side of Cross-Selling, Idea Watch. *Harvard Business Review* (December): 21.

(1) *"Big business can do more to support smaller enterprises in their supply and distribution chains. To* <u>encourage</u> *small and medium-size businesses on the basis of their productivity rather than their experience or size would help establish the idea that everyone has a stake in the capitalist system."*

—de Rothschild, Lynn Forester, and Adam Posen. How Capitalism Can Repair Its Bruised Image, Opinion. *Wall Street Journal*, January 2.

<u>Collocates to: designed, development, efforts, growth, investment, policies, students, teachers</u>

ENCROACH

 (1)   make gradual or stealthy inroads or progress into; trespass

Word Used in Sentence(s)

(1) *"Never give way to melancholy; resist it steadily, for the habit will* <u>encroach</u>*."*

—Sydney Smith, English clergyman, essayist (1771–1845)

<u>Collocates to: land, on upon, rights, territory</u>

ENERGIZE

(1)   active; arouse; brace; excite; pump up; stimulate; to put fourth energy; vigorous

Word Used in Sentence(s)

(1) "The world of the 1990s and beyond will not belong to 'managers' or those who can make the numbers dance. The world will belong to passionate, driven leaders—people who not only have enormous amounts of energy but who can energize those whom they lead."

—Jack Welch, American chemical engineer, business executive, and author

(1) "We look at the dance to impart the sensation of living in an affirmation of life, to energize the spectator into keener awareness of the vigor, the mystery, the humor, the variety, and the wonder of life. This is the function of the American dance."

—Martha Graham, American dancer, teacher, and choreographer (1894–1991)

ENERVATE

(1)   cause to lose energy; debilitate; deplete; devitalize; drain; enfeeble; exhaust; fatigue; undermine; weary; wear out; weaken

Word Used in Sentence(s)

(1) "Reformers sought to strengthen certain measures while their opponents sought to repeal or <u>enervate</u> some provisions of the 1985 Defense Authorization Act. This fight became part of the work on defense authorization in 1986."

—Wirls, Daniel. 1991. Congress and the Politics of Military Reform. *Armed Forces & Society (Transaction Publishers)* 17 (4): 487–512.

ENGAGE

(1)   charter; engross; involve; occupy; participate; pledge; tie up; to bind by a promise

(2)   to arrange for the services of; employ; hire; mesh

(3)   to arrange for the use of; reserve

(4)   to draw into; involve

(5) to attract and hold; to employ and keep busy; to occupy

(6) to mesh together

Word Used in Sentence(s)

(1) "Those who are too smart to engage in politics are punished by being governed by those who are dumber."

—Plato, classical Greek philosopher, mathematician (427 BC–327 BC)

(1) "In motivating people, you've got to engage their minds and their hearts. I motivate people, I hope, by example—and perhaps by excitement, by having productive ideas to make others feel involved."

—Rupert Murdoch, Australian American media mogul (1931–)

(1) "Not to engage in the pursuit of ideas is to live like ants instead of like men."

—Mortimer Adler, American philosopher, educator, and editor (1902–2001)

(1) "Hike to the top floor of Thayer Hall, and you will find Lieutenant Colonel Greg Dardis engaging small groups of firsties in discussions of classical-leadership theory, dissecting such leading-edge thinkers as Morgan McCall and Peter Senge."

—Hammonds, Keith. 2006. *Grassroots Leadership: U.S. Military Academy from: Issue 47, June 2001, Fast Company's Greatest Hits, Ten Years of the Most Innovative Ideas in Business* New York: Penguin, 173.

Collocates to: activities, behavior, conversation, dialogue, likely, students

ENGENDER

(1) begat; create; come into existence; give rise to

Word Used in Sentence(s)

(1) Goodwill engenders good will.

(1) "Test ideas in the marketplace. You learn from hearing a range of perspectives. Consultation helps engender the support decisions need to be successfully implemented."

—Donald Rumsfeld, American politician and businessman (1932–)

(1) "For Mark Leslie, CEO of Veritas Software, it all came down to trust. 'I believe if you want to be trusted, you have to trust'...But the value of <u>engendering</u> trust is greater than the cost of being betrayed sometimes."

—Hann, Christopher. 2012. The Masters. *Entrepreneur* (March): 56.

ENHANCE

(1)   add to; grow; improve; increase; make better; make more desirable

Word Used in Sentence(s)

(1) "For Good Eggs, a San Francisco-based tech start-up aiming to <u>enhance</u> local food systems, a process of self-examination forms the very basis of the company's culture."

—Hann, Christopher. 2012. The Masters. *Entrepreneur* (March): 58.

(1) "It is important to note, however, that on the basis of current research and specific conditions (ophthalmologic or age), appropriate magnification—through the use of low vision devices and large print—can <u>enhance</u> the reading performance of individuals with low vision."

—Russell-Minda, Elizabeth. 2007. The Legibility of Typefaces for Readers with Low Vision: A Research Review. *Journal of Visual Impairment & Blindness* 101 (7): 402–415.

<u>Collocates to: ability, learning, performance, students, understanding, quality</u>

ENLIST

(1)   conscript; count on; engage; enroll; enter; sign up; join; join up; procure; recruit; register; solicit; volunteer

Word Used in Sentence(s)

(1) "A person who doubts himself is like a man who would <u>enlist</u> in the ranks of his enemies and bear arms against himself. He makes his failure certain by himself being the first person to be convinced of it."

—Ambrose Bierce, American writer, journalist, and editor (1842–1914)

(1) Leaders <u>enlist</u> followers by appealing to a common vision, hopes, and dreams.

<u>Collocates to: aid, help military, support, trying, volunteers</u>

ENSURE

(1) follow; guarantee; make certain; make sure

(2) make safe; secure; protect

Word Used in Sentence(s)

> *(1) "Despite genuine efforts to <u>ensure</u> fairness, some business may be inadvertently overlooking bias that creeps in at initial job placement. Others may underestimate early managers' impact on employees' career trajectories. And others may have neglected the topic of gender equality in recent years, considering it an issue of the past."*

—Carter, Nancy, and Christine Silva. 2010. Women in Management: Delusions of Progress, Idea Watch. *Harvard Business Review* (March): 21.

ENMESH

(1) catch; embroil; ensnare; entangle; implicate; involve; trap

Word Used in Sentence(s)

> *(1) "No matter how <u>enmeshed</u> a commander becomes in the elaboration of his own thoughts, it is sometimes necessary to take the enemy into account."*

—Winston Churchill, British politician, best known for his leadership of the United Kingdom during the Second World War (1874–1965)

> *(1) "They come here, they don't know the can'ts because they're fleeing things that are generally worse. And they see this place as the land of opportunity, and they come here and they—they—they <u>enmesh</u> themselves in it, and many of them do quite well—much better, in many cases, than some who are born and raised here."*

—Rush Limbaugh. 1996. Radio discussion. EIB network, January 18.

ENNOBLE

(1) confer dignity; elevate in degree, elegance, or respect

Word Used in Sentence(s)

> *(1) "Good actions <u>ennoble</u> us, and we are the sons of our deeds."*

—Miguel de Cervantes Saavedra, Spanish writer (1547–1616)

ENTAIL

(1)   have as a logical consequence; impose; involve; imply as necessary
accompaniment or result; require

ENVISAGE

(1)   conceive of; consider; contemplate the possibility; foresee; form mental
picture; imagine; visualize

Word Used in Sentence(s)

(1) "I did envisage being this successful as a player, but not all the hysteria around it off the golf course."

—Tiger Woods, American professional golfer

(1) "Running for President is physically, emotionally, mentally and spiritually the most demanding single undertaking I can envisage unless it's World War III."

—Walter F. Mondale, American politician, lawyer, and vice president
(1928–)

Collocates to: ability, difficult, impossible, situation, seems

ENVISION

(1)   conceive; conjure; dream; imagine; fancy; feature; ideate; imagine; picture; see; vision; visualize

Word Used in Sentence(s)

(1) If you could envision the best customer service operation, what would it be like?

(1) "The mind is the limit. As long as the mind can envision the fact that you can do something, you can do it, as long as you really believe 100 percent."

—Arnold Schwarzenegger, Austrian-born American actor and governor
(1947–)

(1) "The heroes of the world community are not those who withdraw when difficulties ensue, not those who can envision neither the prospect

of success nor the consequence of failure—but those who stand the heat of battle, the fight for world peace through the United Nations."

—Hubert H. Humphrey, 38th vice president of the United States, U.S. Senator from Minnesota (1911–1978)

(1) "The world is changing...Networks without a specific branding strategy will be killed...I envision a world of highly niched services and tightly run companies without room for all the overhead the established networks carry."

—Barry Dillar, American media executive (1942–)

ENTREAT

(1)   ask; beg; beseech; implore; plead; pray; request earnestly or emotionally

Word Used in Sentence(s)

(1) "I rather would entreat thy company To see the wonders of the world abroad, Than, living dully sluggardized at home, Wear out thy youth with shapeless idleness."

—William Shakespeare, English poet and playwright (1564–1615)

ESCHEW

(1)   abstain; avoid; distain; give a wide berth; have nothing to do with; shun; steer clear of

Word Used in Sentence(s)

(1) "An important part of Chief Executive Ron Johnson's Strategy at JC Penney has been to eschew sales and promotions in favor of everyday low prices."

—Lahart, Justin. 2012. Penney Must Endure Pain Before Gain, Ahead of Tape. *WSJ Money & Investing*, November 9.

(1) "In their own ways, Mayor Bloomberg and President Obama embody the obsessions of modern liberalism. Each holds an advanced Ivy League degree. Each believes he would make better choices for others that they could for themselves. Each has consequently eschewed the gradual and modest—the unglamorous improvements that might have better prepared Staten Island, for a dangerous storm."

—McGurn, William. 2012. Sandy and the Failures of Blue-Statism, Opinion. *Wall Street Journal*, November 6.

ESPOUSE

(1)   advocate; to support

Word Used in Sentence(s)

(1) Be careful how many causes you <u>espouse</u> because you may have trouble remembering which side of an argument you are supposed to be on.

ESTABLISH

(1)   begin; bring about; create; form; found; inaugurate; launch; set up or start something

(2)   ascertain; authenticate; confirm; corroborate; determine; cause something to be recognized; find out; prove; show; verify

Word Used in Sentence(s)

(1) "Leaders <u>establish</u> the vision for the future and set the strategy for getting there; they cause change. They motivate and inspire others to go in the right direction and they, along with everyone else, sacrifice to get there."

—John Kotter, American, former professor at the Harvard Business School, an acclaimed author (1947–)

(1) "College football ad deals also give marketers the chance to <u>establish</u> a presence on college campuses, notes marketers such as GM's Chevrolet brand."

—Bachman, Rachel, and Mathew Futterman. 2012. College Football's Big-Money, Big-Risk Business Model, Marketplace. *Wall Street Journal*, December 10.

ESTEEM

(1)   admire; appreciate; have great regard; respect; value highly

(2)   hold to be; consider; regard

Word Used in Sentence(s)

(1) "Dozens of recent experiments show that rewarding self-interest with economic incentives can backfire. When we take a job or buy a car, we are not only trying to get stuff we are also trying to be a certain kind

of person. People desire to be <u>esteemed</u> by others and to be seen as ethical and dignified. And they don't want to be taken as suckers."

—Bowels, Samuel. 2009. When Economic Incentives Backfire, Forethought. *Harvard Business Review* (March): 22.

EVOKE

(1)   to bring to mind a memory or feeling, especially from the past; call forth or summon; to provoke a particular reaction or feeling

Word Used in Sentence(s)

(1)   "Every revolutionary idea seems to <u>evoke</u> three stages of reaction. They may be summed up by the phrases: 1) It's completely impossible. 2) It's possible, but it's not worth doing. 3) I said it was a good idea all along."

—Arthur C. Clarke, English writer (1917–)

(1)   "Merchandisers, by embedding subliminal trigger devices in media, are able to <u>evoke</u> a strong emotional relationship between, say, a product perceived in an advertisement weeks before and the strongest of all emotional stimuli—love (sex) and death."

—Unknown

EXALT

(1)   animate; boost; enliven; elevate; glorify; inspire; intensify; invigorate; laud; to praise or worship somebody or something; raise high; proclaim

Word Used in Sentence(s)

(1)   "Whatever enlarges hope will also exalt courage."

—Samuel Johnson, English writer (1709–1784)

(1)   "Just once in a while let us exalt the importance of ideas and information."

—Edward R. Murrow, American broadcast journalist (1908–1965)

EXCEED

(1)   beat; go beyond; surpass what was expected or thought possible; to be more or greater than; outdo; overachieve

Word Used in Sentence(s)

(1) "People expect a certain reaction from a business, and when you pleasantly exceed those expectations, you've somehow passed an important psychological threshold."

—Richard Thalheimer, American business executive

(1) "Rarely do the followers exceed the expectations of the leaders."

—Unknown

EXCEL

(1) shine; stand out; surpass
(2) be better, greater, or superior to others in the same field, profession, endeavor

Word Used in Sentence(s)

(1) "Allow yourself to be inspired. Allow yourself to succeed. Dare to excel."

—Unknown

(1) "Those who are blessed with the most talent don't necessarily outperform everyone else. It's the people with follow-through who excel."

—Mary Kay Ash, American businesswoman, founder of Mary Kay Cosmetics (1915–2001)

(1) "I founded Wang Laboratories to show that Chinese could excel at things other than running laundries and restaurants."

—An Wang, Chinese-born American computer engineer and inventor (1920–1990)

EXCOGITATE

(1) contrive; devise; discover; find; invent; study or think something through carefully and in detail

Word Used with Rhythm and Imagery

- **Vivid imagery**—"By evening, there were still groups fighting in the outlying neighborhoods. Fires and looting were involved and a certain amount of gunfire. Nobody could say when it began to quieten, but by nine P.M. the streets were silent and the fires had been extinguished.

White billowy clothes, sheets mainly, blew around the streets for a few days before they were all picked up. Need I <u>excogitate</u> upon this? (Wayne Wightman, Wayne. 2008. A Foreign Country. *Fantasy & Science Fiction* 115 (6): 7).

EXCULPATE

(1) acquit; clear from blame; excuse; exonerate; free someone from guilt or wrongdoing; let off

Word Used in Sentence(s)

(1) "I'm disappointed we won't get the witnesses, because they <u>exculpate</u> my client."

—Frank Dunhan, American lawyer (1946–2006)

<u>Collocates to: any, also, client, defendants, people, responsibility</u>

EXEMPLIFY

(1) characterize; demonstrate; embody; epitomize; personify; serve as an example; represent; show; typify or model of something

Word Used in Sentence(s)

(1) "It is easier to <u>exemplify</u> values than teach them."

—Theodore Hesburgh, American, priest of the Congregation of Holy Cross, president emeritus of the University of Notre Dame (1917–)

Word Used with Rhythm and Imagery

- **Parallelism**—"There is only one way in which one can endure man's inhumanity to man and that is to try, in one's own life, to <u>exemplify</u> man's humanity to man" (Alan Paton, South African writer and educator, 1903–1988).

<u>Collocates to: activities, character, leadership, spirit, values, ways</u>

EXHORT

(1) encourage; give serious warning; goad; inspire; press; prod; push; spur; urge strongly

Word Used in Sentence(s)

(1) "The most excellent and divine counsel, the best and most profitable advertisement of all others, but the least practiced, is to study and learn how to know ourselves. This is the foundation of wisdom and the highway to whatever is good. God, Nature, the wise, the world, preach man, <u>exhort</u> him both by word and deed to the study of himself."

—Pierre Charron, French 16th-century Catholic theologian and philosopher (1541–1603)

(1) "I <u>exhort</u> you also to take part in the great combat, which is the combat of life, and greater than every other earthly combat."

—Plato, classical Greek philosopher, mathematician (424 BC–327 BC)

EXPATIATE

(1) speak or write at great length or detail

Word Used in Sentence(s)

(1) "Robert E. Lee was generally described as antislavery. This assumption rests not on any public position he took but on a passage in an 1856 letter to his wife. The passage begins: 'In this enlightened age, there are few I believe, but what will acknowledge, that slavery as an institution, is a moral &; political evil in any Country. It is useless to <u>expatiate</u> on its disadvantages."

—Blount, Roy. 2004. Making Sense of Robert E. Lee. *Smithsonian* 34 (4): 58.

EXPIATE

(1) amends; make amends for wrongdoing

Word Used in Sentence(s)

(1) "Some Republicans remain terminally uncomfortable with issues involving race. One can still find those who regard black Americans as a group apart—poor, exotic, faintly criminal, and not fully equipped for life in polite society. In the grips of remorse, these Republicans act like white liberals: anxious, guilt-besotted, stricken by low self-esteem. They

try to <u>expiate</u> their sins by behaving like what Peggy Noonan once called 'low-rent Democrats.'"

—Snow, Tony. 1992. The Race Card. *New Republic* 207 (25): 17–20.

<u>Collocates to: against, desire, helped, sins, guilt</u>

EXPEDITE

(1)   hasten; speed up; ease the progress of

Word Used in Sentence(s)

(1)   "The art of statesmanship is to foresee the inevitable and to <u>expedite</u> its occurrence."

—Charles M. de Talleyrand, French statesman (1754–1838)

EXPLICATE

(1)   clarify; explain; elucidate; expound; illuminate; interpret; make clear; spell out

Word Used in Sentence(s)

(1)   The business plan components should <u>explicate</u> both the vision and mission of the firm.

(1)   The term <u>explicate</u> the quote means tell the whole truth. Make it plain to the reader and don't leave anything out; but also don't leave anything implied.

EXPOSTULATE

(1)   admonish; argue or make a friendly protest; disagree; complain; protest; object

Word Used in Sentence(s)

(1)   "Caroline drew in a breath to <u>expostulate</u>, then let it out again slowly as the necessity for realism overtook her."

—Perry, Anne. 1993. *Farriers' Lane*. New York: Fawcett Crest.

EXPUNGE

(1) efface; eliminate; erase; exercise; delete; destroy; obliterate; to rub or wipe out; strike out

Word Used in Sentence(s)

(1) "There is no man, however wise, who has not at some period of his youth said things, or lived in a way the consciousness of which is so unpleasant to him in later life that he would gladly, if he could, <u>expunge</u> it from his memory."

—Marcel Proust, French novelist, critic, and essayist (1871–1922)

EXPURGATE

(1) abridge; bleep; blue pencil; bowdlerize; castrate; clean up; cut down; purify writing by removing objectionable material; sanitize; scrub; shorten; squash; squelch

Word Used in Sentence(s)

(1) It was clear the outside consultant did not understand our market because I had to <u>expurgate</u> nearly the entire marketing plan he submitted.

EXTOL

(1) admire; command; eulogize; exalt; laud; praise; worship

Word Used in Sentence(s)

(1) "Many are always praising the by-gone time, for it is natural that the old should <u>extol</u> the days of their youth; the weak, the time of their strength; the sick, the season of their vigor; and the disappointed, the spring-tide of their hopes."

—George Caleb Bingham, American realist artist (1811–1879)

(1) "That sign of old age, <u>extolling</u> the past at the expense of the present."

—Sydney Smith, English clergyman, essayist (1771–1845)

EXTRAPOLATE

(1) conclude; deduce; infer; induce; generalize; posit; project; reason; suspect

Word Used in Sentence(s)

(1) "My hope is that I will take the good from my experiences and <u>extrapolate</u> them further into areas with which I am unfamiliar. I simply do not know exactly what that difference will be in my judging. But I accept there will be some based on my gender and my Latina heritage."

—Sonia Sotomayor, Supreme Court justice

Collocates to: can, data, findings, from, motion, results, track

EXTRICATE

(1) extract; disconnect; disengage; disentangle; free; free from difficulty; get out; remove

Word Used in Sentence(s)

(1) "Sometimes accidents happen in life from which we have need of a little madness to <u>extricate</u> ourselves successfully."

—François de la Rochefoucauld, French classical author (1613–1680)

(1) "You know from past experiences that whenever you have been driven to the wall, or thought you were, you have <u>extricated</u> yourself in a way which you never would have dreamed possible had you not been put to the test. The trouble is that in your everyday life you don't go deep enough to tap the divine mind within you."

—Orson Welles, American motion-picture actor, director, producer, and writer (1915–1985)

EXALT

(1) boost; celebrate; elevate; intensify; lift; promote; raise; rejoice

Word Used in Sentence(s)

(1) "Whatever enlarges hope will also <u>exalt</u> courage."

—Samuel Johnson, English poet, critic, and writer (1709–1784)

(1) "Affirmation of life is the spiritual act by which man ceases to live unreflectively and begins to devote himself to his life with reverence in order to raise it to its true value. To affirm life is to deepen, to make more inward, and to <u>exalt</u> the will."

—Albert Schweitzer, German missionary, theologian, 1952 Nobel Peace Prize recipient (1875–1965)

EXEMPLIFY

(1) characterize; demonstrate; epitomize; show or illustrate by being model of; personify; represent; show; typify

Word Used in Sentence(s)

(1) "David Maxwell, like Darwin Smith and Colman Mockler, <u>exemplified</u> a key trait of Level 5 leaders: ambition first and foremost for the company and concern for its success rather than for one's own riches and personal renown."

—Collins, Jim. 2001. *Good to Great*. New York: Harper Collins, 25.

EXPERIMENT

(1) research; test; trial; try something new to gain experience
(2) make or conduct an experiment

Word Used in Sentence(s)

(1) Leaders are not afraid to <u>experiment</u>, take risks, and learn from their mistakes.

EXTEND

(1) cover; encompass; make bigger; open or stretch out into additional space; outrange; spread; spread out; spread
(2) continue something for a time longer than normal; go on; run on; stretch longer than expected

Word Used in Sentence(s)

(2) "Christopher E. Kubasik, 51, Lockheed's president and chief operating officer, has been named to succeed Robert J. Stevens, 60, as chief executive. Kubasik is part of a new crop of contracting executives who have been groomed within their companies and are being tasked with

overseeing a transition that has required layoffs, buyouts and corporate restructuring. 'When I look at future challenges, I recognize they will certainly extend *beyond my mandatory retirement age,' Stevens told reporters Thursday morning."*

—Censer, Marjorie. 2012. Lockheed Latest Contractor to Announce New Leadership. *Washington Post*, April 27.

FACILITATE

(1) accelerate; aid; assist; ease; expedite; help; make easy; make possible; simplify

Word Used in Sentence(s)

(1) The ability to facilitate *and manage meetings are important leadership skills.*

(1) "The essential job of government is to facilitate, *not frustrate, job development."*

—Andrew Cuomo, American, 56th and current governor of New York (1957–)

(1) "Every human being must find his own way to cope with severe loss, and the only job of a true friend is to facilitate *whatever method he chooses."*

—Calab Carr, American novelist and military historian (1955–)

(1) "Boardroom discussions often center on just two questions: How can we sustain innovation? And do we have a plan for developing future leaders who can facilitate *this goal?"*

—Cohn, Jeffery, Jon Katzenbach, and Gus Vlak. 2008. Finding and Grooming Breakthrough Innovators. *Harvard Business Review* (December): 64.

(1) "To be a leader, one has to make a difference and facilitate *positive change."*

—DuBrin, Andrew. 1998. *Leadership Research Findings, Practice, and Skills*. Boston: Houghton Mifflin Company, 2.

Collocates to: communications, development, design, learning, order, process

FASHION

(1)   accommodate; adapt; direct; to give shape or form to; train or influence the state or character

Word Used in Sentence(s)

(1) "At company headquarters, Clint Smith co-founder and CEO of Emma e-mail Marketing, <u>fashioned</u> an open floor plan expressly to inspire a spirit of collaboration among the more than 100 employees."

—Hann, Christopher. 2012. The Masters. *Entrepreneur* (March): 56.

FIGHT ON DEATH GROUND

(1)   deliberately choosing a strategy that leaves no options other than winning

Word Used in Sentence(s)

(1) In the 3rd century the Chinese strategist Sun Tzu...talked of <u>fighting on 'death ground</u>,' a place where an army is backed up against some geographical feature with no escape route. Without a way to retreat, Sun Tzu argued, an army fights with far greater spirit it would have on open terrain because death is viscerally present. Sun Tzu advocated deliberately stationing soldiers on death ground to give them the desperate edge that makes men fight harder. That is what Cortés did in Mexico. He burned his ships and his men knew the only way they could survive was to <u>fight on death ground</u>.

(1) "When it comes to the carbon pricing agenda, PM Gillard and her Labor Government are <u>fighting on death ground</u>—the terrain that the military strategist Sun Tzu described more than 2,000 years ago in The Art of War.*"*

—Eubank. 2011. Carbon Price Fight Price on Death Ground. *ABCnews.net*, March 17.

FINESSE

(1)   ability; assurance; dexterity; discretion; flair; grace; poise; refinement; sensitivity; skill; skillful maneuvering; smooth; subtlety; tact; use of subtle charm

Word Used in Sentence(s)

(1) "Experience is what allows us to repeat our mistakes, only with more finesse!"

—Unknown

(1) Be prepared to finesse what we can do; we need to make some hard decisions.

FIRST MOVE

(1) be first to market; take initial action; take quick action

Word Used in Sentence(s)

(1) An experienced web developer's first move is to get the client's signature on a comprehensive Web site development contract before starting any project.

(1) "The advantages to those who are first movers are three: (1) Technological leadership, (2) preemption of assets and capital, and (3) increase in buyer switching costs."

—Liberman, Marvin, and David Montgomery. 1987. First-Mover Advantages, Research Paper 969, Stanford Business School, October.

FLAUNT

(1) boast; brandish; display ostentatiously; exhibit; flourish; show off; parade; vaunt

Word Used in Sentence(s)

(1) "They flaunt their conjugal felicity in one's face, as if it were the most fascinating of sins."

—Oscar Wilde, Irish poet, novelist, dramatist, and critic (1854–1900)

(1) "Wealth is an inborn attitude of mind, like poverty. The pauper who has made his pile may flaunt his spoils, but cannot wear them plausibly."

—Jean Cocteau, French poet, novelist, and actor (1889–1963)

FLOG

(1)   to offer for sale; hawk; peddle

Word Used in Sentence(s)

(1) I went to the convention and exhibit to flog the software.

FLOUNDER

(1)   move awkwardly or clumsily; make mistakes; become confused

Word Used in Sentence(s)

(1) "Many people flounder about in life because they do not have a purpose, an objective toward which to work."

—George Halas, American football coach (1895–1983)

FLOUT

(1)   disobey openly; mock; express scorn for; disregard something out of disrespect

Word Used in Sentence(s)

(1) To flout regulations, rules, and authority may make you a hero albeit a lonely one.

FOCUS

(1)   center of attention; concentration; direct one's attention to something; effort; focal point; hub; spot light

Word Used in Sentence(s)

(1) "In product development, a popular tool is the quick-and-dirty prototype. Because simple prototypes make the abstract concrete, they can guide innovators' conversations and focus their attention, helping them to move forward."

—Leonardi, Paul. 2011. Early Prototypes Can Hurt a Team's Creativity, Innovations. *Harvard Business Review* (December): 28.

(1) "Examples of business leaders who rise to the heights of corporate power only to be brought down by their egos include Dennis Kozlowski,

former CEO of TYCO, and Carly Fiorina former head of Hewlett-Packard. As leaders of corporate empires they focused on what flattered instead of what mattered."

—Forbes, Steve, and John Prevas. 2009. *Power Ambition Glory.* New York: Crown Business Press, 7.

(1) "Companies that want to make better use of the data they gather should focus on two things: training workers to increase their data literacy and efficiently incorporate information into decision making, and giving those workers the right tools."

—Shah, Shvetank, Andrew Horne, and Jamie Capella. 2012. Good Data Won't Guarantee Good Decisions, Idea Watch. *Harvard Business Review* (April): 24.

Word Used with Rhythm and Imagery

- **Metaphor**—"Concentrate all your thoughts upon the work at hand. The sun's rays do not burn until brought to a <u>focus</u>" (Alexander Graham Bell, American inventor and educator, 1847–1922).

Collocates to: attention, groups, issues, main, primary, on

FOLLOW

(1) abide by; adhere; comply; conform; continue in the direction of another; do as someone else has done; emulate; keep mind; model; obey; observe; pattern; pursue

(2) sign up as one who receives tweet digital messages

Word Used in Sentence(s)

(1) "You cannot be a leader, and ask other people to <u>follow</u> you, unless you know how to <u>follow,</u> too."

—Sam Rayburn, American politician and lawyer (1882–1961)

FORBEAR

(1) abstain; hold back from something; refrain; tolerate

Word Used in Sentence(s)

(1) "Follow then the shining ones, the wise, the awakened, the loving, for they know how to work and <u>forbear.</u>"

—Buddha, a spiritual teacher from the Indian subcontinent, on whose teachings Buddhism was founded

(1) "The wise man... if he would live at peace with others, he will bear and forbear."

—Samuel Smiles, Scottish author (1812–1904)

FORECAST

(1) calculate; predict

Word Used in Sentence(s)

(1) "The ability to forecast sales with more accuracy optimizes the firm's operational plans."

—Hilenrath, Jon. 2012. Fed's Computer Models Pose Problems, The Outlook. *Wall Street Journal*, December, 31.

FORGE

(1) come up with an concept, explanation, idea, principle, or theory; contrive; create

(2) beat; make out of components

(3) move ahead or act with sudden increase in motion or speed

Word Used in Sentence(s)

(1) "People are more inclined to be drawn in if their leader has a compelling vision. Great leaders help people get in touch with their own aspirations and then will help them forge those aspirations into a personal vision."

—John Kotter, former professor at the Harvard Business School, an acclaimed author

(1) "The President's offer is very much in keeping with history of insisting that negotiation consists of the other side giving him everything he wants. That approach has given him the reputation as the modern president least able to forge a consensus."

—Strassel, Kimberley. 2012. This Unserious White House, Opinion. *Wall Street Journal*, November 30.

Word Used with Rhythm and Imagery

- **Metaphor**—"We forge the chains we wear in life" (Charles Dickens, English writer and social critic, 1812–1870).

- **Vivid imagery**—"Bad men cannot make good citizens. It is when a people forget God that tyrants <u>forge</u> their chains. A vitiated state of morals, a corrupted public conscience, is incompatible with freedom. No free government, or the blessings of liberty, can be preserved to any people but by a firm adherence to justice, moderation, temperance, frugality, and virtue; and by a frequent recurrence to fundamental principles" (Patrick Henry, American lawyer, patriot, and orator, symbol of the American struggle for liberty, 1736–1799).

FOREGO

(1) do without; forebear; to do or go before something in time or position

Word Used in Sentence(s)

(1) "To <u>forego</u> even ambition when the end is gained—who can say this is not greatness?"

—William Makepeace Thackeray, English author and novelist (1811–1863)

(1) "Next to knowing when to seize an opportunity, the most important thing in life is to know when to <u>forego</u> an advantage."

—Benjamin Disraeli, British prime minister and novelist (1804–1881)

(1) "The people who are regarded as moral luminaries are those who <u>forego</u> ordinary pleasures themselves and find compensation in interfering with the pleasures of others."

—Bertrand Russell, English logician and philosopher (1872–1970)

FORMULATE

(1) articulate; contrive; create; develop; devise; draft; elaborate; express; frame; put into words or expressions; invent; make; originate; plan; prepare; verbalize; voice

Word Used in Sentence(s)

(1) It is critical to <u>formulate</u> a clear mission statement.

FORSAKE

(1) abandon; cast off; desert; disown; ditch; leave; renounce; relinquish; reject; quit

Word Used in Sentence(s)

(1) "Forsake not God till you find a better master."

—Scottish proverb

(1) "There is not a more repulsive spectacle than on old man who will not forsake the world, which has already forsaken him."

—T. S. Eliot, American-born English editor, playwright, poet, and critic (1888–1965)

FORSWEAR

(1) abandon; abjure; deny; disavow; disclaim; disown; gainsay; to give up; reject; renounce

Word Used with Rhythm and Imagery

- **Vivid imagery**—"Did my heart love till now? Forswear it, sight, For I never saw true beauty till this night" (William Shakespeare, English poet and playwright, 1564–1516).

FOSTER

(1) advance; back; bring up; care for; cherish; encourage; favor; forward; favor; help develop; maintain; promote the growth of; raise; rear; support

Word Used in Sentence(s)

(1) "William Smith founded Euclid Elements…His awareness of his own strengths and weaknesses led him to hire far more experienced managers and engineers… Their hiring, in turn, fostered a culture at Euclid in which Smith does not hesitate to rely on those around him."

—Hann, Christopher. 2012. The Masters. *Entrepreneur* (March): 58.

(1) "Volunteer activities can foster enormous leadership skills. The non-professional volunteer world is a laboratory for self-realization."

—Mae West, American actress (1892–1980)

(1) "It is not my intention to do away with government. It is rather to make it work—work with us, not over us; stand by our side, not ride on our back. Government can and must provide opportunity, not smother it; foster productivity, not stifle it."

—Ronald Reagan, 40th president of the United States (1911–2004)

(1) "Moreover, laudable and beguiling though professional standards and ethics may be, and however appealing professional status is, hanging the mantle 'professional' on business education <u>fosters</u> inappropriate analysis and misguided prescriptions."

—Barker, Richard. 2012. No, Management Is Not a Profession, The Big Idea. *Harvard Business Review* (July/August): 54.

FUEL

(1) stimulate or maintain an idea, emotion, concept, or action; keep something going

Word Used in Sentence(s)

(1) "Why did new business starts plunge during 2008–2012? To write it off as an effect of the recession overlooks key ingredients to <u>fueling</u> the next wave of start-ups."

—Alkarim Nasser, managing partner, BNotions

FULFILL

(1) achieve expected desire; accomplish; bear out; feel satisfied with accomplishment; live out; realize ambition; satisfy; justify

(2) accomplish; carryout an order or request; bring to fruition; complete something started; execute; follow through; implement; make happen; obey; perform

Word Used in Sentence(s)

(1) "Employment in the manufacturing sector contracted for the first time in three years…however production surged, but order backlogs fell, a sign that businesses are <u>fulfilling</u> old orders rather than receiving new ones."

—Neil Shah, Neil. 2012. Slow Hiring, Spending Hit Factories, U.S. News, *Wall Street Journal*, December 4.

(1) "We must make the choices that enable us to <u>fulfill</u> the deepest capacities of our real selves."

—Thomas Merton, American and trappist monk (1915–1968)

(1) "Whenever I hear people talking about liberal ideas, I am always astounded that men should love to fool themselves with empty sounds. An idea should never be liberal; it must be vigorous, positive, and without

loose ends so that it may <u>fulfill</u> its divine mission and be productive. The proper place for liberality is in the realm of the emotions."

—Johann Wolfgang von Goethe, German playwright, poet, novelist, and dramatist (1749–1832)

(1) Consumer products and services are purchased to <u>fulfill</u> certain basic human needs. Whether it is Maslow's hierarchy of needs or the more contemporary Lawrence and Nohria Four Drives that Underline Human Motivation, marketers have to discover the proper need and <u>ful-fill</u> them or there will be no long-term customer relationship.

GALVANIZE

  (1) activate; animate; electrify; fire up; incite; motivate; rouse; spur; stimulate into action; stir up

Word Used in Sentence(s)

(1) "Fear has a lot of flavors and textures. There is a sharp, silver fear that runs like lightning through your arms and legs, <u>galvanizes</u> you into action, power, motion."

—Jim Butcher, in *Grave Peril*

(1) "There are some men whom a staggering emotional shock, so far from making them mental invalids for life, seems, on the other hand, to awaken, to <u>galvanize</u>, to arouse into an almost incredible activity of soul."

—William McFee, English writer (1881–1961)

GARNER

  (1) accumulate; acquire; amass; bring; collect; earn; gather; get; harvest; to lay or place at rest; put away; reap; save; search out; store

Word Used in Sentence(s)

(1) "Work and live to serve others, to leave the world a little better than you found it and <u>garner</u> for yourself as much peace of mind as you can. This is happiness."

—David Sarnoff, Russian-born American inventor (1891–1971)

(1) "Garner up pleasant thoughts in your mind, for pleasant thoughts make pleasant lives."

—John Wilkins, English clergyman, natural philosopher, and author (1614–1672)

GEL

(1) come to useful and firm form; to work out

Word Used in Sentence(s)

(1) If this international merger doesn't gel, the local folks will be left out in the cold.

GENERATE

(1) begat; breed; bring into being; cause; create; develop; engender; hatch; induce; make; produce; provoke; spawn; stir; touch off

Word Used in Sentence(s)

(1) "Tasks outside the core should only be undertaken if they generate excess revenue that can support the core."

—Richard Romano, Looking Behind Community College Budgets for Future Policy Considerations. Community College Review, April 2012, Vol. 40 Issue 2, p. 165–189, 25p

(1) "Under the stewardship of Darwin Clark, Kimberly Clark generated cumulative stock returns 4.1 times the general market, beating its direct rival Scott Paper and Procter & Gamble and outperforming such venerable companies as Coca Cola, Hewlett-Packard, 3M and General Electric."

—Collins, Jim. 2001. *Good to Great.* New York: Harper Collins, 18.

Collocates to: ability, electricity, energy, ideas, income, interest, jobs, power, revenue

GET CROSSWISE WITH SOMEONE

(1) to be in conflict with another

Word Used in Sentence(s)

(1) Tim got himself crosswise with his supervisor over the work rules.

GET UP TO SPEED

(1) adapt and learn quickly

Word Used in Sentence(s)

> *(1) "The stable project management teams we grew up still work in many contexts…Situations that call for teaming are, by contrast, complex and uncertain, full of unexpected events that require rapid changes in course. No two teaming projects are alike, so people must <u>get up to speed</u> quickly on brand-new topics, again and again. Because solutions can come from anywhere, team members do too."*

> —Edmondson, Amy, C. 2012. Teamwork on the Fly, Spotlight. *Harvard Business Review* (April): 74.

GILD THE LILY

(1) add unnecessary decoration or ornamentation that is already pleasing; attempt to improve something that is already okay

GIN UP

(1) create; encourage; produce; increase

Word Used in Sentence(s)

> *(1) Supply-side economics in theory should help in <u>ginning up</u> markets.*

GIVE AUTHORITY AND RESPONSIBILITY

(1) granting subordinates authority and responsibility

Word Used in Sentence(s)

> *(1) A manager must find the correct balance between <u>giving</u> his or her people <u>responsibility and authority</u> to have a healthy, happy, and productive staff.*

GO DOWN THE LINE

(1) all out; all in; compete with dead earnest; do whatever is necessary; give or take no quarter; go balls out; go for broke; go for the fences; go for gold; go down swinging; go for all the marbles; go full bore; go great guns; go the distance; go the limit; go toe to toe; go to the wall; full steam; make the maximum effort; valiant try

Word Used in Sentence(s)

(1) A manager's dream team would include members who would <u>go down the line</u>.

GO ON AN ODYSSEY

(1) to go on a long, arduous journey or mission

GRAPPLE

(1) fight; grab somebody; grab hold of somebody; seize; struggle with somebody; struggle to deal with or comprehend something; tackle; wrestle

Word Used in Sentence(s)

(1) "Tom Enders, CEO of EADS said 'I have mixed feelings about innovation' as his company <u>grappled</u> with cracks inside the wings of newest plane in the skies, the A380 superjumbo."

—Michaels, Daniel. 2013. Innovation Is Messy Business, Marketplace. *Wall Street Journal*, January 24.

GRAVITATE

(1) be inclined; to have a natural inclination toward; move steadily toward

Word Used in Sentence(s)

(1) "Responsibilities <u>gravitate</u> to the man who can shoulder them and the power to him who knows how."

—Elbert Hubbard, American editor, publisher, and writer (1856–1915)

(1) "The excitement factor is a strong one with his top students, says Dr. Zurbuchen. The students tend to have an entrepreneurial spirit, he says, and <u>gravitate</u> toward the opportunities that may be risky in terms of job security, but give them the feeling that, 'hey, we're going to kick in some doors and have an impact,' he says."

—Spotts, Pete. 2011. SpaceX Launch: Private Industry Inspires New Generation of Rocketeers. *Christian Science Monitor*, May 22.

GROUND BREAK

(1) begin; start new project; do something no one else has been able to do; go off into a new direction with a project or idea

GUIDE

(1) conduct; channel; direct; funnel; point

(2) escort; lead; pilot; route; surround; show; steer; supervise; usher

Word Used in Sentence(s)

(1) A true leader both <u>guides</u> and follows.

Word Used with Rhythm and Imagery

- **Metaphor**—"The only <u>guide</u> to man is his conscience; the only shield to his memory is the rectitude and sincerity of his actions. It is very imprudent to walk through life without this shield, because we are so often mocked by the failure of our hopes and the upsetting of our calculations; but with this shield, however the fates may play, we march always in the ranks of honor" (Winston Churchill, British orator, author, and prime minister, 1874–1965).

HARANGUE

(1) accost; to be bellicose; berate or yell at someone or something; loud blustering rant

Word Used in Sentence(s)

(1) "Bay area water agencies seem to be winning their long battle to <u>harangue</u> customers into consuming less."

—John Upton, American writer for *New York Times*

(1) "Ayn Rand's popularity on the street is at odds with her standing in the academic world. Some critics have called her interminable, tone-deaf, blind to human reality, a writer who creates not dialogue but <u>harangue</u>."

—John Timpane, American writer for *Philadelphia Inquirer*

HARNESS

(1) put a harness on an animal

(2) attach with a harness to something

(3) gather or put together resources to accomplish a goal or an objective

Word Used in Sentence(s)

(1) "The person who figures out how to <u>harness</u> the collective genius of his or her organization is going to blow the competition away."

—Walter Wriston, American banker and former chairman and CEO of Citicorp (1919–2005)

Word Used with Rhythm and Imagery

- **Repetition**—"Normal fear protects us; abnormal fear paralyses us. Normal fear motivates us to improve our individual and collective welfare; abnormal fear constantly poisons and distorts our inner lives. Our problem is not to be rid of fear but, rather to <u>harness</u> and master it" (Martin Luther King, Jr., American Baptist minister and civil-rights leader, 1929–1968).

HECTOR

(1) bait; browbeat; bully; heckle; intimidate; push around; swagger; treat with insolence; vituperative

Word Used in Sentence(s)

(1) Political debates are used as opportunities for voters to learn the candidates' views on issues but now the debate time seems to be spent seeing who can heckle and <u>hector</u> their opponent more.

Word Used with Rhythm and Imagery

- **Vivid imagery**—All Troy then moves to Priam's court again
  A solemn, silent, melancholy train;
  Assembled there, from pious toil they rest,
  And sadly shared the last sepulchral feast
  Such honors Ilion to her hero paid,
  And peaceful slept the might <u>Hector's</u> shade
  (Homer, Iliad, trans, Alexander Pope, bk xxiv)

HYPOTHECATE

(1) advance loan; pledge or mortgage; remortgage; secured loan

HYPOTHESIZE

(1) educated guess of some outcome

Word Used in Sentence(s)

(1) "In the last five years, though, an expanding number of computer scientists have embraced developmental psychology's proposal that infants possess basic abilities, including gaze tracking, for engaging with others in order to learn. Social interactions combined with sensory experiences gained as a child explores the world set off a learning explosion, researchers <u>hypothesize</u>."

—Bower, Bruce. 2011. Meet the Growbots. *Science News* 179 (3): 18.

(1) "I <u>hypothesize</u> that the Katrina event has made people think pretty seriously about infrastructure and its vulnerability."

—Stuart Elway, American business executive

Collocates to: might, may, therefore, led, reasonable, researchers, we

IGNITE

(1) burn; combust; conflagrate; flare up; glow; inflame; kindle; light up; stimulate or provoke

Word Used in Sentence(s)

(1) "Leaders can't <u>ignite</u> the flame of passion in others if they don't express enthusiasm for the compelling vision of their group."

—Kouzes, James, and Barry Posner. 1995. *The Leadership Challenge.* San Francisco, CA: Jossey-Bass Publishers, 11.

(1) "Without inspiration the best powers of the mind remain dormant, they is a fuel in us which needs to be <u>ignited</u> with sparks."

—Johann Gottfried Von Herder, German poet, critic, theologian, and philosopher (1744–1803)

Collocates to: fire, help, inflation, passion, spark, war

IMAGINE

(1) assume; conjecture; form a mental image of something; suppose; guess; think, believe, or fancy

Word Used in Sentence(s)

(1) <u>Imagine</u> what our business would be like if we achieved just a fraction of our goals.

(1) He <u>imagined</u> the entire project before committing it to paper.

(1) "The best way to appreciate your job is to <u>imagine</u> yourself without one."

—Oscar Wilde, Irish poet, novelist, dramatist, and critic (1854–1900)

Word Used with Rhythm and Imagery

- **Simile**—"<u>Imagination</u> is everything. It is a preview of life's coming attractions" (Albert Einstein, American theoretical physicist, 1879–1955).

IMBUE

(1) indoctrinate; instill

(2) drink; endow; fill; infuse; permeate or take in moisture

Word Used in Sentence(s)

(1) "Education would be so much more effective if its purpose were to ensure that by the time they leave school every boy and girl should know how much they don't know, and be <u>imbued</u> with a lifelong desire to know it.

—Sir William Haley, British newspaper editor and broadcasting administrator (1901–1987)

(1) "Many companies, of course, benefit greatly from the mental and emotional investment of their creators. They thrive on the founders' passion and on the passion of like-minded employees. Their products or services—born of extreme attention to detail—are often of the highest quality. And founders with strong personalities may <u>imbue</u> their progeny with distinctive identities that can be exploited in marketing."

—Singer, Thea. 2006. Our Companies, Ourselves. *Inc.* 28 (11): 38–40.

<u>Collocates to: consciousness, life, meaning, personality, significance, with</u>

IMPACT

(1) fix firmly; make contact, especially force tightly together; forcefully; wedge

(2) affect

Word Used in Sentence(s)

(1) "I like my job because it involves learning. I like being around smart people who are trying to figure out new things. I like the fact that if people really try they can figure out how to invent things that actually have an impact.*"*

—Bill Gates, American entrepreneur and founder of Microsoft Co. (1955–)

(1) "A serious problem in America is the gap between academe and the mass media, which is our culture. Professors of humanities, with all their leftist fantasies, have little direct knowledge of American life and no impact *whatever on public policy."*

—Camille Paglia, American author, teacher, and social critic (1947–)

IMPEDE

(1) block; delay; encumber; get in the way; hamper; hinder; hold back; hold up; inhibit; obstruct progress; slow down

Word Used in Sentence(s)

(1) "Human folly does not impede *the turning of the stars."*

—Tom Robbins, American novelist (1936–)

(1) It is the manager's job to see that nothing impedes *the progress of the company's objectives.*

Collocates to: ability, development, efforts, growth, investigation, progress

IMPLEMENT

(1) apply; carry out; enforce; execute; fulfill; instigate; put into action, effect, operation, service, or practice; realize

Word Used in Sentence(s)

(1) Sometimes leaders are better at creating new ideas than implementing *them.*

(1) "It is not always what we know or analyzed before we make a decision that makes it a great decision. It is what we do after we make the decision to implement *and execute it that makes it a good decision."*

—William Pollard, American physicist and an Episcopal priest (1911–1989)

(1) "Palestinian President Mahmoud Abbas officially changed his government's name to the 'the State of Palestine' in an attempt to <u>implement</u>—even if only symbolically—a recent United Nations vote to granting it the status of non-observer state."

—Mitnick, Joshua. 2013. Palestinians Adopt Name to Show off New 'State' Status, World News. *Wall Street Journal*, January 7.

<u>Collocates to: changes, develop, measures, necessary, plan, policies, program, reform, strategies</u>

IMPLY

(1) connote; hint; mean; signify; suggest strongly

Word Used in Sentence(s)

(1) "Convictions do not <u>imply</u> reasons."

—Margaret Deland, American novelist, short-story writer, and poet (1857–1945)

Word Used with Rhythm and Imagery

- **Repetition**—"But the fact that some geniuses were laughed at does not <u>imply</u> that all who are laughed at are geniuses. They laughed at Columbus, they laughed at Fulton, they laughed at the Wright brothers. But they also laughed at Bozo the Clown" (Dr. Carl Sagan, American astronomer, writer, and scientist, 1934–1996).

IMPROVE

(1) ameliorate; amend; better; build up; develop; employ; enhance in value; enrich; expand; further; help; get better; increase; make better; meliorate; perfect; raise to a better quality; upgrade use

(2) convalesce; get better; get stronger; get well; make progress; mend; perk up; rally; recover

Word Used in Sentence(s)

(1) "The research shows that in almost every case, a bigger opportunity lies in <u>improving</u> your performance in the industry you're in, by fixing your strategy and strengthening the capabilities that create value for customers and separate you from your competitors. This conclusion was

reached after analyzing shareholder returns for 6,138 companies in 65 industries worldwide from 2001 to 2011."

—Hirsh, Evan, and Kasturi Rangan. 2013. The Grass Isn't Greener, Idea Watch. *Harvard Business Review* (January/February): 23.

(1) Sam found two ways of <u>improving</u> the efficiency of the CAD software.

(1) Engineering <u>improved</u> upon the original design of the device.

(1) "When you are through <u>improving</u>... you are through."

—Arab proverb

(1) "The 'Inside-Out' approach to personal and interpersonal effectiveness means to start first with self; even more fundamentally, to start with the most inside part of self / with your paradigms, your character, and your motives. The inside-out approach says that private victories precede public victories, that making and keeping promises to ourselves precedes making and keeping promises to others. It says it is futile to put personality ahead of character, to try to <u>improve</u> relationships with others before <u>improving</u> ourselves."

—Stephen R. Covey, American educator, author, businessman, and keynote speaker (1932–2012)

IMPUGN

(1) attack; express doubts about truth or honesty

Word Used in Sentence(s)

(1) "I am thankful to God for this approval of the people. But while deeply grateful for this mark of their confidence in me, if I know my heart, my gratitude is free from any taint of personal triumph. I do not <u>impugn</u> the motives of any one opposed to me. It is no pleasure to me to triumph over any one."

—Abraham Lincoln

<u>Collocates to: anybody, character, might, motives, patriotism</u>

IMPUTE

(1) accredit; attribute; ascribe a result or quality to anything or anyone; assign; fix

(2) accuse; allege; assert; challenge; charge; cite; implicate

Word Used in Sentence(s)

(1) "Steve Jobs wanted customers to have a tactile experience when opening the box of an iPhone or iPad. Sometimes Jobs used the design of a machine to 'impute' a signal rather than to be merely functional."

—Isaacson, Walter. 2012. The Real Leadership Lessons of Steve Jobs. *Harvard Business Review* (April): 98.

INAUGURATE

(1) begin officially; induct; initiate; install; instate; invest; swear in

Word Used in Sentence(s)

(1) "The republic has been on a collision course with the Kremlin ever since Gamsakhurdia's nationalist coalition won an election victory last October. The first acts of the new parliament were to drop the words Soviet and Socialist from the republic's name and <u>inaugurate</u> a transitional to full independence."

—Editors. 1991. Hastening the End of the Empire. *Time.* January 28.

INCORPORATE

(1) absorb; assimilate; combine, join or include with; encompass; include; integrate; merge; fill in; slip in; slot in; unite

Word Used in Sentence(s)

(1) "Natural science will in time <u>incorporate</u> into itself the science of man, just as the science of man will <u>incorporate</u> into itself natural science: there will be one science."

—Karl Marx, German political philosopher and revolutionary (1818–1883)

(1) "Companies that want to make better use of the data they gather should focus on two things: training workers to increase their data literacy and efficiently <u>incorporate</u> information into decision making, and giving those workers the right tools."

—Shah, Shvetank, Andrew Horne, and Jamie Capella. Good Data Won't Guarantee Good Decisions, Idea Watch. *Harvard Business Review* (April): 24.

Word Used with Rhythm and Imagery

- **Vivid imagery**—"Organizations that most creatively <u>incorporate</u> diversity of thinking will reap the rewards of innovation, growth, and progress" (Joel Barker, American independent scholar and futurist).

INCENTIVIZE

(1) encourage; provide one with a reason to work harder; provide with an incentive

Word Used in Sentence(s)

(1) The argument over the best way to <u>incentivize</u> salespeople continues without conclusive empirical data proving any one argument.

INCREASE

(1) add to; amplify; augment; boost; enhance; enlarge; improve; multiply; raise; swell

(2) encourage; foster; fuel; intensify; redouble; strengthen

(3) escalate; expand; grow; mushroom; multiply; proliferate; rise; soar; spread; swell

Word Used in Sentence(s)

(1) "Think of an investment portfolio, there are methods of managing risk and <u>increasing</u> efficiency, but you cannot get away from the fundamental fact that you need to diversity for the overall portfolio to win."

—Wang, Jennifer. 2012. Radicals & Visionaries. *Entrepreneur* (March): 52.

(1) "Difficulties <u>increase</u> the nearer we approach the goal."

—Johann Wolfgang von Goethe, German playwright, poet, novelist, and dramatist (1749–1832)

INCULCATE

(1) to impress a belief or idea on someone by repeating it over and over again until the idea is accepted

(2) teach by persistent urging

(3) implant ideas through constant admonishing

Word Used in Sentence(s)

(1) "When schools fail to <u>inculcate</u> American values, giving short shrift to the history of the American Revolution, the American Civil War, and the American Civil Rights Movement, while emphasizing the history of Africa, Latin America, or Asia, they are severing the ties that bind Americans together in the name of diversity."

—Braceras, Jennifer. 2005. Not Necessarily in Conflict: Americans Can Be Both United and Culturally Diverse. *Harvard Journal of Law & Public Policy.*

(1) "As a researcher, I am interested in the behavior of digital natives. The question of privacy—even the illusion of it—does not appear to be a concern. Research indicates that the early <u>inculcation</u> to a digital interface (for example, children using iPads) may result in people never even thinking about privacy."

—Lee Sr., Jim. 2012. Knowledge Management Practice Leader, The Best Leaders Have Short Résumés, Interaction. *Harvard Business Review* (December): 19.

INCULPATE

(1) to blame; charge; incriminate

Word Used in Sentence(s)

(1) If you don't process a piece of biological material properly, you've lost or at least run the risk of losing that piece of evidence as something which potentially can either <u>inculpate</u> or exculpate any particular person.

INDEMNIFY

(1) protect from loss; provide compensation for loss; save from loss; secure

Word Used in Sentence(s)

(1) "Insurance is defined as 'coverage by contract whereby one party undertakes to <u>indemnify</u> or guarantee another against loss by a specified contingency or peril.' Implicit in this is that the contingency or peril comes subsequent to the contract."

—Letters to the editor. 2008. Open Forum, Letters to the Editor. *Denver Post*, August 23.

INDUCE

(1) bring about some action; cause; effect; encourage; make; move by persuasion or influence; tempt

(2) bring about; bring on; cause; generate; produce; provoke; stimulate

Word Used in Sentence(s)

(1), (2) *"When an idea reaches critical mass there is no stopping the shift its presence will <u>induce</u>."*

—Marianne Williamson, American author and lecturer (1952–)

INFER

(1) assume; conclude or suppose; conjecture; deduce; extrapolate; gather; judge; reckon; reason; surmise; understand

Word Used in Sentence(s)

(1) *"From a drop of water a logician could <u>infer</u> the possibility of an Atlantic or a Niagara without having seen or heard of one or the other."*

—Arthur Conan Doyle, Sr., Scottish writer (1859–1930)

(1) *"It is long ere we discover how rich we are. Our history, we are sure, is quite tame: we have nothing to write, nothing to <u>infer</u>. But our wiser years still run back to the despised recollections of childhood, and always we are fishing up some wonderful article out of that pond; until, by and by, we begin to suspect that the biography of the one foolish person we know is, in reality, nothing less than the miniature paraphrase of the hundred volumes of the Universal History."*

—Ralph Waldo Emerson, American poet, lecturer, and essayist (1803–1882)

INFLUENCE

(1) authority; clout; drag; effect; induce; leverage; manipulate; prestige; pull; talk into; sway; weight; win over

(2) affect; change; have a bearing on; have an effect on; inspire; shape

Word Used in Sentence(s)

(1) *The HR consultant's report will be <u>influencing</u> a large number of people.*

(1) The CEO was <u>influenced</u> in a positive way by her work ethic.

(1) The most important person you have to <u>influence</u> is your direct supervisor.

(1) Leaders and managers are much more effective and productive when they apply <u>influence</u> rather than force to accomplish tasks and objectives.

INFUSE

(1) bathe; fill; fix an emotion or feeling; fortify; imbue; immerse; impart; implant; inculcate; inspire; instill; introduce; penetrate; permeate

(2) brew; saturate; steep; soak; souse; suffuse

Word Used in Sentence(s)

(1) "Words mean more than what is set down on paper. It takes the human voice to <u>infuse</u> them with shades of deeper meaning."

—Maya Angelou, American poet (1928–)

(1) "An occupation earns the right to be a profession only when some ideals, such as being an impartial counsel, doing no harm, or serving the greater good, are <u>infused</u> in to the conduct of people in that occupation. In like vein, a business school becomes a professional school only when in <u>infuses</u> those ideal into its graduates."

—Barker, Richard. 2012. No, Management Is Not a Profession. The Big Idea. *Harvard Business Review* (July/August): 54.

INGRATIATE

(1) work hard to gain someone's favor

Word Used in Sentence(s)

(1) "Politicians are aiming to <u>ingratiate</u> themselves with Hispanics."

—Meadows, Bob. 2010. Race (Still) Matters. *Essence* 41 (7):132.

(1) "No book is perfect. But Sleeper's citation of minor mistakes, especially when accompanied by his crude and pejorative ideological labeling, is where the real dishonesty resides. His effort represents one of the more unfortunate things a book critic can do: use a review to <u>ingratiate</u>

himself with a certain ideological camp or to be more strongly identified with that camp's views."

—Anonymous. 2011. Letter to the Editors. *The Washington Monthly*, Jul/Aug.

Collocates to: herself, himself, myself, themselves, trying, with

INITIATE

(1) begin; create; commence; inaugurate; induct; install; instate; instigate; introduce; invest; kick off; open; set off; start

(2) coach; instruct; mentor; teach; train; tutor

Word Used in Sentence(s)

(1) "Without change there is no innovation, creativity, or incentive for improvement. Those who initiate change will have a better opportunity to manage the change that is inevitable."

—William Pollard, American physicist and an Episcopal priest (1911–1989)

(1) "Advertising generally works to reinforce consumer trends rather than to initiate them."

—Michael Schudson, American academic sociologist (1946–)

Collocates to: action, conversation, discussion, process, program, sex

INNOVATE

(1) begin with something new create; derive; devise; coin; commence; introduce something new; instigate; invent; make; modernize; originate; remodel; renew; renovate; transform; update; revolutionize

Word Used in Sentence(s)

(1) Because we were able to innovate the production process, our costs fell 20 below our top competitors.

(1) "To turn really interesting ideas and fledgling technologies into a company that can continue to innovate for years, it requires a lot of disciplines. "

—Steve Jobs, American entrepreneur; cofounder, chairman, and CEO of Apple, Inc. (1955–2011)

(1) "Sometimes when you <u>innovate</u>, you make mistakes. It is best to admit them quickly, and get on with improving your other innovations.

—Steve Jobs, American entrepreneur; cofounder, chairman, and CEO of Apple, Inc. (1955–2011)

INSINUATE

(1) allude; creep in; hint; imply; indicate; intimate; suggest indirectly at something unpleasant; whisper

Word Used in Sentence(s)

(1) "This commission has rule-making power that carries the force of law. The Senate, it is true, will have the power to override its decisions— but only with a three-fifths majority. There are no procedures that allow citizens or doctors to appeal the Board's decisions. The administrative state—here in the guise of providing health care for all—surely will reduce the people under a kind of tyranny that will <u>insinuate</u> itself into all aspects of American life, destroying liberty by stages until liberty itself becomes only a distant memory."

—Erler, Edward. 2011. SUPREME Decisions Ahead. *USA Today*, November.

(1) "It is precisely the purpose of the public opinion generated by the press to make the public incapable of judging, to <u>insinuate</u> into it the attitude of someone irresponsible, uninformed."

—Walter Benjamin, German theologian, writer, and essayist (1892–1940)

Collocates to: herself, himself, into, itself, themselves, tried, trying

INSOURCE

(1) assign tasks to someone inside the organization rather than a vendor; keep within an organization; subcontract work

Word Used in Sentence(s)

(1) After years of outsourcing our industrial waste removal, we began to <u>insource</u> it to our own employees.

INSPIRE

(1) breathe life into; encourage, give inspiration; have an exalting influence; influence or impel; invigorate; motivate; produce or arouse a feeling in others; stimulate

Word Used in Sentence(s)

(1) "Shawn Kent Hayashi asks a profound question—'are you inspiring?' Then through practical, real life examples, she demonstrates, how leaders can develop from being motivational to inspirational through the power of conversations."

—Seybold, Meghan. 2012. *Praise for Conversations for Creating Star Performers*. New York: McGraw Hill.

(1) Her courage inspired the other employees to work even harder.

(1) "Our chief want is someone who will inspire us to be what we know we could be."

—Ralph Waldo Emerson, American poet, lecturer, and essayist (1803–1882)

(1) "To inspire others, you have to know what motivates them, and you have to be inspired yourself about the topic you are discussing. To be a leaders and developer of others, you have to be inspiring."

—Hayashi, Shawn Kent. 2012. *Conversations for Creating Star Performers*. New York: McGraw Hill, 7.

(1) "Leadership is the ability to inspire confidence and support among people who are needed to achieve organizational goals."

—DuBrin, Andrew. 1998. *Leadership Research Findings, Practice, and Skills*. Boston: Houghton Mifflin Company, 2.

(1) "Few business narratives are more evocative that that of the inspired leader boldly pursuing and extraordinary innovative idea."

—Gaovondarajan, Vijay, and Chris Trimbla. 2005. Building Breakthrough Businesses Within Established Organizations. *Harvard Business Review* (May): 58.

Collocates to: ability, awe, confidence, continue, educate, fear, generation, helped, motivate, others, trust

INSTIGATE

(1) cause a process to start; enkindle action; ignite; initiate change; enkindle; spark

(2) cause trouble; provoke; stir up things

Word Used in Sentence(s)

(1) Change is inevitable. This much we know. But don't we occasionally feel the urge to <u>instigate</u> change rather than simply let it happen, as if we had no say in the matter?"

—Editors. 2010. Time for a Change. *Town and Country* 164 (5360).

Word Used with Rhythm and Imagery

- **Vivid images**—Indeed heresies are themselves <u>instigated</u> by philosophy (Quintus Septimius Florens Tertullian, Christian author from Carthage in the Roman province of Africa, AD 160–AD 225).

Collocates to: change, conflicts, investigation, social, reform

INSTITUTE

(1) be first; found; get established; inaugurate; introduce; organize; originate; set some origination or activity in motion; set up; start

Word Used in Sentence(s)

(1) "There is nothing more difficult to carry out, nor more doubtful of success, nor more dangerous to handle, that to <u>institute</u> a new order of things."

—Niccolo Machiavelli, Italian writer and statesman (1469–1527)

(1) "Whenever any form of government becomes destructive of these ends life, liberty, and the pursuit of happiness it is the right of the people to alter or abolish it, and to <u>institute</u> new government..."

—Thomas Jefferson, third president of the United States (1762–1826)

INTEGRATE

(1) amalgamate; assimilate; combine two; concatenate; fit in; incorporate; join in; make part of; mix; open up; take part; participate; put together; unify

Word Used in Sentence(s)

(1) <u>Integrate</u> the existing standards rather than create new specifications.

(1) The new technology will be <u>integrated</u> into the syllabus in both the course content and the teaching methodology.

(1) "You must <u>integrate</u> before you can have independence."

—Noam Chomsky, American linguist, philosopher, cognitive scientist, logician, historian, and political critic (1928–)

INTERJECT

(1) introduce; butt in; cut in; exclaim; interpose; interrupt; put or set into between another or other things; speak; throw in

INTERLARD

(1) intersperse; diversify; mix together

INTERMESH

(1) come or bring together; engage

Word Used in Sentence(s)

(1) "Educators need to consider global learning in terms of the conditions necessary for it to emerge, the requisite attributes and processes that <u>intermesh</u> with the content during global-learning activities, and finally the characteristics and responsibilities of the world citizen in relation to the attributes and processes developed through global learning."

—Editors. 2008. Developing Global Awareness and Responsible World Citizenship With Global Learning. *Roeper Review* 30 (1): 11–23.

INTERPOLATE

(1) introduce something foreign between parts

INTERPOSE

(1) aggressive; arbitrate; insert; intercept; interfere; intermediate; meddle; mediate; unsolicited opinion; offer assistance or presence; put between

Word Used in Sentence(s)

(1) The chairman <u>interposed</u> a point of order into the discussion.

INTERSPERSE

(1) combine; comingle; disburse; distribute; intermingle; interpose; pepper; scatter here and there; spread; sprinkle

Word Used in Sentence(s)

(1) "A collection of anecdotes and maxims is the greatest of treasures for the man of the world, for he knows how to <u>intersperse</u> conversation with the former in fit places, and to recollect the latter on proper occasions."

—Johann Wolfgang von Goethe, German playwright, poet, novelist, and dramatist (1749–1832)

INTERVENE

(1) get involved, so as to alter or change an action through force, influence, or power; interfere; interpose; come between points of time, issues, people, ideas, or events; to occur between two things

Word Used in Sentence(s)

(1) "One man has built his career around trying to help people track their conversational interactions, understand the hidden dynamics in them, and learn how to <u>intervene</u> effectively."

—Art Kliener, Building the Skills of Insight. *Strategy + Business*, http://www.strategy-business.com/article/00154?gko=d4421&cid=TL20130117&utm_campaign=TL20130117 (accessed January 17, 2013).

INUNDATE

(1) deluge; engulf; fill to overflow; flood; overwhelm; saturate; swamp

INURE

(1) accustom; habituate

INVEST

(1)   gift; initiate; spend resources; infuse endow with a special quality

Word Used in Sentence(s)

(1) "Companies should <u>invest</u> in workers and business relationships, just as they did a century ago in response to mounting inequality and public dissatisfaction. Back then Robert Bosch in Germany, William Hesketh Lever in Britain, and the Houghton family of Corning Glass in the United States, among many other leaders of large companies, took initiatives in this direction."

—de Rothschild, Lynn Forester, and Adam Posen. 2013. How Capitalism Can Repair Its Bruised Image, Opinion. *Wall Street Journal*, January 2, A17.

(1) "<u>Investing</u> in apprenticeships and other training programs means a more productive and engaged workforce and better aligns worker's motivations with the success of their employers."

—de Rothschild, Lynn Forester, and Adam Posen. 2013. How Capitalism Can Repair Its Bruised Image, Opinion. *Wall Street Journal*, January 2.

(1) "Some firms are taking steps to expand the talent pool—for example, by <u>investing</u> in apprenticeships and other training programs."

—Hancock, Bryan, and Dianna Ellsworth. 2013. Redesigning Knowledge Work. *Harvard Business Review* (January/February): 60.

(1) "If you <u>invest</u> in improving your employees' view of your firm's corporate character, those positive attitudes will rub off and boost customer's opinions of the company. That will drive growth.

—Davis, Gary, and Rosa Chun. 2007. To Thine Own Staff Be Agreeable, Organizational Character. *Harvard Business Review* (June): 30.

(1) "Professor Katz of Harvard said it would make sense to create a more progressive tax system when corporations and the top 1 percent are commanding more of the economic pie. He said those on top should agree to some redistribution and to <u>invest</u> in the next generation."

—Greenhouse, Steve. 2013. Our Economic Pickle. *New York Times*, January 13.

INVIGORATE

(1) animate; energize; enliven; galvanize; increase; liven; refresh; revitalize; strengthen; stimulate

Word Used in Sentence(s)

(1) "Four years ago we said we would <u>invigorate</u> our economy by giving people greater freedom and incentives to take risks and letting them keep more of what they earned. We did what we promised, and a great industrial giant is reborn."

—Ronald Reagan, 40th president of the United States (1911–2004)

(1) "In our drive to comprehend we want very much sense of the world around us and we are frustrated when things seem senseless, and we are <u>invigorated</u>, typically, by the challenge of working out answers."

—Nohria, Nitin, Boris Groysberg, and Linda-Eling Lee. 2008. Employee Motivation a Powerful New Tool, Honing Your Competitive Edge. *Harvard Business Review* (July/August): 81.

ITERATE

(1) say or utter again; repeat

Word Used in Sentence(s)

(1) To <u>iterate</u> a point made previously, customer retention is our main marketing priority.

JACK IT

(1) loaf; malinger; work half-heartedly

Word Used in Sentence(s)

(1) If a dissatisfied worker demonstrates his or her discontentment by <u>jacking it</u> or other visible signs, it is symbolic of a deeper character flaw.

JETTISON

(1) abandon; discard; throw away; toss aside

Word Used in Sentence(s)

(1) "What seems to gall reformers most is the recent pattern of big companies using Chapter 11 of the bankruptcy code to <u>jettison</u> the debt of underfunded pension plans, then exit bankruptcy and survive."

—Adams, Marilyn. 2005. 'Fundamentally broken' pension system in 'crying need' of a fix. *MONEY, USA Today*, November 15.

JIBE WITH

(1) agree with

JOCKEY

(1) contend; jostle; skillfully change positions; maneuver in order to gain an advantage; manipulate; position oneself for better position

Word Used in Sentence(s)

(1) "Steve Jobs took his top 100 people on an annual retreat for the purpose of strategic planning. The main activity was the list of ten things Apple should do. There was a lot of <u>jockeying</u> to get one's favorite item on that list."

—Isaacson, Walter. 2012. The Real Leadership Lessons of Steve Jobs. *Harvard Business Review* (April): 95.

JOIN FORCES

(1) combine resources or efforts with another

Word Used in Sentence(s)

(1) In the value chain model producers, vendors, suppliers, key customers, NGOs, key stakeholders and even some competitors with similar interests <u>join forces</u> in a coopitive venture.

JUDGE

(1) adjudge; adjudicate; arbitrate; decide; decree; determine; form an opinion; govern; infer; referee; rule on something; umpire

Word Used in Sentence(s)

(1) "You can easily <u>judge</u> the character of a man by how he treats those who can do nothing for him."

—James D. Miles, American, associate professor of Psychology at Purdue University

(1) "We are not afraid to entrust the American people with unpleasant facts, foreign ideas, alien philosophies, and competitive values. For a nation that is afraid to let its people <u>judge</u> the truth and falsehood in an open market is a nation that is afraid of its people."

—John Fitzgerald Kennedy, 35th president of the United States (1917–1963)

(1) "While weight remains a taboo conversation topic in the workplace, it's hard to overlook. A heavy executive is <u>judged</u> to be less capable because of assumptions about how weight affects health and stamina says Berry Posner, a professor at Santa Clara University's Leavey School of Business."

—Kwoh, Leslie. 2013. Marketing. *Wall Street Journal*, January 16.

JUMP ONBOARD

(1) bustle; decide to join; full of activity; hustle; energetically move on something; obey or decide quickly; rise suddenly or quickly; join in enthusiastically

Word Used in Sentence(s)

(1) "Aspiring entrepreneurs are increasingly <u>jumping on board</u> with sites like Kickstarter, IndieGoGo, Peerbackers, and ChipIn."

—Moran, Gwen. Mob Money. *Entrepreneur* (March): 84.

(1) Job seekers should give serious consideration to the move before <u>jumping onboard</u> start-ups if they have never been in that kind of business environment.

JUMP THROUGH HOOPS

(1) accommodate without question; exert oneself in frantic way; obey; serve

Word Used in Sentence(s)

(1) Alice <u>jumped through hoops</u> to please her manager.

(1) I had to <u>jump through hoops</u> to get you this opportunity.

JUSTIFY

(1) explain why something is the way it is

JUXTAPOSE

(1) place side by side to compare and contrast

Word Used in Sentence(s)

> *(1) "I'm very interested in the color of sound. And I'm very interested in the juxtaposition of different things, ethnic instruments juxtaposed with symphonic instruments, and I'm interested in the ancient and the modern. I don't know why, but it has always been something that's fascinated me, from when I first heard a symphony orchestra I wanted to know how those sounds were made."*

—Anne Dudley, English composer and pop musician (1956–)

KEEP ON KEEPING ON

(1) doing one's best; keep trying; maintain; persist

Word Used in Sentence(s)

> *(1) In these trying economic times, sometimes all we can do is keep driving, keep moving forward, keep on keeping on.*

KICK-START

(1) advantage; get a jump; head start

Word Used in Sentence(s)

> *(1) "Yes, investment flows have slowed in the green-tech sector, but the promise of new money in the stimulus package for solar, wind, electric cars, and smart grids engendered lively debates about which new technologies will help kick-start the economy and generate the most green-collar jobs."*

—Dumaine, Brian. 2009. Getting the Economy Back on Track. *Fortune* 159 (11): 25.

Collocates to: economy, effort, fat, help metabolism

KICK SOMEONE TO THE CURB

(1) do away with; disregard; dump someone; eliminate; fire someone; reject someone; throw under the bus

Word Used in Sentence(s)

(1) "Only hang around people that are positive and make you feel good. Anybody who doesn't make you feel good <u>kick them to the curb</u> and the earlier you start in your life the better. The minute anybody makes you feel weird and non included or not supported, you know, either beat it or tell them to beat it."

—Amy Poehler, American actress, comedienne, producer, and writer (1971–)

Word Used with Rhythm and Imagery

- **Vivid imagery**—"<u>Kicked to the Curb</u>" (Headline *New York Post Sunday*, November 11, 2012).

KICK THE TIRES

(1) cursory check; do grassroots investigation on an investment; superficial check; make a quick check or inspection of the fundamentals

Word Used in Sentence(s)

(1) Individual investors and fund managers both participate in <u>tire kicking</u> before investing.

KINDLE

(1) arouse; fire; light; provoke; stir to action

Word Used with Rhythm and Imagery

- **Metaphor**—"The fire you <u>kindle</u> for your enemy often burns yourself more than them" (Chinese proverb).
- **Metaphor**—"Originality is nothing but judicious imitation. The most original writers borrowed from one another. The instruction we find in books is like fire. We fetch it from our neighbors, <u>kindle</u> it at home, communicate it to others, and it becomes the probe" (Voltaire, French philosopher and writer, 1694–1778).

LAMENT

(1) be sad; cry; dirge; howl; express grief or sorrow; lament; mourn; weep

(2) annoyance; express regret, or disappointment about something

Word Used in Sentence(s)

(1), (2) "The public generally applauds recent 'Shock of Order' policing and commercial revitalization, although critics <u>lament</u> the loss of traditional freedoms for informal beach vendors and casual sports. These paradoxes highlight enduring tensions between social order and hierarchy on one hand, and democratic rights and equality on the other."

—Godfrey, Brian, and M. Oliva Arguinzoni. 2012. Regulating Public Space on the Beachfronts of Rio De Janeiro. *Geographical Review* 102 (1): 17–34.

LAMPOON

(1) satirize; charade; mockery; parody

LAUD

(1) acknowledge; applaud; celebrate; praise; extol

Word Used with Rhythm and Imagery

- **Metaphor**—"And give to dust that is a little gilt More <u>laud</u> than gilt o'er-dusted" (William Shakespeare, English dramatist, playwright, and poet, 1564–1616).

LAUNCH

(1) begin; commence; dispatch; embark; get under way; hurl; introduce; initial steps; release something; let loose something; send off; shoot; start or kick off something

(2) introduce something; inaugurate; reveal; present; start marketing; unleash; unveil

Word Used in Sentence(s)

(1), (2) I plan to <u>launch</u> the new advertising plan during the Christmas season.

(1) "Many companies react to competitors' acquisition sprees reflex-ively, by <u>launching</u> bids of their own. Smart managers should consider other moves."

—Keil, Thomas, and Tomi Laamanen. 2011. When Rivals Merge, Think Before You Follow Suit, Idea Watch. *Harvard Business Review* (December): 25.

Word Used with Rhythm and Imagery

•*"Yesterday, the Japanese government also <u>launched</u> an attack against Malaya.*

Last night, Japanese forces attacked Hong Kong.

Last night, Japanese forces attacked Guam.

Last night, Japanese forces attacked the Philippine Islands.

Last night, the Japanese attacked Wake Island.

And this morning, the Japanese attacked Midway Island."

—President Franklin Roosevelt, Pearl Harbor Address to the nation, Washington, D.C., 12/08/1941.

LEAD

(1) to be first; captain; command; conduct; control; direct; head; direct the operations, activity, or performance; escort; go ahead; go in front; guide on a way especially by going in advance; manage; officer; pilot; show the way

Word Used in Sentence(s)

(1) I will <u>lead</u> the task force looking into ways to cut costs

(1) "A company at the forefront of this effort is Tyco. Instead of simply offering training to employees in emerging markets, Tyco has compliance personnel <u>lead</u> focus group-like sessions with its employees.

—Currell, Dan, and Tracy D. Bradley. 2012. Greased Palms, Giant Headaches, Idea Watch. *Harvard Business Review* (September): 23.

(1) "Many rising stars trip when they shift from <u>leading</u> a function to <u>leading</u> an enterprise and for the first time taking responsibility for P&L and oversight of executive decisions across corporate functions."

—Watson, Michael. 2012. How Managers Become Leaders. *Harvard Business Review* (June): 68.

(1) "<u>Leading</u> is one of the four functions of management instilling enthusiasm by communicating with others, motivating them to work hard, and maintaining good interpersonal relations."

—Schermerhorn, John, Richard Osborn, Mary UHL-Bien, and James Hunt. 2012. *Organizational Behavior*. 12th ed. New York: John Wiley & Sons, Inc.

LEARN

(1) acquire knowledge through study and experience; add to one's store of facts; ascertain; become informed; check; detect; discover; find out; gain by exposure, experience or example; imply

Word Used in Sentence(s)

(1) "Who dares to teach must never cease to <u>learn</u>."

—John Cotton Dana, American librarian and museum director (1856–1929)

(1) "Live as if you were to die tomorrow. <u>Learn</u> as if you were to live forever."

—Unknown

LEVERAGE

(1) control; force; influence; power; pull; weight

Word Used in Sentence(s)

(1) "We must develop knowledge optimization initiatives to <u>leverage</u> our key learnings."

—Scott Adams, American cartoonist (1957–)

LIQUIDATE

(1) convert assets into cash

(2) pay off debt; settle

(3) eliminate or kill the competition

Word Used in Sentence(s)

(1) "Hostess owners have decided to <u>liquidate</u> rather than ride out a nationwide strike by one of the largest of its dozen unions, the Bakery,

Confectionary, Tobacco Workers and Grain Millers International Union. The Texas-based company owned by the private- equity shop Ripplewood Holdings and other hedge funds essentially gave up."

—WSJ Editors. 2012. Opinion. *Wall Street Journal*, November 18.

(1) "Let me live onward; you shall find that, though slower, the progress of my character will <u>liquidate</u> *all these debts without injustice to higher claims. If a man should dedicate himself to the payment of notes, would not this be an injustice? Does he owe no debt but money? And are all claims on him to be postponed to a landlord's or a banker's?"*

—Ralph Waldo Emerson, American essayist, poet, philosopher (1802–1883)

(1) "The death tax causes one-third of all family-owned small businesses to <u>liquidate</u> *after the death of the owner. It is also an unfair tax because the assets have already been taxed once at their income level."*

—Ric Keller, American, Member of U.S. House (1964–)

LISTEN

(1) attend; hark; hear; hearken; list; lend an ear; make an effort to hear and understand something; pay attention; respond to advice, request, or command

Word Used in Sentence(s)

(1) If you <u>listen</u> *to your customers, you will become a marketing expert.*

(1) "Leaders who take organizational conversation seriously know when to stop talking and start <u>listening</u>*. Few behaviors enhance conversational intimacy as much as attending to what people say…Duke Energy's president and CEO, James Rogers, instituted a series of what he called '<u>listening</u> sessions' when he was the CEO of Cinergy which later merged with Duke."*

—Groysberg, Boris, and Michael Slind. 2012. Leadership Is a Conversation. *Harvard Business Review* (June): 79.

(1) To <u>listen</u> *is a communications skill and is very different from hearing, which is not a communications skill.*

LITIGATE

(1) try in court; engage in legal proceedings

LOATH

(1) detest; disinclined; reluctant; unwilling

Word Used in Sentence(s)

(1) "But the tide (which says for no man) calling them away, that were thus loath to depart, their Reverend Pastor, falling down on his knees, and they all with him, with watery cheeks commended them with the most fervent prayers unto the Lord and his blessing."

—Nathaniel Morton, Keeper of Records, Plymouth Colony, 1620

MACERATE

(1) drip; make or become soft; pulp; saturate; soften; soak; steep

(2) break up; separate; waste away

MALINGER

(1) duck; pretend to be ill; shirk duty or work; shun; side step; skive

MANAGE

(1) administer; be in charge of; conduct or direct affairs; oversee; regulate; run; supervise

(2) do; fare; fend; get along; get by; make do; muddle through

(3) succeed in dealing with, control the behavior of; handle

(4) succeed despite difficulties

Word Used in Sentence(s)

(1) Managing is a skill that involves allocating limited resources to accomplish specific objectives.

(1) "It's self-evident that an entrepreneur's ability to hire talented people is vital to a company's success. But how the entrepreneur manages those people helps define the company culture."

—Hann, Christopher. 2012. The Masters. *Entrepreneur* (March): 58.

(1) "Business executives don't manage information as well as they manage talent, capital, and brand."

—Shah, Shvetank, Andrew Horne, and Jamie Capella. 2012. Good Data Won't Guarantee Good Decisions, Idea Watch. *Harvard Business Review* (April): 24.

(1) To effectively <u>manage</u>, it is generally recognized one should be skilled in four functions—planning, organizing, leading, and controlling.

(1) There are three types of skills necessary to <u>manage</u> skillfully—technical, human, and conceptual.

<u>Collocates to: ability, able, affairs, difficulty, effectively, how, resources, somehow, stress</u>

MANEUVER

(1) carefully manipulate in order to achieve an end; specific tactic; finagle; jockey; manipulate; navigate; pilot; steer

Word Used in Sentence(s)

(1) "What makes the issue so difficult is trying to <u>maneuver</u> around controversial past US actions at Guantanamo—harsh interrogations and alleged torture, bypassing the Geneva Conventions, use of coerced statements to justify further detention, military commissions with stripped-down due process protections."

—Warren, Richey. 2009. Sorting Out Guant Mo Detainees. *Christian Science Monitor,* January 22.

MARSHAL

(1) arrange; array; gather; put together; set in order

Word Used in Sentence(s)

(1) "Of Ernest Hemingway, for example, I feel that he was unable to <u>marshal</u> any adequate defense against the powerful events of his childhood, and this despite his famous toughness and the courage he could call upon in war, in hunting, in all the dangerous enterprises that seduced him."

—Dianna Trilling, American literary critic and author (1905–1996)

MAXIMIZE

(1) make best use of; make as great or as large as possible; raise to the highest possible degree

Word Used in Sentence(s)

(1) *"We must expect to fail...but fail in a learning posture, determined not to repeat the mistakes, and to <u>maximize</u> the benefits from what is learned in the process."*

—Ted W. Engstrom, American evangelical leader and author (1919–2006)

(1) *"Superior business performance requires striking a healthy balance between customer value and cost structure. The goal is neither to <u>maximize</u> customer benefit—which would entail giving away your product—nor to minimize costs in isolation but rather to optimize the relationship between the two. Marketing and Finance both have important insights to offer, so the goal is to manage the tension between them, not to eliminate it."*

—*Harvard Business Review* (June, 2007): 24.

MEASURE

(1)   appraise; assess; calculate; compute; determine; evaluate; gauge; mete; rate; quantify

Word Used in Sentence(s)

(1) *"Managing a nonprofit and working with people is a totally different <u>measure</u> of success."*

—Healy, Wendy Stark. 2011. Ten Years Later, the Wounds Remain Open. *USA Today*, September.

(1)"Just how do constituents <u>measure</u> a characteristic as subjective as honesty, though? In our discussions with survey respondents, we learned that the leader's behavior provided the evidence. In other words, regardless of what the readers say about their own integrity, people with to be shown they observe behavior."

—Kouzes, James, and Barry Posner. 1999. *The Leadership Challenge.* San Francisco, CA: Jossey-Bass Publisher, 23.

Collocates to: ballot, design, distance, items, pass, performance, progress, scale, success, tape

MEDIATE

(1) arbitrate; act as a go between; help settle difference of opinion; intercede; intervene; judge; reconcile; referee; umpire

Word Used in Sentence(s)

(1) Mediating disputes in their early stages can prevent them from escalating into more serious matters.

MELIORATE

(1) improve; make something better

MILITATE

(1) have substantial effect; weigh heavily

MITIGATE

(1) appease; make less intense or severe; less serious or important; moderate

Word Used in Sentence(s)

(1) "The GOP would have to swallow hard on the defense cuts, though Mr. Obama will be under huge pressure to take action to mitigate the damage to the military."

—Strassel, Kimberly. 2012. Potomac Watch, Opinion. *Wall Street Journal*, December 7.

MOBILIZE

(1) activate; assemble; call up; drum up support for; generate support for something; gather people and resources for something; marshal; muster; organize; rally

Word Used in Sentence(s)

(1) I plan to mobilize the entire staff for the fund drive.

(1) "Big companies face the challenge of how to mobilize vast forces such as employees and new market strategies."

—Bussey, John. 2012. What Price Salvation, The Business, Marketplace. *Wall Street Journal*, November 30.

(1)   "It is a new world of management where managers aren't the only leaders and where part of every manager's success is based on how well he or she <u>mobilizes</u> leadership contributions from others."

—Schermerhorn, John, Richard Osborn, Mary UHL-Bien, and James Hunt. *Organizational Behavior.* 12th ed. New York: John Wiley & Sons, Inc., 4.

MODEL THE WAY

(1)   archetype; design; facsimile; hold up as an example; use an example to demonstrate meaning or prototype purpose; mold; original; representation; standard

MONITOR

(1)   check the quality or content; keep track systematically with a view to collecting information; observe or record; watch attentively

Word Used in Sentence(s)

(1)   "As soon as the boss decides he wants his workers to do something, he has two problems: making them do it and <u>monitoring</u> what they do."

—Robert Krulwich, American radio and television journalist

(1)   "To reach that level of maturity, companies need to focus on (1) raising accountability for risk management to the board and executive levels; (2) embedding and en enterprise approach in to risk assessment and <u>monitoring</u>; optimizing risk function by breaking down silos and coordinating risk-related infrastructure, people, practices and technology across the enterprise..."

—Herrington, Michael. 2012. American Advisory Risk Leader. *Ernst & Young, Interaction to HBR* (September): 18.

MOTIVATE

(1)   cause; egg on; encourage; incentivize; induce; inspire; provide with a motive; prompt; provoke; stimulate; trigger

Word Used in Sentence(s)

(1) There is more to <u>motivating</u> employees than compensation.

(1) "Offering ownership opportunities is still a great way to lure and <u>motivate</u> top-notch employees."

—Caggiano, Christopher. 2002. The Right Way to Pay. *Inc.* 24 (12): 84.

<u>Collocates to: ability, action, behavior, employee, factor, inspire, learn, students, teachers, ways</u>

MOLLIFY

(1) soften; sooth; pacify

Word Used in Sentence(s)

(1) One of the issues that has continued to allude managers is the answer to the question: Is there any way to <u>mollify</u> an employee whose job has been eliminated through no fault of theirs?

MULCT

(1) take money away as in a fine

NATTER

(1) chat; chatter idly; confab; confabulate; gossip; grumble; be peevish

NAVIGATE

(1) plan or direct; find the way; follow the route; guide; map read; plot the course; plot a route; steer

Word Used in Sentence(s)

(1) "What I found is that to make the transition successfully, executives must <u>navigate</u> a tricky set of changes in their leadership focus and skills, which I call the seven seismic shifts."

—Watson, Michael. 2012. How Managers Become Leaders. *Harvard Business Review* (June): 68.

NET DOWN

(1) amount to; to be equivalent to

Word Used in Sentence(s)

(1) Hostile takeovers <u>net down</u> to a power grab.

NETWORK

(1) building personal relationships for mutual benefit; connecting with people with similar interests; exchange cards; interpersonal contacts; make friends; meeting people; reciprocal connections; schmooze

Word Used in Sentence(s)

(1) "Research shows that today's most sought-after-early-career professionals are constantly <u>networking</u> and thinking about their next career step."

—Hamari, Monika. 2012. Why Top Young Mangers Are in a Nonstop Job Hunt, Talent. *Harvard Business Review* (July/August): 28.

(1) <u>Networking</u> through either one's strong or weak network remains the most effective tool for the job search.

(1) "<u>Networking</u> is an important strategy for career management, including becoming an influential person. The ability to establish a network and call on support when needed helps a manager or professional exert influence."

—DuBrin, Andrew. 1998. *Leadership, Research Findings, Practice, and Skills.* Boston: Houghton Mifflin Company, 201.

OBJURGATE

(1) berate; castigate; chasten; chide; correct; decry; denounce; reprobate; reprove; revile; scold; take to the wood shed; upbraid harshly

OBFUSCATE

(1) befog; befuddle; cloud; complicate; confuse; darken; make unclear; muddy; mystify; obscure

Word Used in Sentence(s)

(1) "It's <u>obfuscation</u>. There is no attempt to be clear and concise and to describe the product for what it is."

—Don Catlin, American scientist and one of the founders of modern drug testing in sports (1938–)

OBSECRATE

(1)   beg; beseech; plead; supplicate

OBTRUDE

(1)   to force oneself on others; thrust forth; push

Word Used in Sentence(s)

(1) "As a theory of mass communication, agenda setting asserts that while media may not tell us exactly what to think, they frequently tell us what to think about, when the issues at hand do not otherwise <u>obtrude</u> into our lives."

—Denham, Bryan. 2006. Effects of Mass Communication on Attitudes Toward Anabolic Steroids: An Analysis of High School Seniors. *Journal of Drug Issues.* 36 (4): 809–829.

Word Used with Rhythm and Imagery

- **Vivid imagery**—"I can't do with mountains at close quarters—they are always in the way, and they are so stupid, never moving and never doing anything but <u>obtrude</u> themselves" (D. H. Lawrence, British poet, novelist, and essayist, 1885–1930).

OBVIATE

(1)   make unnecessary

Word Used in Sentence(s)

(1) The legal department found a solution and they were able to <u>obviate</u> the problem thus preventing a major crisis.

OCCLUDE

(1)   close; obstruct; stop up; shut in

OPEN THE KIMONO

(1) to expose or reveal secrets or proprietary information

Word Used in Sentence(s)

(1) "Look, I will let you invest a million dollars in Apple if you will sort of open the kimono at Xerox PARC."

—Steve Jobs, American entrepreneur, cofounder, chairman, and CEO of Apple, Inc. (1955–2011)

OPEN PANDORA'S BOX

(1) to open a can of worms; unleash a stream of unforeseen problems

Word Used in Sentence(s)

(1) "At some point, this century or next, we may well be facing one of the major shifts in human history—perhaps even cosmic history—when intelligence escapes the constraints of biology, nature didn't anticipate us, and we in our turn shouldn't take artificial general intelligence (AGI) for granted. We need to take seriously the possibility that there might be a 'opening of Pandora's box' moment with AGI that, if missed, could be disastrous. With so much at stake, we need to do a better job of understanding the risks of potentially catastrophic technologies."

—Shedlock, Mike. 2012. Rise of Intelligent Machines Will Open "Pandora's Box" Threatening Human Extinction, Business News. *Favstocks.com*, November 29.

OPINE

(1) harangue; discourse; go on; hold, express, or give an opinion; lecture; make one's opinion known; orate; preach; rant; stress something; speak out; suppose; think

OPPUGN

(1) battle; call into question; challenge the accuracy; fight against; probity of

Word Used in Sentence(s)

(1) Jorge had the audacity to oppugn the merits of the data privacy research, which is a subject he knows nothing about.

OPTIMIZE

(1) make the best or most effective use of a situation or resource

Word Used in Sentence(s)

(1) "Fully understanding a company requires knowledge of its social structure and informal networks, and <u>optimizing</u> performance requires social investments."

—Kanter, Rosabeth. 2011. How Great Companies Think Differently. *Harvard Business Review* (November): 75.

(1) "I've heard claims that we can wish our way to perfect, permanent wellness, but I haven't seen any proof of that. Sickness and death are part of life. But you can <u>optimize</u> your life. You can make progress as you strive toward perfection."

—Unknown

(1) "India and China developed by being involved in the far end of the value chain. Instead Africa will meet and may exceed the Asian experience by <u>optimizing</u> its resources and focusing on massive agricultural and energy (solar) projects that will primarily aid the food crisis."

—Femi-Ishola, Olusegun. 2012. Human Resource Executive, The Best Leaders Have Short Résumés, Interaction. *Harvard Business Review* (December): 19.

—Lee Sr., Jim. 2012. Knowledge Management Practice Leader, The Best Leaders Have Short Résumés, Interaction. *Harvard Business Review* (December): 19.

ORCHESTRATE

(1) combine and adapt in order to obtain a particular outcome

(2) to arrange or organize surreptitiously so as to achieve a desired effect

Word Used in Sentence(s)

(1), (2) "U.S. intelligence officials say Zadran helped the Haqqanis <u>orchestrate</u> attacks on troops in Kabul and southeastern Afghanistan."

—Gannon, Kathy, Adam Goldman, and Lolita C. Baldor. 2011. Top U.S. Delegation to Enlist Pakistan's Help. INTERNATIONAL NEWS, Associated Press, November 11.

(1) Our goal is to <u>orchestrate</u> a partnership with a Chinese manufacturing firm.

(1) "Digital convergence has created new opportunities for hitherto separate markets and feed the growing desire among customers for integrated solutions and services. This calls for the development of integrated—or at least commonly <u>orchestrated</u>—strategies and actions across business units."

—Doz, Yves, and Mikko Kosonen. 2007. The New Deal at the Top. *Harvard Business Review* (June): 100.

<u>Collocates to: ability, arrange, attacks, campaign, help, trying</u>

ORDER

(1) directive, demand; edict; give a command; give instructions to so something; imperative; mandate

Word Used in Sentence(s)

(1) "The art of giving <u>orders</u> is not to try to rectify the minor blunders and not to be swayed by petty doubts."

—Sun Tzu, Chinese general and author (500 BC)

ORGANIZE

(1) arrange systematically; categorize; make arrangements, plans, or preparations for; order; put in order; sort out; systematize
(2) control; coordinate; fix; manage; take charge

Word Used in Sentence(s)

(1) "Do you know what amazes me more than anything else? The impotence of force to <u>organize</u> anything."

—Napoleon Bonaparte, French general, politician, and emperor (1769–1821)

(1) "It is essential that there should be organization of labor. This is an era of organization. Capital organizes and therefore labor must <u>organize</u>."

—Theodore Roosevelt, 26th president of the United States (1858–1919)

(1) "<u>Organizing</u> is one of the four main functions of management—creating work structures and systems, and arranging resources to accomplish goals and objectives."

—Schermerhorn, John, Richard Osborn, Mary UHL-Bien, and James Hunt. *Organizational Behavior*. 12th ed. New York: John Wiley & Sons, Inc., 4.

OVERCOME

(1) achieve in spite of great obstacles; get the better of; defeat obstacles

Word Used in Sentence(s)

(1) "During the Great Depression, officials doubted monetary policy's ability to <u>overcome</u> the forces that had wrecked the economy."

—Derby, Michael, and Kristina Peterson. 2013. Is the Fed Doing Enough—or Too Much—to Aid Recovery, U.S. News. *Wall Street Journal*, January 7.

OVERSEE

(1) administer; direct; keep an eye on; manage; mastermind; run; supervise; watch over

Word Used in Sentence(s)

(1) "Harald's first challenge as head of the plastics resins unit was shifting from leading a single function to <u>overseeing</u> the full set of business functions."

—Watson, Michael. 2012. How Managers Become Leaders. *Harvard Business Review* (June): 68.

OVERLOOK

(1) look over and beyond and not see
(2) ignore; neglect
(3) pass over indulgently; excuse

Word Used in Sentence(s)

(1) "While weight remains a taboo conversation topic in the workplace, it's hard to <u>overlook</u>. A heavy executive is judged to be less capable because of assumptions about how weight affects health and stamina

says Berry Posner, a professor at Santa Clara University's Leavey School of Business."

—Kwoh, Leslie. 2013. Marketing. *Wall Street Journal*, January 16.

PACIFY

(1)   appease; assuage; calm; mollify; placate; soothe

Word Used in Sentence(s)

(1) The latest pension enhancement management is offering should pacify the union representatives.

Word Used with Rhythm and Imagery

* **Simile**—"The wrath of a king is as messenger of death: but a wise man will pacify it"

—Proverbs 16:14

PALLIATE

(1)   alleviate or calm the problem but not rid the problem; ameliorate; cure; heal; improve; relieve

Word Used in Sentence(s)

(1) "Friends are often chosen for similitude of manners, and therefore each palliate the other's failings because they are his own."

—Samuel Johnson, English poet, critic, and writer (1709–1784)

PARLAY

(1)   to build or increase from a small start; exploit an asset successfully; take a winning position and stake all on a subsequent effort

(2)   talk or negotiate with someone

Word Used In Sentence(s)

(1) "It was Ismail's first big order—$12,000. The money was enough to parlay into his first store, which opened in Dallas a year later."

—Simons, John. 2002. Living in America. *Fortune* 145 (1): 92.

Collocates to: able, experience, hopes, into, success, trying

PARODY

(1) apery; burlesque; mimicry; mock; pun; satirize; spoof; take off

Word Used in Sentence(s)

(1) "To provide meaningful architecture is not to <u>parody</u> history but to articulate it."

—Daniel Libeskind, American architect, artist, and set designer (1946–)

(1) "I think a lot of the time you just <u>parody</u> yourself."

—Dylan Moran, Irish stand-up comedian, writer, actor, and filmmaker (1971–)

PARSE

(1) analyze or break down in detail; analyze a sentence grammatically; describe a word grammatically to make a point

Word Used in Sentence(s)

(1) "Constitutional Scholars <u>Parse</u> Pay Measures"

—*Wall Street Journal*, U.S. News Headlines, January 24, 2012

PARTNER

(1) ally; common cause; confederate; team; join; work or perform together

Word Used in Sentence(s)

(1) "Courage makes change possible…Verizon's leaders saw growth limits in traditional telecom, so they invested billions in fiber optics to speed up landlines and <u>partnered</u> with Google to deploy Android smartphones, requiring substantial changes in the firm's practices."

—Kanter, Rosabeth. 2011. Courage in the C-Suite. *Harvard Business Review* (December): 38.

<u>Collocates to: business, firm, former, law, longtime, managing, partner, senior, sexual, trading</u>

PASS THE BUCK

(1) pass something along to another, especially as a means of avoiding responsibility or blame; shift responsibility or blame to another person

Word Used in Sentence(s)

(1) Never one to admit error, he <u>passed the buck</u> to his subordinates.

(1) <u>Passing the buck</u> is a way of life for government employees.

PATRONIZE

(1) belittle; condescend; demean; denigrate; talk down to; treat one in inferior manner

(2) be a regular customer of a store or business; frequent; sponsor; use; utilize

Word Used in Sentence(s)

(1) "Preferential affirmative action <u>patronizes</u> American blacks, women, and others by presuming that they cannot succeed on their own. Preferential affirmative action does not advance civil rights in this country."

—Alan Keyes, American conservative political activist, author, and former diplomat (1950–)

(1) "Too many people grow up. That's the real trouble with the world, too many people grow up. They forget. They don't remember what it's like to be 12 years old. They <u>patronize</u>, they treat children as inferiors. Well I won't do that.

—Walt Disney, American motion-picture producer, pioneer of animated cartoon films (1901–1966)

PERMEATE

(1) penetrate; seep or spread through

Word Used in Sentence(s)

(1) "Three-quarters of about 10 million students at four-year colleges and universities in the U.S. take at least one internship before graduating, according to the College Employment Research Institute. Interns <u>permeate</u> most every corner of the economy, from Disney World to

Capitol Hill, the Fortune 500 to the nonprofit sector, Main Street to Silicon Valley."

—Italie, Leanne. 2011. New Book Takes Critical Look at Internships. DOMESTIC NEWS. Associated Press, April 20.

Collocates to: air, aspect, culture, entire, every, must, seem, space, society

PERPETUATE

(1)   continue; carry on; keep up; maintain; make everlasting; preserve; prolong memory or use of; spread

Word Used in Sentence(s)

(1)   "When a government becomes powerful it is destructive, extravagant and violent; it is an usurer which takes bread from innocent mouths and deprives honorable men of their substance, for votes with which to perpetuate itself."

—Marcus Tullius Cicero, Ancient Roman lawyer, writer, scholar, orator, and statesman (106 BC–43 BC)

(1)   One of the problems with American management isn't the desire to perpetuate their positions since the average position expectancy of a CEO is less than 36 months.

(1)   "No monuments are erected for the righteous; their deeds perpetuate their memory."

—Unknown

Collocates to: continue, help, itself, myth, status, serve, stereotypes, system, violence

PERSEVERATE

(1)   repeat something insistently; do over and over again

PERSONIFY

(1)   embody; represent something in human form or characteristics

PERSUADE

(1)   cause someone to believe something; convince; induce someone to do something through reasoning or argument; reason; urge

Word Used in Sentence(s)

(1) By <u>persuading</u> his boss to take that step, Jeff demonstrated his skill in managing upwards.

(1) "Companies work hard to <u>persuade</u> existing customers to buy additional products. Often that is a money losing proposition."

—Shah, Denish, and V. Kumar. 2012. The Dark Side of Cross-Selling, Idea Watch. *Harvard Business Review* (December): 21.

(1) "<u>Persuading</u> institutional investors to actively exercise oversight control would be useful—and would reduce fixations on quarterly results."

—de Rothschild, Lynn Forester, and Adam Posen. 2013. How Capitalism Can Repair Its Bruised Image, Opinion. *Wall Street Journal*, January 2.

(1) "We need to try harder to <u>persuade</u> one another—to try to get people to change their minds. There isn't nearly enough persuasion going on in America today, and there was too little, in the view of many citizens, in the past presidential campaign."

—Jenkins, John. 2013. Persuasion as the Cure for Incivility. *Wall Street Journal*, January 9.

PERUSE

(1) check; examine or read through; scan

PERVADE

(1) defuse; infuse; permeate; saturate; spread throughout; suffuse; tranfuse

Word Used in Sentence(s)

(1) "Sincerity is impossible, unless it <u>pervades</u> the whole being, and the pretense of it saps the very foundation of character."

—James Russell Lowell, American poet, critic, essayist, editor, and diplomat (1819–1891)

(1) "The illusion that times that were are better than those that are, has probably <u>pervaded</u> all ages."

—Horace Greeley, American newspaper editor (1811–1872)

PETTIFOG

(1) argue, bicker, or quibble over unimportant manners

PIGEONHOLE

(1) buttonhole; classify; identify; separate into compartments

PIONEER

(1) initiate or participate in the development of something new; open or pre-pare new ventures or activities; prepare or open up

Word Used in Sentence(s)

(1) "You can surmount the obstacles in your path if you are determined, courageous and hard-working. Never be fainthearted. Be resolute, but never bitter.... Permit no one to dissuade you from pursuing the goals you set for yourselves. Do not fear to pioneer*, to venture down new paths of endeavor."*

—Ralph J. Bunche, American political scientist, academic, and diplomat (1903–1971)

PIVOT

(1) revolve; rotate; spin around; turn or cause change in direction

Word Used in Sentence(s)

(1) "Many conservative House Republicans opposed last week's fiscal-cliff measures... 'Now it's time to pivot *and turn to the real issue which is our spending addition' Mr. McConnell said."*

—Gorman, Siobhan, and Peter Nicholas. 2013. Battle Lines Drawn on Budget. *Wall Street Journal*, January 7.

PLACATE

(1) appease; make one less angry; pacify; soothe

Word Used in Sentence(s)

(1) "Successful politicians are insecure and intimidated men. They advance politically only as they placate, appease, bribe, seduce,

bamboozle, or otherwise manage to manipulate the demanding and threatening elements in their constituencies."

—Walter Lippmann, American journalist (1889–1974)

PLAN

(1) arrange; design; have in mind a project or purpose; intend; prepare; purpose; set up

(2) arrangement of strategic ideas in diagrams, charts, sketches, graphs, tables, maps, and other documents

Word Used in Sentence(s)

(1) "In order to plan your future wisely, it is necessary that you understand and appreciate your past."

—Jo Coudert, American author

(1) "Planning will help you think in terms of laying down a foundation of the particular experiences you need to create a résumé to move you into senior management."

—Wellington, Sheila. 2001. *Be Your Own Mentor*. New York: Random House, 33.

(1) "One of the four functions of management is planning—setting specific performance objectives, and identifying the actions needed to achieve them."

—Schermerhorn, John, Richard Osborn, Mary UHL-Bien, and James Hunt. 2012. *Organizational Behavior*. 12th ed. New York: John Wiley & Sons, Inc., 4.

Word Used with Rhythm and Imagery

• Metaphor—"Do you wish to rise? Begin by descending. You plan a tower that will pierce the clouds? Lay first the foundation of humility" (Saint Augustine, Ancient Roman Christian theologian and bishop of Hippo, AD 354–AD 430).

POLARIZE

(1) break into opposing camps; divide by opinion or belief

Word Used in Sentence(s)

(1) "As <u>polarized</u> as we have been, we Americans are locked in a cultural war for the soul of our country."

—Patrick Buchanan, American conservative political commentator, author, syndicated columnist, politician, and broadcaster (1938–)

POSIT

(1) assume or state fact; conceive; conjecture; hypothesize; imagine; postulate; put forward; speculate; suggest; state or assume as fact; theorize

Word Used in Sentence(s)

(1) "Government, for the past 80 years or so, has seen its purpose as mainly to 'respond' to society's failures the moment they occur or whenever they are imagined. Adam Lanza killed with guns, so modern policy making logic <u>posits</u> that government must pass a law. Whether that law will accomplish its goal is…irrelevant."

—Henninger, Daniel. 2012. The Biggest Cliff of All, Opinion. *Wall Street Journal*, December 27.

Word Used with Rhythm and Imagery

- **Antithesis**—"It is the duty of the human understanding to understand that there are things which it cannot understand, and what those things are. Human understanding has vulgarly occupied itself with nothing but understanding, but if it would only take the trouble to understand itself at the same time it would simply have to <u>posit</u> the paradox" (Soren Kierkegaard, Danish philosopher and theologian, 1813–1855).

PRECLUDE

(1) bar; disqualify; exclude; forestall; debar; impede; prevent; prohibit; rule out; stop

Word Used in Sentence(s)

"You look back and you say you've done everything you can. It doesn't <u>preclude</u> someone from coming forward and enabling it to be done better."

—Michael Wolf, German artist and photographer (1954–)

<u>Collocates to: action, any, does, limitations, necessarily, not, possibility</u>

PREDICT

(1) achieve; acquire; arrive at; attain; come into possession of; find; gain; get; get hold of; take

(1) Analysts predict the firm would exceed last year's sales figures.

(1) Jessie was the only person willing to predict we would make our sales projections.

(1) "No model or human can perfectly predict the future. But the FED models have a more specific problem. Despite all their complexity and sophistication, they have long been plagued by gaps in how they read and project the economy."

—Hilenrath, Jon. 2012. Fed's Computer Models Pose Problems, The Outlook. *Wall Street Journal*, December 31.

PREPONDERATE

(1) be a majority; dominate; intensify; prevail; lead; outweigh; surpass others in numbers

Word Used in Sentence(s)

(1) "The prudent see only the difficulties, the bold only the advantages, of a great enterprise; the hero sees both; diminishes the former and makes the latter preponderate, and so conquers."

—Johann Kaspar Lavater, Swiss theologian (1741–1801)

PRESENT

(1) communicate; convey or offer something; display; expound; give or hand something to someone; introduce; offer; organize; put forward; put on; stage; state; submit

(2) award; bestow

Word Used in Sentence(s)

(1) "As more games air, the audience becomes more fragmented when presented with more viewing options across both traditional television outlets and digital platforms, which can ultimately lead to smaller audiences for any given broadcast."

—Bachman, Rachel, and Mathew Futterman. 2012. College Football's Big-Money, Big-Risk Business Model, Marketplace. *Wall Street Journal*, December 10.

PRECIPITATE

(1) careless or reckless action; cause to happen; be rash or impulsive

PREEMPT

(1) seize; stop from occurring

PREPOSSESS

(1) to preoccupy; influence beforehand; prejudice; make a good impression beforehand

PRESIDE

(1) act as chairperson, leader, or person of authority; chair; govern; have control; head; honcho; manage; reign; run; supervise; oversee

Word Used in Sentence(s)

(1) "For starters Mark Leslie, founding chairman and CEO of Veritas Software, wanted to make the firm's decision making process more transparent. Early on he <u>presided</u> over a weekly meeting with employees at which, all of the issues of the day were discussed."

—Hann, Christopher. 2012. The Masters. *Entrepreneur* (March): 54.

PREVAIL

(1) to triumph; win; overcome; preserver

PRODUCE

(1) achieve; accomplish; finish a task
(2) bring forth; produce; yield

Word Used in Sentence(s)

(1) "One obvious difference between coaches in business and licensed therapists is that coaches have to <u>produce</u> results. Managers who don't <u>produce</u> positive performance results will be out of job in short order."

—Nigro, Nicholas. 2002. *The Everyday Coaching and Mentoring Book.* Avon, MA: Adams Media, 12.

(1) "My research also indicates that the process that <u>produces</u> great leaders are similar or perhaps even identical to those that <u>produce</u> awful ones and this is true in domains ranging from politics to business to science. Unfiltered leaders can be domain experts—such expertise is rarely company specific. What they are not is evaluated by their new organizations, so, whatever their expertise, it is difficult to know what they will do in power and impossible to be sure that one is the right person for the job."

—Kader, Abdul. 2012. Regional Health and Wellness Director (NC) Walmart, US, The Best Leaders Have Short Résumés, Interaction. *Harvard Business Review* (December): 18.

(1) Creating and <u>producing</u> product line extensions will add 10 percent new revenue.

PROJECT

(1) estimate; expect; forecast; plan; proposal; scheme

(2) extend outward toward something else

(3) cause a light shadow to fall on a surface

(4) attribute an emotion to another person

Word Used in Sentence(s)

(1) Tammy's <u>projecting</u> a mid-year gain of 5 percent.

(1) We <u>project</u> the sales of our new product will lift our market share by 15 percent.

(1) "No model or human can perfectly predict the future. But the FED models have a more specific problem. Despite all their complexity and sophistication, they have long been plagued by gaps in how they read and <u>project</u> the economy."

—Hilenrath, Jon. 2012. Fed's Computer Models Pose Problems, The Outlook. *Wall Street Journal*, December 31.

PROPITIATE

(1) appease; calm; conciliate; mollify; pacify; placate; sooth; win favor or forgiveness of

PROFESS

(1) declare; proclaim; declaim

PROLIFERATE

(1) multiply; spread; grow rapidly

PROMULGATE

(1) proclaim; declare publically

PROSCRIBE

(1) prohibit; outlaw

PROTOTYPE

(1) copy; example; model; pattern; sample; type

Word Used in Sentence(s)

(1) "...prototyping not only speeds up the design of solutions but helps solicit valuable input and get buy-in from diverse constituents."

—Vossoghi, Sohrab. 2011. Is the Social Sector Thinking Small Enough? *Harvard Business Review* (December): 40.

PURLOIN

(1) make off with the possessions or belongings of others; steal

Word Used with Rhythm and Imagery

- **Metaphor**—"It is curious how sometimes the memory of death lives on so much longer than the memory of the life it purloined" (Roy Arundhati, *The God of Small Things*).

PURSUE

(1) hunt; seek to obtain; continue to discuss or investigate

(2) attempt to overtake

(3) devote one's self to something

Word Used in Sentence(s)

(1) The question today for most midsized and above American firms is not just which markets are the most attractive and should be <u>pursued</u> but which global markets.

QUALIFY

(1) modify; restrict

Word Used in Sentence(s)

(1) "Learning is pedantry, wit, impertinence, virtue itself looked like weakness, and the best parts only <u>qualify</u> a man to be more sprightly in errors, and active to his own prejudice."

—Joseph Addison, English essayist, poet, dramatist, and statesman (1672–1719)

QUANTIFY

(1) express something in quantifiable terms

(2) numerical expression or explanation

(3) determine or express or explain the quantity of, numerical measure of, or extent of

Word Used in Sentence(s)

(1) "We should not forget, no matter how we <u>quantify</u> it: 'Freedom is not free.' It is a painful lesson, but one from which we have learned in the past and one we should never forget."

—Unknown

QUASH

(1) abate; annul; beat down; crush; dash forcibly; extinguish summarily; reject as not valid; suppress; overthrow

Word Used in Sentence(s)

(1) Sales managers should <u>quash</u> the concept of the written sales quote or bid unless the product is an undifferentiated commodity.

RAISE

(1) hold or lift up; lift or move to higher position; increase the amount, level, or strength of something

(2) wake from sleeping

(3) establish contact with someone by communications device

Word Used in Sentence(s)

(1) "Congress and President Obama last week <u>raised</u> income tax rates on high earners as part of legislation to avoid the series of spending cuts and broad tax increases known as the fiscal cliff."

—Gorman, Siobham, and Peter Nicholas. 2013. Battle Lines Drawn on Budget. *Wall Street Journal*, January 7.

RAISE THE BAR

(1) demand more; expect more; increase standards; raise demands or quota

Word Used in Sentence(s)

(1) "He proceeded to clear his calendar, force himself to delegate tasks that were less central to success, and focus on <u>raising the bar</u> in each of the areas we discussed."

—Kaplan, Robert. 2008. Reaching Your Potential, Managing Yourself. *Harvard Business Review* (July/August): 47.

RANGE

(1) extend reach or lie within a certain direction

(2) wander about; roam; saunter

(3) vary the stated limits

(4) move about an area

(5) put data in proper classes

Word Used in Sentence(s)

(1) "Mayor Bloomberg's performance during the aftermath of hurricane Sandy has <u>ranged</u> from mediocre to awful."

—Goodwin, Michael. 2012. Blueblood Bloomberg Has Ice in His Veins. *New York Post*, November 11.

RATIOCINATE

(1) be deductive in determining the answer to; offer reason or argument; reason deductively

RAZE

(1) destroy completely; tear down

REASSESS

(1) estimate the value or character of; fix or determine

Word Used in Sentence(s)

(1) To make a proper career evaluation, you need to <u>reassess</u> the path from your first position to your current and past decisions, values, long-range goals, and interests.

REBUKE

(1) admonish; criticize

Word Used in Sentence(s)

(1) "We tolerate without rebuke the vices with which we have grown familiar."

—Publilius Syrus, Roman author, 1st century BC

REBUT

(1) argue against; contradict

RECANT

(1) publically take back

Word Used in Sentence(s)

(1) "They may attack me with an army of six hundred syllogisms; and if I do not <u>recant</u>, they will proclaim me a heretic."

—Desiderius Erasmus, Dutch priest, humanist, and editor of the New Testament (1469–1536)

RECOGNIZE

(1) be aware of; identify a thing or person; distinguish; know

(2) acknowledge somebody's achievement; appreciate; show appreciation of another's achievement; understand; value

Word Used in Sentence(s)

> *(1) "The essence of management risk is <u>recognizing</u> patterns. There are positions in chess that appear safe to the beginner but to a more experienced player are full of risk and opportunity."*

—Konstadindis, Alexandros. 2012. Strategy Consultant, Interaction. *Harvard Business Review* (September): 18.

RECOGNIZE AND SUPPORT GOOD IDEAS

(1) acknowledge somebody's achievement; appreciate; show appreciation of, or give credit to and support another's achievement; understand; value

REFURBISH

(1) renovate; rebuild; repair

REFUTE

(1) disprove; prove to be false

Word Used in Sentence(s)

> *(1) "Silence is one of the hardest arguments to refute."*

—Josh Billings, American humorist (1818–1885)

REIN IN

(1) check; control; curb; cut back; contain; decrease; hold in; inhabit; limit; reduce; restrain; slow; stop; temper

Word Used in Sentence(s)

> *(1) "...This 'new economy' era saw a tremendous misallocation of resources as firms built paper empires, not sustainable value. Now corporate America has become far too cautious when it comes to growth. A misguided shift in compensation design is causing this. In the name of*

reigning in corporate risk-taking, boards have disconnected CEO pay from the enhancement of equity value across all industries..."

—Ubben, Jeff. 2012. How to Revive Animal Sprits in CEOs, Opinion. *Wall Street Journal*, November 30.

REINFORCE

(1) confirm; expand; give added strength

(2) increase the number or amount of

(3) add or make stronger by construction techniques

Word Used in Sentence(s)

(1) "After brainstorming and formalizing our instincts, we commissioned a consulting firm to provide us with competitor benchmarketing. Our instincts confirmed, we clearly saw the way forward; We would reinforce our Burberry heritage, our Brutishness, by emphasizing and growing our core luxury products, innovating them and keeping them at the heart of everything we do."

—Ahrendts, Angele. 2013. Turning an Aging British Icon into a Global Luxury Brand, How I Did It. *Harvard Business Review* (January/February): 41.

REINTEGRATE

(1) make whole again; reestablish; renew

Word Used in Sentence(s)

(1) "If you don't want to have to kill or capture every bad guy in the country, you have to reintegrate those who are willing to be reconciled and become part of the solution instead of a continued part of the problem."

—David Petraeus, retired American military officer and public official

REITERATE

(1) say again; repeat

Word Used in Sentence(s)

(1) "Mr. Obama plans to <u>reiterate</u> Monday at an event in Michigan his call for the House to pass an extension of the Bush-era tax cuts for households making under $250,000 in annual income."

—Bendavid, Naftali, and Carol Lee. 2012. Obama, Boehner Meet as Urgency Over Talks Increases, U.S. News. *Wall Street Journal*, December 10.

RELATE

(1) apply to someone or something; associate; attach; be relevant to; concern; connect; convey; correlate; get on; give an account to; have a relationship to; have a bearing on; involve; join; link; logical or casual connection; share

Word Used in Sentence(s)

(1) "Indra Nooya, Chairman and CEO of Pepsico, has been called a deeply caring person who can <u>relate</u> to people from the boardroom to the front line."

—Editors. 2012. Role Models. *Entrepreneur* (March): 63.

RELEGATE

(1) banish; send away

RELINQUISH

(1) let go; release; surrender

REMONSTRATE

(1) argue against; protest; raise objections

RENOUNCE

(1) disown; give formal notice

REPINE

(1) be disconnected; fret

REPLENISH

(1) fill again; restore

REPOSE

(1) to lay or place at rest; to stop

Word Used in Sentence(s)

(1) "Consider the peaceful <u>repose</u> of the sausage compared with the aggressiveness and violence of the bacon."

—Tim Robbins, in *Another Roadside Attraction*

REPROACH

(1) blame; scold

REPROVE

(1) criticize mildly

REPUDIATE

(1) disown; have nothing to do with; reject; renounce

REQUIRE

(1) ask or insist upon by authority; be necessary or appropriate; consider obligatory; demand; expect; have need of; make someone do something; require as useful or proper; specify as compulsory

Word Used in Sentence(s)

(1) "While marathon training and predawn workouts aren't explicitly part of a senior manager's job description, leadership experts and executive recruiters say that staying trim is now virtually <u>required</u> for anyone on track for the corner office."

—Kwoh, Leslie. 2013. Marketing. *Wall Street Journal*, January 16.

RESHAPE

(1) change or restore; reform; reformat; remake; remodel; restructure; rewrite; shape anew or again

Word Used in Sentence(s)

(1) "On October 25, 2005, the Swedish telecommunications equipment maker Erickson announced the acquisition of key parts of Marconi's telecom business—thus starting a wave of deals that would <u>reshape</u> the global industry."

—Keil, Thomas, and Tomi Llmanen. 2011. When Rivals Merge, Think Before You Follow Suit, Idea Watch. *Harvard Business Review* (December): 25.

(1) "Business model innovations have <u>reshaped</u> entire industries and redistributed billions of dollars of value."

—Johnson, Mark, Clayton Christensen, and Henning Kagermann. 2008. Reinventing Your Business Model. *Harvard Business Review* (December): 51.

REVERBERATE

(1) echo back; rebound; recoil

Word Used in Rhythm and Imagery

- **Visual imagery**—"These lonely channels would frequently <u>reverberate</u> with the falls of ice, and so often would great waves rush along their coasts; numerous icebergs, some as tall as cathedrals, and occasionally loaded with 'no inconsiderable blocks of rock,' would be stranded on the outlying islets; at intervals violent earthquakes would shoot prodigious masses of ice into the waters below" (Charles Darwin, English naturalist, *The Tale of the Beagle,* 1809–1839).

REVERE

(1) honor; respect highly

Word Used in Sentence(s)

(1) "'I do not understand that Latin,' answered Don Quixote, 'but I know well I did not lay hands, only this pike; besides, I did not think I was committing an assault upon priests or things of the Church, which,

like a Catholic and faithful Christian as I am, I respect and <u>revere</u>, but upon phantoms and spectres of the other world; but even so, I remember how it fared with Cid Ruy Diaz when he broke the chair of the ambassador of that king before his Holiness the Pope, who excommunicated him for the same; and yet the good Roderick of Vivar bore himself that day like a very noble and valiant knight.'"

—Miguel Cervantes, Spanish novelist, poet, and playwright (1547–1616), *Don Quixote*

RISK

(1) chance; exposure to danger; hazard

Word Used in Sentence(s)

(1) "There is no <u>risk</u> and the reward is great."

—Edgar Rice Boroughs, American author (1875–1950), *The Warlords of Mars*

ROISTER

(1) act boisterously; revel loudly or noisily

Word Used with Rhythm and Imagery

- **Repetition**—"With the out-of-door world he had no understanding nor tolerance. In food and drink he was abstemious as a monk, while exercise was a thing abhorrent. Daylight's friendships, in lieu of anything closer, were drinking friendships and <u>roistering</u> friendships" (Jack London, American author, journalist, and social activist (1876–1915), *Burning Daylight*).

RUMINATE

(1) chew over; cogitate; contemplate; mull over; ponder; reflect on; think over

Word Used in Sentence(s)

(1) "I may revolve and <u>ruminate</u> my grief."

—William Shakespeare, English poet and playwright (1564–1516), *King Henry VI, Part 1*

(1) "'True,' replied Danglars; 'the French have the superiority over the Spaniards, that the Spaniards <u>ruminate</u>, while the French invent.'"

—Alexandre Dumas, French writer (1802–1870), *The Count of Monte Cristo*

SATIATE

(1) satisfy fully

Word Used in Sentence(s)

(1) "But, emulating the patience and self-denial of the practiced native warriors, they learned to overcome every difficulty; and it would seem that, in time, there was no recess of the woods so dark, nor any secret place so lovely, that it might claim exemption from the inroads of those who had pledged their blood to <u>satiate</u> their vengeance, or to uphold the cold and selfish policy of the distant monarchs of Europe."

—James Fennimore Cooper, American writer (1789–1851), *The Last of the Mohicans*

SCINTILLATE

(1) sparkle

Words Used with Rhythm and Imagery

- **Visual imagery**—"When the waves <u>scintillate</u> with bright green sparks, I believe it is generally owing to minute crustacea" (Charles Darwin, English naturalist, 1809–1882, *The Voyage of the Beagle*).

SCREW THE POOCH

(1) {slang} foul up; make a mistake; mess up

SCURRY

(1) bustle; dart; dash; hurry; move briskly; move around in an agitated manner; scuttle

Word Used in Sentence(s)

(1) "As super storm Sandy bore down on the East Coast last week, employees of Great Lakes Dredge & Dock Corp. <u>scurried</u> to move 15

giant dredging machines into ports in New York, New Jersey and Maryland."

—Thurm, Scott. 2012. Putting the Storm Behind Them, Marketplace. *Wall Street Journal*, November 19.

SCRUTINIZE

(1) analyze; dissect; examine very carefully; inspect; pore over; search; study

Word Used in Sentence(s)

(1) "The blow had struck home, and Danglars was entirely vanquished; with a trembling hand he took the two letters from the count, who held them carelessly between finger and thumb, and proceeded to <u>scrutinize</u> the signatures, with a minuteness that the count might have regarded as insulting, had it not suited his present purpose to mislead the banker."

—Alexandre Dumas, French writer (1802–1870), *The Count of Monte Cristo*

SEARCH OUT

(1) discover; catch on; get to know something, especially by asking somebody or searching in an appropriate source, or just by chance; get wind; hear about; learn; note; notice; observe; realize; uncover

Word Used in Sentence(s)

(1) Leadership involves <u>searching out</u> new opportunities, ways to innovate, change, ideas for growth, and improvement.

SELECT

(1) choose; pick; vote

(2) choose one in preference over another; pick out one based on some quality of excellence

(3) limit to certain groups based on some standard

Word Used in Sentence(s)

(1) "In every survey we conducted, honesty was <u>selected</u> more often than any other leadership characteristic; it consistently emerged as the single most important ingredient in the leader-constituent relationship."

—Kouzes, James, and Barry Posner. 1999. *The Leadership Challenge.* San Francisco, CA: Jossey-Bass Publisher, 17.

SET UP

(1)   erect or prepare something; establish something, or bring something into being; make necessary arrangements for something; found; inaugurate; institute; organize; prepare

SEQUESTER

(1)   set or keep apart; separate

Word Used in Sentence(s)

(1) "Oh to have been able to discharge this monster, whom John now perceived, with tardy clear-sightedness, to have begun betimes the festivities of Christmas! But far from any such ray of consolation visiting the lost, he stood bare of help and helpers, his portmanteau <u>sequestered</u> in one place, his money deserted in another and guarded by a corpse; himself, so sedulous of privacy, the cynosure of all men's eyes about the station; and, as if these were not enough mischances, he was now fallen in ill-blood with the beast to whom his poverty had linked him! In ill-blood, as he reflected dismally, with the witness who perhaps might hang or save him!"

—Robert Lewis Stephenson, Scottish novelist, poet, essayist, and travel writer (1850–1894), *Tales and Fantasies*

SERVE

(1)   aid; assist; be of use; help; do services for; perform duties; treat in a certain way

Word Used in Sentence(s)

(1) "Leadership is an opportunity to <u>serve</u>. It is not a trumpet call to self-importance."

—J. Donald Walters, Romanian author, lecturer, and composer

SHAPE

(1)   become suited or conformed for

(2)   arrange; fix; devise; form; fashion; express or devise a plan or an idea

(3) adapt or adjust

Word Used in Sentence(s)

(1) "We know, however, that leaders with no patience for history are missing a vital truth: A sophisticated understanding of the past is one of the most powerful tools we have for <u>shaping</u> the future."

—Seaman, John T., and George David Smith. 2012. Your Company's History as a Leadership Tool. *Harvard Business Review* (December): 46.

SHARE

(1)   carve up; divide something equally between people; have or use something in common with other people; divvy; go halves; split

SHOOT THE MOON

(1)   to work a high-risk strategy where you gain everything and your opponent loses everything; in *Hearts*, you end the game with zero points and your opponent ends with 26 points

(2)   to plan and work toward achieving a highly improbable goal

SHORE UP

(1)   make someone or something stronger where support is needed; prop up; reinforce; support

Word Used in Sentence(s)

(1) "Mr. Hagel <u>shored up</u> support from another senate Democrat who is a prominent voice on foreign policy, Barbara Boxer of California."

—Grossman, Andrew, and Sara Murry. 2013. Hagel Wins Backing of Key Senator. U.S. News, *Wall Street Journal*, January 16.

SOLVE

(1)   find a solution; settle

(2)   provide or find a suitable answer to problem

Word Used in Sentence(s)

(1) "We can't <u>solve</u> problems by using the same kind of thinking we used when we created them."

—Albert Einstein, American physicist (1879–1955)

SOW DRAGON'S TEETH

(1) to plant seeds of future conflict

SPAWN

(1) bring forth; produce

SPEARHEAD

(1) be in front of something; head up; lead or initiate; be the point person; take the lead

Word Used in Sentence(s)

(1) She <u>spearheaded</u> the company-sponsored civic fund drive.

(1) A leader will step forward to <u>spearhead</u> the writing of the company's strategic mission statement.

(1) In the commercial real estate business, brokers <u>spearhead</u> major accounts. But they wouldn't have customers without the people who oversee construction.

STANDARDIZE

(1) even out; homogenize; normalize; order; regiment; regulate; remove variations; stereotype; systematize

Word Used in Sentence(s)

(1) "In a society that tries to <u>standardize</u> thinking, individuality is not highly prized."

—Alex Grey, American artist (1953–)

(1) "If you now go off and develop new standard, and <u>standardize</u> certain processes, you don't have to worry about IBM coming in and asserting our patents. We are not going to be a roadblock. What we hope this encourages people to do is bring health care and educational standards up a notch"

—Bob Sutor, American researcher (1950–)

<u>Collocates to: across, data, efforts, equipment, order, procedures</u>

START-UP

(1) begin; commence; dawn; inaugurate; instigate; onset; originate

STREAMLINE

(1) improve the appearance or efficiency of; modernize; organize; rationalize; simplify

Word Used in Sentence(s)

(1) "Since taking over the CEO job I had been talking with my top leadership team about how to <u>streamline</u> operations, but that meeting required me to think quickly."

—Babe, Gregory. 2011. On Creating a Lean Growth Machine, How I Did It. *Harvard Business Review* (July/August): 42.

STRENGTHEN

(1) bolster; buttress; make stronger

(2) increase the strength of

Word Used in Sentence(s)

(1) "The research shows that in almost every case, a bigger opportunity lies in improving your performance in the industry you're in, by fixing the your strategy and <u>strengthening</u> the capabilities that create value for customers and separate you from your competitors. This conclusion was reached after analyzing shareholder returns for 6,138 companies in 65 industries worldwide from 2001 to 2011."

—Hirsh, Evan, and Kasturi Rangan. 2013. The Grass Isn't Greener, Idea Watch. *Harvard Business Review* (January/February): 23.

STRIKE THE RIGHT NOTE

(1) say or do something suitable or appropriate

STULTIFY

(1) impair or make ineffective

Word Used in Sentence(s)

(1) "Lucas waited until the company had stopped laughing over this; then he began again: 'But look at it from the point of view of practical politics, comrade. Here is an historical figure whom all men reverence and love, whom some regard as divine; and who was one of us—who lived our life, and taught our doctrine. And now shall we leave him in the hands of his enemies—shall we allow them to stifle and <u>stultify</u> his example?"

—Upton Sinclair, American author (1878–1978), *The Jungle*

STYMIE

(1) get in the way of; hinder; thwart

Word Used in Sentence(s)

"President Harry Cotterell said: 'We have long campaigned for the closure of the loophole whereby residents try to have development land suddenly designated inappropriately as a village green to <u>stymie</u> un-sustainable building projects.'"

—*Huddersfield Daily Examiner*, October 19, 2012.

SUBJUGATE

(1) dominate; subdue

Word Used in Sentence(s)

(1) "Strange as may be the historical account of how some king or emperor, having quarreled with another, collects an army, fights his enemy's army, gains a victory by killing three, five, or ten thousand men, and <u>subjugates</u> a kingdom and an entire nation of several millions, all the facts of history (as far as we know it) confirm the truth of the statement that the greater or lesser success of one army against another is the cause, or at least an essential indication, of an increase or decrease in the strength of the nation—even though it is unintelligible why the defeat of an army—a hundredth part of a nation—should oblige that whole nation to submit."

—Leo Tolstoy, Russian writer (1828–1910), *War and Peace*

SUPERANNUATE

(1)   retire an employee; discard something as too old or out of style or use

Word Used in Sentence(s)

> *(1) "I wondered what that worthy sea-dog had found to criticize in my ship's rigging. And I, too, glanced aloft anxiously. I could see nothing wrong there. But perhaps that <u>superannuated</u> fellow-craftsman was simply admiring the ship's perfect order aloft, I thought, with some secret pride; for the chief officer is responsible for his ship's appearance, and as to her outward condition, he is the man open to praise or blame. Meantime the old salt ('ex-coasting skipper' was writ large all over his person) had hobbled up alongside in his bumpy, shiny boots, and, waving an arm, short and thick like the flipper of a seal, terminated by a paw red as an uncooked beef-steak, addressed the poop in a muffled, faint, roaring voice, as if a sample of every North-Sea fog of his life had been permanently lodged in his throat: "Haul 'em round, Mr. Mate!" were his words."*

—Herman Melville, American novelist, short story writer, essayist, and poet (1818–1891), *Moby Dick*

SUPERVISE

(1)   administer; control; direct; handle; observe; organize; oversee; look after and direct work of others; manage; run; superintend; take charge of; watch

SUPPLANT

(1)   displace; replace; take the place of; set aside

Word Used in Sentence(s)

> *(1) "In the case of varieties of the same species, the struggle will generally be almost equally severe, and we sometimes see the contest soon decided: for instance, if several varieties of wheat be sown together, and the mixed seed be resown, some of the varieties which best suit the soil or climate, or are naturally the most fertile, will beat the others and so yield more seed, and will consequently in a few years quite <u>supplant</u> the other varieties."*

—Charles Darwin, English naturalist (1809–1882), *The Origin of the Species*

SUPPORT

(1) aid; encourage, help or comfort

(2) carry or bear the weight for; to keep from falling slipping or dropping

(3) give approval; uphold

Word Used in Sentence(s)

(1) A manager's job is to directly <u>support</u> the work efforts of others by providing them with the resources, training, and backing they need.

SUPPLY THE LACK

(1) provide or supply what is missing or needed

SUSTAIN

(1) bare; brook; carry on; continue; encounter; endure; hold, maintain, or keep in position; keep up; prolong; prop up; put up with; stand; suffer; tolerate; uphold; weather

Word Used in Sentence(s)

(1) "Boardroom discussions often center on just two questions: How can we <u>sustain</u> innovation? And do we have a plan for developing future leaders who can facilitate this goal?"

—Cohn, Jeffery, Jon Katzenbach, and Gus Vlak. 2008. Finding and Grooming Breakthrough Innovators. *Harvard Business Review* (December): 64.

SYNCHRONIZE

(1) to cause to take place at the same time; in unison; make agree in time

SYSTEMATIZE/SYSTEMIZE

(1) arrange according to a system; make into a system; make more systematic; organize; prioritize; put in place some organized and written plan

TAILOR

(1) adjust; create; customize; fashion; fit; specify; style to fit

Word Used in Sentence(s)

(1) "Rather than assuming that there is one 'best' or universal answer to questions about such things as job design, resistance to change, the best compensation plans, how to design teams, what are the causes of unethical behavior, organizational behavior recognizes that management practices must be <u>*tailored*</u> *to fit the exact nature of each situation…"*

—Schermerhorn, John, Richard Osborn, Mary UHL-Bien, and James Hunt. 2012. *Organizational Behavior*. 12th ed. New York: John Wiley & Sons, Inc., 4.

(1) "The Federal Reserve's decision to tie interest rate increases to specific unemployment and inflation levels…are decisions most <u>*tailored*</u> *to the specific situation the economy is in."*

—Derby, Michael, and Kristina Peterson. 2013. Is the Fed Doing Enough—or Too Much—to Aid Recovery, U.S. News. *Wall Street Journal*, January 7.

TAKE RISKS

(1) put oneself in danger or in hazard; take or run the chance of; venture upon

TAKE UP THE CUDGEL FOR

(1) defend something or someone strongly

TARGET

(1) aim; focus; reduce effort or cost to achieve objective

(2) establish as a target or goal

Word Used in Sentence(s)

(1) <u>*Targeting*</u> *new markets for existing products creates more profitable sales opportunities.*

(1) "Scientists and the National Aeronautics and Space Administration's Jet Propulsion Laboratory in California said Tuesday that they have <u>*targeted*</u> *a fine grained fractured slab of bedrock for the Mars rover's first drilling attempt."*

—Hotz, Robert Lee. 2013. Mars Rover Ready to Dig In. U.S. News, *Wall Street Journal*, January 16.

TEAM BUILD

(1) to create cooperative group dynamics

Word Used in Sentence(s)

(1) We team built our success.

(1) It took four years of team building and some personnel changes before we could say we were successful in creating just the right infrastructure.

TEAMING

(1) gather and use experts in temporary work groups to solve problems that may only be encountered once; use of teamwork on the fly

Word Used in Sentence(s)

(1) "The stable project management teams we grew up still work in many contexts…Situations that call for teaming are, by contrast, complex and uncertain, full of unexpected events that require rapid changes in course. No two teaming projects are alike, so people must get up to speed quickly on brand-new topics, again and again. Because solutions can come from anywhere, team members do too."

—Edmondson, Amy C. 2012. Teamwork on the Fly, Spotlight. *Harvard Business Review* (April): 74.

(1) "The concept of teaming helps individuals acquire knowledge, skills, and networks. And it lets companies accelerate the delivery of current products of services while responding to new opportunities. Teaming is a way to get work done while figuring how to do it better; it's executing and learning at the same time."

—Edmondson, Amy C. 2012. Teamwork on the Fly, Spotlight. *Harvard Business Review* (April): 74.

TEMPORIZE

(1) gain time by being evasive or indecisive

(2) suit one's actions to the situation

(3) parlay or deal so as to gain time

(4) effect a compromise; negotiate

TENDER

(1) bid; present an offer; make offer; propose a payment in offer of an obligation

TERGIVERSATE

(1) change one's attitude or opinions with respect to a cause or subject

(2) turn one's back on one's cause; make evasive or conflicting statements; equivocate over one's calling; apostatize; renegade; shift; evade

THE GOOSE HANGS HIGH

(1) the prospects are good; good luck

TOPLINE

(1) to feature; to cover the most important issues

TOUT

(1) praise highly

TRAIN

(1) coach; educate; guide; inform; instruct; mentor; prepare; school; teach

Word Used in Sentence(s)

(1) "Companies that want to make better use of the data they gather should focus on two things: training workers to increase their data literacy and efficiently incorporate information into decision making, and giving those workers the right tools."

—Shah, Shvetank, Andrew Horne, and Jamie Capella. 2012. Good Data Won't Guarantee Good Decisions, Idea Watch. *Harvard Business Review* (April): 24.

(1) New hires are trained on all the production equipment.

(1) There are times, my dear Harvard, when I feel as if I were really capable of everything—capable de tout, as they say here—of the greatest excesses as well as the greatest heroism."

—James Henry, American writer (1843–1916), *A Bundle of Letters*

TRANSACT

(1)   conduct affairs; do business; cause to happen

TRANSCEND

(1)   exceed; excel; surpass

Word Used in Sentence(s)

> *(1) "An ELECTIVE DESPOTISM was not the government we fought for; but one which should not only be founded on free principles, but in which the powers of government should be so divided and balanced among several bodies of magistracy, as that no one could <u>transcend</u> their legal limits, without being effectually checked and restrained by the others."*

—James Madison, American statesman and political theorist, the fourth president of the United States (1751–1836), *The Federalist Papers*

TRANSFORM

(1)   alter; change the structure; convert from one form to another; make over; transmute; undergo total change

Word Used in Sentence(s)

> *(1) "My conversation with customers gave me three insights into how we should <u>transform</u> our business to become more competitive: One, we had to reduce the size of our stores. They were too large and too difficult to shop in. Two, we had to dramatically improve the in-store experience for our customers. That meant retraining our associates to stop focusing on the things our existing systems had incentivized them to do and focus on customer instead. Three, we had to look beyond office products to provide other services our customers wanted. They wanted copying, printing, and shipping. They wanted help installing software and fixing computer. We needed to expand our offering if we were to remain relevant to our customers."*

—Peters, Kevin. 2011. Office Depot's President on How Mystery Shopping Helped Spark a Turnaround. *Harvard Business Review* (November): 48.

(1) "Zhongxing Medical transformed the medical equipment business by focusing on direct digital radiography in a novel way."

—Williamson, Peter, and Ming Zeng. 2009. Value-for-Money Strategies for Recessionary Times. *Harvard Business Review* (March): 70.

(1) "In 2003, Apple introduced the iPod with the iTunes store, revolutionizing portable entertaining, creating a new market, and transforming the company."

—Johnson, Mark, Clayton Christensen, and Henning Kagermann. 2008. Reinventing Your Business Model. *Harvard Business Review* (December): 51.

(1) "In his life time, Steve Jobs transformed seven industries."

—Isaacson, Walter. 2012. The Real Leadership Lessons of Steve Jobs. *Harvard Business Review* (April): 94.

TRANSITION

(1) alteration; change; changeover; conversion; evolution; make or undergo a transition; process or period in which something undergoes a change and passes from one state, stage, form, or activity to another; move; switch

Word Used in Sentence(s)

(1) "Walt Disney Co. posted a 14% increase in quarterly profit and Chief Executive Robert Iger said the company is 'transitioning out of an investment mode and transitioning in a more-compelling growth mode', having completed several multibillion dollar acquisitions in recent years."

—Orden, Erica. 2012. ESPN, Parks Propel Disney, Corporate News, December 9, 2012, p. B3.

UNBOSOM

(1) disclose a secret; reveal

Word Used in Sentence(s)

(1) "Don Quixote wrapped the bedclothes round him and covered himself up completely, leaving nothing but his face visible, and as soon as they had both regained their composure he broke silence, saying, 'Now, Senora Dona Rodriguez, you may unbosom yourself and out with everything you have in your sorrowful heart and afflicted bowels; and by me

you shall be listened to with chaste ears, and aided by compassionate exertions.'"

—Miguel Cervantes, Spanish novelist, poet, and playwright (1547–1616), *Don Quixote*

UNDERSTAND

(1) assume that something is present or is the case; believe to be the case; know and comprehend something; infer from information received; interpret or view in a particular way; perceive the intended meanings of something

Word Used in Sentence(s)

(1) Marketing and Finance have a famously fractious relationship, with each accusing the other of failing to <u>understand</u> how to create value. That tension may seem to be dysfunctional, but when channeled right, it can actually be productive."

—*Harvard Business Review* (June, 2007): 25.

(1) "<u>Understanding</u> the values of the person or team you are developing will enable you to build rapport and create meaningful connections."

— Hayashi, Shawn Kent. 2012. *Conversations for Creating Star Performers.* New York: McGraw Hill, 41.

(1) "For the past three years we have undertaken in-depth case study research on the strategy and leadership of a dozen large global companies…Our goal was to <u>understand</u> what makes a company strategically agile, able to change its strategies and business models rapidly in response to major shifts in its market space."

—Doz, Yves, and Mikko Kosonen. 2007. The New Deal at the Top. *Harvard Business Review* (June): 100.

UNDERTAKE

(1) begin something; take on; assume duties, roles, or responsibilities

(2) promise; guarantee; to give a pledge

Word Used in Sentence(s)

(1) Career development is not something someone should <u>undertake</u> just when they become unhappy in their position or lose their job.

(1) He always volunteered to <u>undertake</u> the most difficult tasks on the team.

(1) <u>Undertaking</u> difficult tasks demonstrates a willingness to take risks—a leadership trait.

UNDERWRITE

(1)   assume responsibility or liability; guarantee something

(2)   agree to buy at a given price on a certain date

(3) subscribe or agree to by contract

UNIFY

(1)   bring together; blend; federate; merge; tie; solidify; unite

Word Used in Sentence(s)

(1) The unforeseen problems and difficulties <u>unified</u> the project management team like nothing else could.

(1) <u>Unifying</u> a demoralized and self-interested staff is a very difficult management task.

UNLEASH

(1)   turn loose or let go of the restraints so that all power, resources, and forces can be directed toward something

UPGRADE

(1)   get latest version; apply updates

(2)   promote to a more skilled level or position; raise to higher salary

(3) raise in importance, value, or esteem

Word Used in Sentence(s)

(1) <u>Upgrading</u> the equipment made everyone more effective.

USURP

(1)   wrongly seize

Word Used in Sentence(s)

(1) "If a single member should attempt to <u>usurp</u> the supreme authority, he could not be supposed to have an equal authority and credit in all the confederate states."

—Alexander Hamilton, American founding father, soldier, economist, political philosopher (1755–1804), *The Federalist Papers*

VACILLATE

(1) be indecisive; waver

Word Used in Sentence(s)

(1) "'At this moment,' said Porthos, 'I feel myself pretty active; but at times I <u>vacillate</u>; I sink; and lately this phenomenon, as you say, has occurred four times. I will not say this frightens me, but it annoys me. Life is an agreeable thing. I have money; I have fine estates; I have horses that I love; I have also friends that I love: D'Artagnan, Athos, Raoul, and you.'"

—Alexandre Dumas, French writer (1802–1870), *The Man in the Iron Mask*

VALIDATE

(1) confirm; make valid

Word Used in Sentence(s)

(1) "This is all that is necessary to <u>validate</u> the use of images to be made in the sequel."

—Bertrand Russell, British philosopher, logician, mathematician, historian, and social critic (1872–1970), *The Analysis of Mind*

VENTURE OUT

(1) explore; move out; take chances

VEX

(1) annoy; bother; irate; pester

Word Used in Sentence(s)

(1) "Nuclear Options Vex Europe"

—Headline of article in *Wall Street Journal*, December 21, 2012.

(1) "Delays in Medicaid Pay Vex Hospitals"

—Headline of article in *Wall Street Journal*, January 16, 2013.

Words Used with Rhythm and Imagery

• **Repetition**—"Action and affection both admit of contraries and also of variation of degree. Heating is the contrary of cooling, being heated of being cooled, being glad of being vexed. Thus they admit of contraries. They also admit of variation of degree: for it is possible to heat in a greater or less degree; also to be heated in a greater or less degree. Thus action and affection also admit of variation of degree. So much, then, is stated with regard to these categories" (Aristotle, Greek philosopher and polymath, 384 BC–322 BC, *The Categories*).

VIE

(1) compete for something; contend; contest, fight; rival; oppose; struggle; strive

Word Used in Sentence(s)

(1) "Hannibal was a leader caught in a conflict between two ancient superpowers for control of the western Mediterranean. Carthage and Roam were vying for power when Hannibal seized the initiative and turned the ancient world upside down."

—Forbes, Steve, and John Prevas. 2009. *Power Ambition Glory*. New York: Crown Business Press, 7.

(1) "Facebook and Google are vying to become the primary gateway to the internet. Google has long served as a destination to find websites and information; Facebook, to share gossip and photos with friends. But those distinctions are increasingly blurring, and billions in advertising dollars are at stake."

—Rusli, Evelyn, and Anir Efrati. 2013. Apple vs. Google vs. Facebook vs. Amazon. *Wall Street Journal*, January 16.

VILIFY

(1)   defame; say vile things about

Word Used in Sentence(s)

(1) "Now, as both of these gentlemen were industrious in taking every opportunity of recommending themselves to the widow, they apprehended one certain method was, by giving her son the constant preference to the other lad; and as they conceived the kindness and affection which Mr. Allworthy showed the latter, must be highly disagreeable to her, they doubted not but the laying hold on all occasions to degrade and <u>vilify</u> him, would be highly pleasing to her; who, as she hated the boy, must love all those who did him any hurt."

—Henry Fielding, English novelist and dramatist (1707–1754), *The History of Tom Jones, A Foundling*

VINDICATE

(1)   clear of blame or suspicion

Word Used in Sentence(s)

(1) "Then why—since the choice was with himself—should the individual, whose connexion with the fallen woman had been the most intimate and sacred of them all, come forward to <u>vindicate</u> his claim to an inheritance so little desirable?"

—Nathaniel Hawthorne, American novelist and short-story writer (1804–1864), *The Scarlet Letter*

VITALIZE

(1)   provide resources; materials or assets

(2)   make vital; provide life to; give vigor and animation to

VITIATE

(1)   debase; impair the quality of; make ineffectual; weaken; invalidate

Word Used in Sentence(s)

(1) "The fact is that we had absolutely incompatible dispositions and habits of thought and action, and our danger and isolation only accentuated the incompatibility. At Halliford I had already come to hate the

curate's trick of helpless exclamation, his stupid rigidity of mind. His endless muttering monologue <u>*vitiated*</u> *every effort I made to think out a line of action, and drove me at times, thus pent up and intensified, almost to the verge of craziness."*

—H.G. Wells, English writer (1866–1946), *The War of the Worlds*

VOUCH SAFE

(1)   deign to do or give; give or grant in a gracious manner

Word Used in Sentence(s)

(1) "The Trojans were scared when they saw the two sons of Dares, one of them in fright and the other lying dead by his chariot. Minerva, therefore, took Mars by the hand and said, 'Mars, Mars, bane of men, bloodstained stormer of cities, may we not now leave the Trojans and Achaeans to fight it out, and see to which of the two Jove will <u>*vouchsafe*</u> *the victory? Let us go away, and thus avoid his anger.'"*

—Homer, author of the *Iliad* and the *Odyssey*, and revered as the greatest of ancient Greek epic poets, *The Iliad*

VOYAGE

(1)   go somewhere; take a trip or journey; travel

Word Used in Sentence(s)

(1) "The NASA Mars rover spacecraft <u>*voyaged*</u> *352 million miles to reach Mars this past August, but the next step will be measured in fractions of an inch. The Rover's drill can chip about 2 inches in to the interior of Mars to extract a small spoonful of powdery rock for analysis in an onboard chemistry kit."*

—Hotz, Robert Lee. 2013. U.S. News. Mars Rover Ready to Dig In. *Wall Street Journal*, January 16.

WADE IN

(1)   get directly involved in something

WALK THE WALK

(1)   do what one says they are going to do; do what one promises; follow through; follow up on promise

WANE

(1) to become less intense, bright, or strong; to decline in power, dim; importance and posterity; to grow gradually less in extent

(2) to approach the end

Word Used in Sentence(s)

(1) The fire of the regiment had begun to <u>wane</u> and drip. The robust voice, that had come strangely from the thin ranks, was growing rapidly weak."

—Stephen Crane, American novelist, short-story writer, poet, and journalist (1871–1900), *The Red Badge of Courage*

(1) "So the one went off with one group of scholars, and the other with another. In a little while the two met at the bottom of the lane, and when they reached the school they had it all to themselves. Then they sat together, with a slate before them, and Tom gave Becky the pencil and held her hand in his, guiding it, and so created another surprising house. When the interest in art began to <u>wane</u>, the two fell to talking."

—Mark Twain, American author and humorist (1832–1910), *Tom Sawyer*

WANGLE

(1) to get, make, or bring about by persuasion or adroit manipulation

(2) to wriggle

WEIGH IN

(1) join in a cause; argument; discussion; take part

WHEEDLE

(1) cajole; coax; persuade by flattery; smooth talk

Word Used in Sentence(s)

(1) "L. Frank Baum, <u>The Ozma of Oz</u>" For Cocky had a way with him, and ways and ways. He, who was sheer bladed steel in the imperious flashing of his will, could swashbuckle and bully like any over-seas roisterer, or <u>wheedle</u> as wickedly winningly as the first woman out of Eden or the last woman of that descent. When Cocky, balanced on one leg, the other leg in the air as the foot of it held the scruff of Michael's neck,

leaned to Michael's ear and <u>wheedled</u>, Michael could only lay down silkily the bristly hair-waves of his neck, and with silly half-idiotic eyes of bliss agree to whatever was Cocky's will or whimsey so delivered."

—Jack London, American author, journalist, and social activist (1876–1916), *Michael, Brother of Jerry*

WHITEBOARD

(1) brainstorming; getting ideas down

WINDOW DRESS

(1) to cut debt just before quarterly reports to make a firm's financial outlook better than it actually is

WILDCAT

(1) search or work without a plan

Word Used in Sentence(s)

(1) "After months of trial runs, NASA's Curiosity rover is ready to scratch the surface of Mars, positioning itself this week to drill in to the crust of the red planet and <u>wildcat</u> for evidence of life for the first time."

—Hotz, Robert Lee. 2013. U.S. News. Mars Rover Ready to Dig In. *Wall Street Journal*, January 16.

WINNOW

(1) separate the desirable from the worthless; sort out

Word Used in Sentence(s)

(1) "Skeptical scrutiny is the means, in both science and religion, by which deep thoughts can be <u>winnowed</u> from deep nonsense."

—Carl Sagen, American astronomer, astrophysicist, cosmologist, author (1934–1996)

WHERE THE SHOE PINCHES

(1) the source of the actual problem; where the real trouble or difficulty lies

WHITTLE

(1)   carve; cut; fashion; sculpt; shape

Word Used in Sentence(s)

(1) *"The 94-word intelligence summary emerged from a daylong email debate between more than two dozen intelligence officials, in which they contested and* <u>whittled</u> *the available evidence into a bland summary with no reference to al Qaeda."*

—Gorman, Sobhan, and Adam Entous. 2012. Bureaucratic Battle Blunted Libia Attack, Talking Points. *Wall Street Journal*, December 4.

WITH AN EYE TO

(1)   for consideration; extra attention to be paid

WORK ON

(1)   give attention to; put special attention toward; try to persuade or influence

WRITE

(1)   give in writing; mark with letters, words, etc.; record

WRITE-OUT

(1)   cancel; do away with; eliminate

WRITE-UP

(1)   bring up to date in writing; write a description or an account of; write in detail

YIELD

(1)   give way to another

(2)   to produce or bear

(3)   to submit, surrender; give up to another

(4)   to give way to physical force

(5)   to give up willingly a right, possession, privilege

Word Used in Sentence(s)

(1) "Assuming the blubber to be the skin of the whale; then, when this skin, as in the case of a very large Sperm Whale, will <u>yield</u> the bulk of one hundred barrels of oil; and, when it is considered that, in quantity, or rather weight, that oil, in its expressed state, is only three fourths, and not the entire substance of the coat; some idea may hence be had of the enormousness of that animated mass, a mere part of whose mere integument <u>yields</u> such a lake of liquid as that."

—Herman Melville, American novelist, short-story writer, essayist, and poet (1919–1891), *Moby Dick*

(1) "You appear to me, Mr. Darcy, to allow nothing for the influence of friendship and affection. A regard for the requester would often make one readily <u>yield</u> to a request, without waiting for arguments to reason one into it. I am not particularly speaking of such a case as you have supposed about Mr. Bingley. We may as well wait, perhaps, till the circumstance occurs before we discuss the discretion of his behaviour thereupon. But in general and ordinary cases between friend and friend, where one of them is desired by the other to change a resolution of no very great moment, should you think ill of that person for complying with the desire, without waiting to be argued into it?"

—Jane Austen, English novelist (1775–1817), *Pride and Prejudice*

(1) "A TROUBLESOME CROW seated herself on the back of a Sheep. The Sheep, much against his will, carried her backward and forward for a long time, and at last said, 'If you had treated a dog in this way, you would have had your deserts from his sharp teeth.' To this the Crow replied, 'I despise the weak and <u>yield</u> to the strong. I know whom I may bully and whom I must flatter; and I thus prolong my life to a good old age.'"

—Aesop, a fabulist or story teller credited with a number of fables now collectively known as Aesop's Fables (620 BC–560 BC), *The Crow and the Sheep*

YIELD THE PALM TO

(1) admit defeat to; give up; give way; grant; pay reward; surrender; yield to another

ZERO IN

(1) laserlike focus on something

Word Used in Sentence(s)

"Steve Jobs' Zen like ability to focus was accompanied by the related instinct to simplify things by zeroing in on their essence and eliminating the unnecessary components."

—Isaacson, Walter. 2012. The Real Leadership Lessons of Steve Jobs. *Harvard Business Review* (April): 94.

ZERO OUT

(1) eliminate; reduce

Word Used in Sentence(s)

(1) When the Republicans say they want to zero out tax payer funding for PBS, there is a very good reason to believe the threat.

SOURCES

400 Words You Should Know. 2010. New York: Houghton Mifflin Harcourt Publishing Co.

Adams, Marilyn. 2005. "Fundamentally Broken" Pension System in "Crying Need" of a Fix. *MONEY, USA Today*, November 15.

Ahrendts, Angele. 2013. Turning an Aging British Icon into a Global Luxury Brand, How I Did It. *Harvard Business Review* (January/February).

Anonymous. 2011. Letter to the Editors. *The Washington Monthly*, Jul/Aug.

Anonymous. THE NEXT GENERATION OF TECHNOLOGY: 35 Innovators Under 35.

Anthony, Scott D. 2012. The New Corporate Garage. *Harvard Business Review* (September).

Armijo, Leslie Elliott. 1996. Inflation and Insouciance: The Peculiar Brazilian Game. *Latin American Research Review* 31 (3).

Babe, Gregory. 2011. On Creating a Lean Growth Machine, How I Did It. *Harvard Business Review* (July/August).

Bachman, Rachel, and Mathew Futterman. 2012. College Football's Big-Money, Big-Risk Business Model, Marketplace. *Wall Street Journal*, December 10.

Barker, Richard. 2012. No, Management Is Not a Profession, The Big Idea. *Harvard Business Review* (July/August).

Bayles, Martha. 2008. The Return of Cultural Diplomacy. *Newsweek*, December 31.

Bendavid, Naftali, and Carol Lee. 2012. Obama, Boehner Meet as Urgency Over Talks Increases, U.S. News. *Wall Street Journal*, December 10.

Bennsinger, Greg. 2012. Poison Pill at Netflix, Corporate News. *Wall Street Journal*, November 6.

Beyer Thomas, Jr., Ph.D. 2007. *501 English Verbs*. 2nd ed. New York: Baron's Educational Series.

Bhide, Amar. 1988. *Bootstrap Finance, The Art of Start Ups, Harvard Business Review on Entrepreneurship*. Boston: HBR Press.

Blount, Roy. 2004. Making Sense of Robert E. Lee. *Smithsonian* 34 (4).

Bluestein, Greg. 2012. Uneven Results for Tax Districts. *Atlanta Journal Constitution, NEWS*, June 13.

Bly, Robert. 2009. *The Words You Should Know to Sound Smart*. Avon, MA: Adams Media.

Bowels, Samuel. 2009. When Economic Incentives Backfire, Forethought. *Harvard Business Review* (March).

Bower, Bruce. 2011. Meet the Growbots. *Science News* 179 (3).

Braceras, Jennifer. 2006. Not Necessarily in Conflict: Americans Can Be Both United and Culturally Diverse. *Harvard Journal of Law & Public Policy*, Fall 2005, Vol. 29 Issue 1, Fall 2006.

Bussey, John. 2012. What Price Salvation, The Business, Marketplace. *Wall Street Journal*, November 30.

Caggiano, Christopher. 2002. The Right Way to Pay. *INC.* 24 (12): 84.

Calunic, Charles, and Immanuel Hermerck. 2012. How to Help Employees "Get" Strategy, Communications. *Harvard Business Review*.

Carter, Nancy, and Christine Silva. 2010. Women in Management: Delusions of Progress, Idea Watch. *Harvard Business Review* (March).

Censer, Marjorie. 2012. Lockheed Latest Contractor to Announce New Leadership. *Washington Post*, April 27.

Choi, Thomas, and Tom Linton. 2011. Don't Let Your Supply Chain Control Your Business. *Harvard Business Review* (December).

Cohn, Jeffery, Jon Katzenbach, and Gus Vlak. 2008. Finding and Grooming Breakthrough Innovators. *Harvard Business Review* (December).

Collier, Robert. 1997. Tequila Temptation. *San Francisco Chronicle*, November 19.

Collins, Jim. 2001. *Good to Great*. New York: Harper Collins.

Conway, Colleen. 2008. The Implementation of the National Standards in Music Education: Capturing the Spirit of the Standards. *Music Educators Journal* 94 (4).

Crystal, David. 1995. *The Cambridge Encyclopedia of the English Language.* Cambridge: Cambridge University Press.

Currell, Dan, and Tracy D. Bradley. 2012. Greased Palms, Giant Headaches, Idea Watch. *Harvard Business Review* (September).

Daley, Jason. 2012. New Market Opportunities. *Entrepreneur* (March).

Daly, Suzanne. 1998. A Post-Apartheid Agony: AIDS on the March. *New York Times*, July 23.

Darmody, Stephen. 1993. The Oil Pollution Act's Criminal Penalties: On a Collision Course with the Law of the Sea. *Boston College Environmental Affairs Law Review* 21 (1).

Davis, Gary, and Rosa Chun. 2007. To Thine Own Staff Be Agreeable, Organizational Character. *Harvard Business Review* (June).

de Rothschild, Lynn Forester, and Adam Posen. 2013. How Capitalism Can Repair Its Bruised Image, Opinion. *Wall Street Journal*, January 2.

Denham, Bryan. 2006. Effects of Mass Communication on Attitudes Toward Anabolic Steroids: An Analysis of High School Seniors. *Fall 2006* 36 (4).

Dictionary by Hampton, application on iphone, 2013.

Dodds, Paisley. 2011. Murdoch Rejects Blame for Hack Scandal at Hearing, Associated Press, International News, July 20.

Doz, Yves, and Mikko Kosonen. 2007. The New Deal at the Top. *Harvard Business Review* (June).

DuBrin, Andrew. 1998. *Leadership Research Findings, Practice, and Skills.* Boston: Houghton Mifflin Company.

Dumaine, Brian. 2009. Getting the Economy Back on Track. *Fortune* 159 (11).

Editors. 2008. Developing Global Awareness and Responsible World Citizenship with Global Learning. *Roeper Review* 30 (1).

Editors. 1991. Hastening the End of the Empire, *Time*. January 28.

Editors. 1993. Inside the Heart of Marital Violence. *Psychology Today* 26 (Iss).

Editors. 1992. Power of Russian Parliament's Leader Is Becoming Vexing Issue for Yeltsin. *New York Times*, November 25.

Editors. 2005. The Ethnicity of Caste. *Anthropological Quarterly* 78 (3).

Editors. 2010. Time for a Change. *Town and Country* 164 (5360).

Edmondson, Amy C. 2012. Teamwork on the Fly, Spotlight. *Harvard Business Review* (April).

Erler, Edward. 2011. SUPREME Decisions Ahead. *USA Today*, November.

Femi-Ishola, Olusegun. Human Resource Executive, The Best Leaders Have Short Résumés, Interaction. *Harvard Business Review* (December).

Fenell, Barabara, A. 2001. *A History of the English*. Oxford, England: Blackwell Publishers.

Fisher, Julie. 2003. Local and Global: International Governance and Civil Society. *Journal of International Affairs* 57 (1).

Forbes, Steve, and John Prevas. 2009. *Power Ambition Glory*. New York: Crown Business Press.

Fritzon, Art, Lloyd Howell, and Dov Zakheim. 2000. Military of Millennials. *Strategy +Business* Issue 9, Winter 2000.

Gannon, Kathy Adam Goldman, and Lolita C. Baldor. 2011. Top U.S. Delegation to Enlist Pakistan's Help, INTERNATIONAL NEWS, Associated Press, November 11.

Gaovondarajan, Vijay, and Chris Trimbla. 2005. Building Breakthrough Businesses Within Established Organizations. *Harvard Business Review* (May).

Ghadar, Fariborz, John Sviokla, and Dietrich Stephan. 2012. Why Life Science Needs Its Own Silicone Valley, Idea Watch. *Harvard Business Review* (July/August).

Godfrey, Brian, and M. Oliva Arguinzoni. 2012. Regulating Public Space on the Beachfronts of Rio de Janeiro. *Geographical Review* 102 (1).

Goldberg, Dan. 2012. Responses to Sandy: From Great to Galling, In Perspective, Middlesex Edition. *Star Ledger*, November 11.

Gorman, Siobhan, and Peter Nicholas. 2013. Battle Lines Drawn on Budget. *Wall Street Journal*, January 7.

Grantham, Russell. 2009. Traditional Pensions All But Retired; Financial Crisis Forces Firms to Freeze Plans. *Atlanta Constitution and Journal, NEWS*, July 5.

Greenhouse, Steve. 2013. Our Economic Pickle. *New York Times*, January 13.

Grey, John. 1992. The Road from Serfdom. *The National Review* 44 (8).

Grossman, Andrew. 2013. Fiscal Cliff's Shadow Stills Sandy Aid Bill. *Wall Street Journal*, January 2.

Grossman, Mindy. 2011. HSN's CEO on Fixing the Shopping Networks Culture. *Harvard Business Review* (December).

Groysberg, Boris, and Michael Slind. 2012. Leadership Is a Conversation. *Harvard Business Review* (June).

Hall, Joseph, and M. Eric Johnson. 2009. When Should a Process Be an Art and Not a Science? *Harvard Business Review* (March).

Hammonds, Keith. 2006. *Grassroots Leadership: U.S. Military Academy from: Issue 47, June 2001, Fast Company's Greatest Hits, Ten Years of the Most Innovative Ideas in Business.* New York: Penguin.

Hancock, Bryan, and Dianna Ellsworth. 2013. Redesigning Knowledge Work. *Harvard Business Review* (January/February).

Hann, Christopher. 2012. The Masters. *Entrepreneur* (March).

Hayashi, Shawn Kent. 2012. *Conversations for Creating Star Performers.* New York: McGraw Hill.

Henninger, Daniel. 2012. The Biggest Cliff of All, Opinion. *Wall Street Journal*, December 27.

Herrington, Michael. 2012. American Advisory Risk Leader, Ernst & Young, Interaction to HBR, September 2012.

Hilenrath, Jon. 2012. Fed's Computer Models Pose Problems, The Outlook. *Wall Street Journal*, December 31.

Hill, Charles. 2012. Notable & Quotable, Opinion. *Wall Street Journal*, December 1.

Hirsh, Evan, and Kasturi Rangan. 2013. The Grass Isn't Greener, Idea Watch. *Harvard Business Review* (January/February).

Hocutt, Max. 1990/1991. Humanities? No. Liberal arts? Yes. *Academic Questions* 4 (1).

Hodge, Nathan. 2013. Kabul to Seek More Control Over U.S. Aid, World News. *Wall Street Journal*, January 7.

Horst, Gary. 2012. Business Advisor, CEOs Need a NEW Set of Beliefs. *HBR Blog*, September 21.

Hotz, Robert Lee. 2013. U.S. News. Mars Rover Ready to Dig In. *Wall Street Journal*, January 16.

Isaacson, Walter. 2012. The Real Leadership Lessons of Steve Jobs. *Harvard Business Review* (April).

Italie, Leanne. 2011. New Book Takes Critical Look at Internships, DOMESTIC NEWS, Associated Press, April 20.

Jacobs, James B. 1993. Should Hate Be a Crime? *Public Interest* Fall 93 (113).

Janet Hook, Corey Boles, and Patrick O'Connor. 2013. Passing DEBT Bill, GOP Pledges End to Deficits, US News. *Wall Street Journal*, January 24.

Jenkins, John. 2013. Persuasion as the Cure for Incivility. *Wall Street Journal*, January 9.

Johnson, Mark, Clayton Christensen, and Henning Kagermann. 2008. Reinventing Your Business Model. *Harvard Business Review* (December).

Johnson, W. Brad, and Charles R. Ridley. 2004. *The Elements of Mentoring*. New York: Palgrave Macmillan.

Kanter, Rosabeth. 2011. How Great Companies Think Differently. *Harvard Business Review* (November).

Karkau, Betty. Senior Consultant, Career Systems International, Stopping the Mid-Career Crisis.

Keil, Thomas, and Tomi Laamanen. 2011. When Rivals Merge, Think Before You Follow Suit, Idea Watch. *Harvard Business Review* (December).

Kliener, Art. Building the Skills of Insight. *Strategy + Business*. http://www.strategy-business.com/article/00154?gko=d4421&cid=TL20130117&utm_campaign=TL20130117 (accessed January 17, 2013).

Kouzes, James, and Barry Posner. 1995. *The Leadership Challenge*. San Francisco, CA: Jossey-Bass Publishers.

Kwoh, Leslie. 2013. Marketing. *Wall Street Journal*, January 16.

Lahart, Justin. 2012. Penney Must Endure Pain Before Gain, Ahead of Tape. *WSJ Money & Investing*, November 9.

Lee Sr., Jim. 2012. Knowledge Management Practice Leader, The Best Leaders Have Short Résumés, Interaction. *Harvard Business Review* (December).

Leonardi, Paul. 2011. Early Prototypes Can Hurt a Team's Creativity, Innovations. *Harvard Business Review* (December).

Letters to the editor, Open Forum. 2008. *Denver Post*, August 23.

Letters to the editor. 1995. *San Francisco Chronicle, EDITORIAL*, May 17.

Liberman, Marvin, and David Montgomery. 1987. First-Mover Advantages, Research Paper 969, Stanford Business School, October.

Long, David Wessel. 2012. Term Economic To-Do List. *WSJ Capital*, November 8.

Lucas, Stephen. 1983. *The Art of Public Speaking*. 9th ed. Boston: McGraw Hill.

Lucchetti, Aaron, and Brett Phibin. 2013. Bankers Get IOUs Instead of Bonus Cash. *Wall Street Journal*, January 16.

Macroow, Athena Vongalis. 2011. Blog. *Harvard Business Review* (September).

Malpass, David. 2012. Romney, Obama and the Economic Choice, Opinion. *Wall Street Journal*, November 6.

Marquand, David. 1991. IX: Big Ends or Little Ends. *History Today* 41 (9): 38–41.

McGurn, William. 2012. Sandy and the Failures of Blue-Statism, Opinion. *Wall Street Journal*, November 6.

Meadows, Bob. 2010. Race (Still) Matters. *Essence* 41 (7): 132.

Michaels, Daniel. 2013. Innovation Is Messy Business, Marketplace. *Wall Street Journal*, January 24.

Mikotaj, Jan Pisorski. 2011. Social Strategies That Work. *Harvard Business Review* (November).

Mitnick, Joshua. 2013. Palestinians Adopt Name to Show off New 'State' Status, World News. *Wall Street Journal*, January 7.

Montefiore, Simon Sebag. 2005. *Speeches That Changed the World*. London: Quercus Publishing.

Moon, Youngme. 2005. Break Free from the Product Life Cycle. *Harvard Business Review* (May).

Moran, Gwen. 2012. Mob Money. *Entrepreneur* (March).

Morganfield, Robbie. 1995. Faith and Finances; Power Center Seen as Model for Urban Life. Houston Chronicle, September 10.

Murray, Pamela. 1997. Diverse Approaches to Nineteenth-Century Mexican History. *Latin American Research Review* 32 (3).

Nicholas, Peter. 2012. CIA Chief Struggled to Deflect Criticism of Agency, US News. *Wall Street Journal*, November 15.

Nigro, Nicholas. 2003. *The Everything Coaching and Mentoring Book*. Avon, MA: Adams Media Corp.

Nohria, Nitin, Boris Groysberg, and Linda-Eling Lee. 2008. Employee Motivation a Powerful New Tool, Honing Your Competitive Edge. *Harvard Business Review* (July/August).

Noonan, Peggy. 2009. To-Do List: A Sentence, Not 10 Paragraphs, Opinion. *Wall Street Journal*, June 26.

Orden, Erica. 2012. How to Train Your Branding, Media. *Wall Street Journal*, December 10.

Orwell, George. 2012. Politics and the English Language – essay, http://georgeorwellnovels.com/essays/notes-for-politics-and-the-english-language/ (accessed October 20-24, 2012).

Paletta, Damiah. 2012. Fiscal Cliff Talks at Stalemate, US News. *Wall Street Journal*, December 3.

Parkinson, Joe. 2012. Winning Move: Chess Reigns as Kingly Pursuit in Armenia. *Wall Street Journal*, December 4.

Peters, Kevin. 2011. Office Depot's President on How Mystery Shopping Helped Spark a Turnaround. *Harvard Business Review* (November).

Pfeffer, Jeffrey. 2010. Power Play. *Harvard Business Review* (July/August).

Pink, Daniel. 2012. A Radical Prescription for Sales. *Harvard Business Review* (July/August).

Randler, Christopher. 2012. The Early Bird Really Does Get the Worm, Defend Your Research. *Harvard Business Review* (July/August).

Reprint F0706D. 2007. *Harvard Business Review* (June).

Roget's II The New Thesaurus, Editors, The American Heritage Dictionary, Houghton Mifflin Co., Boston, 1980

Romano, Richard. 2012. Looking Behind Community College Budgets for Future Policy Considerations. *Community College Review* 40 (2).

Rossman, Jim. 2010. *DallasNews.com*, August.

Rusli. Evelyn, and Anir Efrati. 2013. Facebook on a Collision Course with Google. *Wall Street Journal*, January 16.

Russell-Minda, Elizabeth. 2007. The Legibility of Typefaces for Readers with Low Vision: A Research Review. *Journal of Visual Impairment & Blindness* (July).

Sabeti, Heerad. 2011. The For-Benefit Enterprise. *Harvard Business Review* (November).

Saunders, Laura, and Hanna Karp. 2012. Fiscal Talks Spur Charitable Giving. *Wall Street Journal*, December 7.

Schachner, Jill Chanen. 1997. Constructing Team Spirit. *ABA Journal* 83 (8).

Schermerhorn, John, Richard Osborn, Mary UHL-Bien, and James Hunt. 2012. *Organizational Behavior*. 12th ed. New York: John Wiley & Sons, Inc.

Seaman, John T., and George David Smith. 2012. Your Company's History as a Leadership Tool. *Harvard Business Review* (December).

Seybold, Meghan. 2012. *Praise for Conversations for Creating Star Performers*. New York: McGraw Hill.

Shah, Denish, and V. Kumar. 2012. The Dark Side of Cross-Selling, Idea Watch. *Harvard Business Review* (December).

Shah, Neil. 2012. Slow Hiring, Spending Hit Factories, U.S. News. *Wall Street Journal*, December 4.

Shah, Shvetank, Andrew Horne, and Jamie Capella. 2012. Good Data Won't Guarantee Good Decisions, Idea Watch. *Harvard Business Review* (April).

Shedlock, Mike. 2012. Rise of Intelligent Machines Will Open "Pandora's Box" Threatening Human Extinction, Business News. *Favstocks.com*, November 29.

Sherman, Mark, Ken Herman, and Cox Washington Bureau. 2000. Now the Work Begins; President-Elect Bush Faces Big Building Job with Little Time, News. *Atlanta Journal Constitution*, December 14.

Singer, Thea. 2006. Our Companies, Ourselves. *Inc.* 28 (11).

Sisson, A. R. 1979. *Sisson's Word and Expression Locator.* West Nyak, NY: Parker Publishing Co.

Smith, George D. 2012. Your Company's History as a Leadership Tool. *Harvard Business Review* (December).

Smith, Jennifer. 2012. With CROSS-Border Mergers, Law Firms Enter Arms Race, MarketPlace. *Wall Street Journal,* December 10.

Snow, Tony. 1992. The Race Card. *New Republic* 207 (25).

Spotts, Pete. 2011. SpaceX Launch: Private Industry Inspires New Generation of Rocketeers. *Christian Science Monitor,* May 22.

Steenburgh, Thomas, and Michael Ahearne. 2012. Motivating Salespeople: What Really Works. *Harvard Business Review* (July/August).

Strassel, Kimberley. 2012. This Unserious White House, Opinion. *Wall Street Journal,* November 30.

Thurm, Scott. 2012. Putting the Storm Behind Them, Marketplace. *Wall Street Journal,* November 19.

Tierney, Thomas. 2011. Collaborating for the Common Good. *Harvard Business Review* (July/August).

Trout, Jack, and Steve Rivikin. 2006. *Differentiate or Die, by, The Marketing Gurus, Editor, Chris Murray.* New York: Penguin Books.

Vossoghi, Sohrab. 2011. Is the Social Sector Thinking Small Enough? *Harvard Business Review* (December).

Wang, Jennifer. 2012. Radicals & Visionaries. *Entrepreneur* (March).

Warren, Richey. 2009. Sorting Out Guant Mo Detainees. *Christian Science Monitor,* January 22.

Watkins, Michael. 2007. Help Newly Hired Executives Adapt Quickly, Corporate Culture. *Harvard Business Review* (June).

Watson, Michael. 2012. How Managers Become Leaders. *Harvard Business Review* (June).

Weldon, Fay. 1992. A "Profile" of the Creator, OUTLOOK. *Washington Post,* July 19.

Wellington, Sheila. 2001. *Be Your Own Mentor.* New York: Random House.

Wessel, David. 2013. Checking the Economy's Pulse, Agenda 2013: US. *Wall Street Journal,* January 2.

Wheeler, Steven, Walter McFarland, and Art Kleiner. 2007. A Blueprint for Strategic Leadership. *Strategy+Business* Winter (49): 46.

Wiggins, Ovetta. 2012. Doubling Up on Education, Metro. *Chicago Sun-Times*, June 14.

Wightman, Wayne. 2008. A Foreign Country. *Fantasy & Science Fiction* 115 (Iss).

Wilfred, Funk, Dr., and Norman Lewis. 1942. *30 Days to a More Powerful Vocabulary*. New York: Simon & Schuster.

Williamson, Peter, and Ming Zeng. 2009. Value-for-Money Strategies for Recessionary Times. *Harvard Business Review* (March).

Wirls, Daniel. 1991. Congress and the Politics of Military Reform. *Armed Forces & Society (Transaction Publishers)* 17 (4).

www.rfp-templates.com/List-of-Action-Verbs.html (accessed August 2-12, 2008).

www.writeexpress.com/action-verbs.html (accessed August 2-12, 2008).

York, Michael Howard. 2012. Gas Rationing Put in Place in New York. *Wall Street Journal, Greater New York*, November 19.

Index

F

G–H

Q–R